READING
THE GLOBAL PAST

READING
THE GLOBAL PAST

Selected Historical Documents

Volume II
1500 to the Present

EDITED BY
RUSSELL J. BARBER
California State University—San Bernardino

LANNY B. FIELDS
California State University—San Bernardino

CHERYL A. RIGGS
California State University—San Bernardino

Bedford Books ☙ **Boston**

For Bedford Books
President and Publisher: Charles H. Christensen
General Manager and Associate Publisher: Joan E. Feinberg
History Editor: Katherine E. Kurzman
Developmental Editor: Jane Betz
Managing Editor: Elizabeth M. Schaaf
Production Editor: Ara Salibian
Copyeditor: India Koopman
Text Design: DeNee Reiton Skipper
Cover Design: Hannus Design Associates
Cover Art: "Head of Victory," 1907 or after, by Augustus Saint-Gaudens (detail). Helen and Alice Colburn Fund. Courtesy of the Museum of Fine Arts, Boston. Dance shield, early twentieth century (detail of back view). Kikuyu, Kenya. Photo by Heini Schneebeli. Courtesy of Marc L. Ginzberg.

Library of Congress Catalog Card Number: 97–80446

Copyright © 1998 by Bedford Books
(A Division of St. Martin's Press, Inc.)

All Rights Reserved. No part of this book may be reproduced, stored in a retrieval system, or transmitted by any form or by any means, electronic, mechanical, photocopying, recording, or otherwise, except as may be expressly permitted by the applicable copyright statutes or in writing by the Publisher.
Manufactured in the United States of America.

2   1   0   9   8
f   e   d   c   b   a

For information, write: Bedford Books,
75 Arlington Street, Boston MA 02116
(617–426–7440)

ISBN 0–312–17192–7

Acknowledgments and copyrights appear at the back of the book, on pages 201–203, which constitute an extension of the copyright page. It is a violation of the law to reproduce these selections by any means whatsoever without the written permission of the copyright holder.

C O N T E N T S

PREFACE

The study of global history is made difficult by the magnitude of the subject. Modern human beings have been on the earth for about 100,000 years, and their ancestors can be traced back to a period over 3 million years earlier. There are six inhabited continents and thousands of inhabited islands. And whenever and wherever there have been people, their activities have comprised part of the composite past that is the subject of global history. Studying such a massive subject is daunting.

To make sense of this vast sweep of time and space, scholars have to find some way to select from the details of history and produce a simpler picture. One way to do that is to seek general patterns that recur at various times and places: that approach has guided the selection of documents in *Reading the Global Past*. Recognizing the impossibility of including every document of significance, we have focused on a few themes of special global significance and selected documents that shed light on those themes. As a result, some old standbys of world history anthologies have been left out, while some unusual documents have been included.

A textbook and an anthology serve very different purposes in a course on the global past. The job of the textbook is to make sense out of the bewildering welter of details that composes the raw material of history. Ideally, the picture presented in the textbook is coherent, consistent, and clear. The job of an anthology of readings that accompany a textbook, in contrast, is to reintroduce some of the detail and conflicting information that was de-emphasized in the textbook. These readings inject complexity and contradiction into the course, as well as life and interest.

The 96 readings that make up *Reading the Global Past* were selected to present a cross section of the major kinds of sources used in global history. Each part contains mostly primary sources along with a few scholarly works. The primary sources present information through the words of participants in, or direct observers of, historic events or processes; they reveal the concerns and conceptions of the place and time in a more vivid manner than any later scholar possibly could do. They provide the raw material that can support minute reconstructions of the past and can give a "feel" for the period that usually is lost in the more sterile accounts of textbooks. The scholarly works are interpretations of historical or archaeological evidence by scholars at a later period; they provide a framework for the assessment and understanding of the primary sources.

The scholarly works we have selected cut across the disciplines that study the past. Many were written by historians, but others were written by archaeologists, anthropologists, geographers, sociologists, and economists. The study of the global past is too complicated and difficult to leave in the hands of any single discipline.

The readings in this anthology span the globe, treating the human past on all the inhabited continents. In recognition of the accomplishments of peoples around the world and of their contributions to the modern world, it is only appropriate that coverage should be truly global.

Finally, the readings have been selected with an eye toward readability. Readings should be understandable by the beginning history student, but in cases where technical vocabulary or other background might be required, we have added notes and introductory material to assist the student.

While *Reading the Global Past* can be used along with any world history text, it was designed to be used with *The Global Past*, the world history text written by the same authors. Accordingly, its emphases and organization are similar. Each part of the text (with the exception of the final part of each volume, which is given over to broad perspectives) has a corresponding part in this reader, with a common theme and title. Organizing the reader by part, rather than chapter, emphasizes thematic comparison among the geographical and cultural areas that form the basis for chapter divisions. The instructor's manual, *Teaching the Global Past*, provides suggestions on how the use of text and reader can be coordinated profitably.

Dividing the readings of each part into scholarly works and primary sources underscores how these two categories of documents differ from and complement one another. The scholarly works provide students with a framework in which they can evaluate and critically use the primary sources. The primary sources, in turn, shed light on the evidence that led scholars to their conclusions. Organizing primary sources into small thematic groups provides case studies of important issues that could be referred to only briefly in *The Global Past*.

Reading the Global Past was conceived with the intention of encouraging habits of good historical scholarship in students. A full bibliographic citation for each reading is included on its first page to encourage recognition of the obligation to cite one's sources. Each reading is introduced by a discussion of the author and, as appropriate, the circumstances of writing; these permit the student to exercise some evaluation of the source for bias and credibility. Each part ends with a set of questions to consider, which are designed to guide students toward a critical evaluation of the readings and a recognition of their significance.

For all these reasons, *Reading the Global Past* forms a valuable complement to a global history textbook, particularly *The Global Past*. The readings interject detail, controversy, and the personalities of writers who participated in some of the great events and processes of history.

PART SIX

THE COLLISION OF WORLDS

INTRODUCTION

One of the most significant processes of the centuries following 1400 was the expansion of European voyaging, which resulted in the reuniting of the peoples of the Old and New Worlds. Separated for tens of thousands of years, the peoples of the Americas had developed differently from the peoples of Eurasia and Africa. When they finally came into contact, each had developed distinctive ideologies, technologies, and cultural practices that seemed exotic and alien to the other. The collision of these two worlds, then, became in part an encounter of fundamentally different ways of life and the transmission of elements of those ways of life from one people to another.

The acquisition of cultural characteristics that results from contact with members of another society is called *acculturation*. There are various degrees of acculturation, ranging from complete replacement of one's traditional culture to merely a few trivial and superficial changes. The degree of acculturation usually is affected profoundly by the attitudes toward one another held by the participants in contact. *Deculturation,* in contrast to acculturation, is the simple loss of cultural elements as a result of contact with another society. Both of these processes were important in the collision of worlds that took place when the Old and New Worlds were reunited. While all parties in the interaction experienced some acculturation, acculturation of Native Americans typically was much more extensive, and deculturation as a result of this contact was largely restricted to Native Americans. Technology, religion, and ways of life all were profoundly changed by the processes set into motion by contact.

Additionally, the contact of peoples of the Americas with Europeans and Africans led to the transmission of diseases, which proved more disastrous for Native Americans than for the Old World peoples. Lacking genetic resistance to many devastating Old World diseases, American Indians died by the millions from smallpox, yellow fever, influenza, and other diseases introduced by explorers, colonists, and slaves. This demographic collapse, coupled with conquest of Native Americans and their subsequent exploitation as a labor force, led to the destruction of much of Native American culture.

The process of interaction between Old World and New World peoples was shaped by a multitude of factors. The various colonial European powers had different agendas, different goals in their colonial enterprises; individual colonists accepted the official agendas to varying degrees, and brought personal agendas with them. The Native Americans, too, had a variety of goals in their interactions with colonists, ranging from an aim of expelling invaders to an aim of encouraging foreign trading partners. How well these goals were attained depended on many factors, particularly demography and access to economic and military resources.

The interaction between peoples that followed the European voyages to the Americas is a complex story, and the readings in this part of the book explore aspects of it. The first essay, by Herman J. Viola, provides an overview of some of the important issues and outcomes of contact between Native Americans, Europeans, and Africans in the Americas. The subsequent readings discuss the transportation of African culture to the Americas by slaves and its persistence there, Native American and European attitudes toward one another, incentives for European colonization, and the effects of contact between peoples from the two halves of the world. Confusion, miscommunication, and attempts to fit new information into old ideas plagues the individuals caught up in the contact; greed, self-preservation, ethnocentrism, and parochialism were among the factors that motivated the actions of these individuals.

SCHOLARLY WORKS

Seeds of Change
Herman J. Viola

This essay by Herman Viola, a historian and curator at the Smithsonian Institution, was originally written as the introduction to the catalogue for an exhibit celebrating the five hundredth anniversary of Christopher Columbus's discovery of the Americas. Here, it provides an overview of the complex interactions and large-scale contact between the Old World peoples of Europe and Africa with Native Americans. Viola finds the demographic and cultural effects of this contact to have been profound and predominantly negative for Native Americans.

Herman J. Viola and Carolyn Margolis, eds., *Seeds of Change: A Quincentennial Commemoration* (Washington, D.C.: Smithsonian Institution, 1991), 11–16.

Every schoolchild knows that in 1492 Christopher Columbus, a Genoese seaman sailing under the flag of Spain, captained a fleet of three tiny ships and discovered a land unknown to the peoples of Europe. His was a remarkable feat despite his inability, even after three more trips to the Americas, to comprehend the true significance of his explorations. He was not alone in this lack of understanding, of course, for it took decades for the peoples of Europe to appreciate the extent of his accomplishments. No better example of this need be noted than the failure of European cartographers to call these newfound lands Columbia, in honor of Columbus. Instead, they named them for Amerigo Vespucci, a Florentine clerk with a yen for travel whose widely circulated letter *Mundus Novus,* written in 1503, publicized the discovery of the New World long before Columbus's journals were available to European readers.

Columbus did more than force the cartographers of Europe to revise their maps of the earth. His voyages of discovery were pivotal in world history. The Western Hemisphere was rapidly and profoundly transformed biologically and culturally by seeds of change—plants, animals, and diseases—that were introduced, sometimes deliberately, sometimes accidentally, by Columbus and those who followed him. Eventually the processes of encounter and exchange that Columbus initiated affected the Old World as well, altering flora and fauna, reordering the ethnic composition of countries, changing the diet and health of peoples everywhere. They continue to this day.

Columbus could not have sailed at a more opportune time. Affairs in Europe in 1492 were in disarray. At the head of the Catholic church, which dominated the political as well as religious life of much of Europe, was the corrupt pope Rodrigo Borgia. Bickering with the church as well as among themselves were the monarchs of England, France, Spain, and the Germanies. Peasants were crushed by a legacy of incessant warfare and excessive taxation. Intellectuals were drifting in a sea of restlessness and uncertainty, lacking the rudder of religious faith and royal authority that had characterized the Middle Ages but heeding the siren call of the Renaissance, which dared man to believe in himself, to create new art and question old gods, to seek knowledge based on facts instead of dogma.

The Renaissance was an unexpected legacy of the crusades, the failed attempt to wrest the Holy Land from its infidel occupants. Although the crusades had military and religious objectives, they produced marked and unexpected cultural, intellectual, and economic benefits for the people of Europe. Returned crusaders had been exposed to new ideas, unfamiliar technologies, strange foods. They had developed a taste for Eastern spices, precious gems, silks and satins, and other exotic attractions from the Orient. Contact with Arab civilization also inspired a revival of interest in other Mediterranean cultures, a rebirth of the classical learning of ancient Greece and Rome. The Renaissance promoted the rise of nationalism, the growth of cities, interstate commerce, a monied economy, and a merchant class. Printing presses and universities flourished as did the teaching of subjects long neglected—astronomy, chemistry, cartography, and navigation. Newly built seaworthy vessels combined with the development of new navigational aids such as the compass, astrolabe, and quadrant, sailing charts, and a rising spirit of adventure and enterprise caused Europeans to break free of physical as well as psychological boundaries.

It was then that a united Spain burst upon the world scene, unleashing forces of radical change. In addition to sponsoring Columbus's first voyage of discovery, Ferdinand and Isabella in 1492 completed seven centuries of conflict on Spanish soil with the Moorish invaders by capturing Granada. Flush with patriotic and religious fervor, the monarchs chose to expel not only the Moors but also the Jews, thereby dispersing across Europe many of the people who were to become the intellectual architects, financiers, and artisans of the global transformation begun by Columbus and continued by Spain's rivals in the decades that followed.

What Columbus had really discovered was, however, another old world, one long populated by numerous and diverse peoples with cultures as distinct, vibrant, and worthy as any to be found in Europe. Tragically, neither Columbus nor those who followed him recognized this truth. The Europeans regarded the peoples whom they encountered in North and South America more as natural objects—another form of the fauna to be discovered and exploited—than as human beings with histories as rich and ancient as their own. They could not imagine that these peoples could offer anything of aesthetic or cultural value. Only recently, in fact, have we come to realize that what Columbus did in 1492 was to link two old worlds, thereby creating one new world.

Another tragedy of 1492 was the failure of the Europeans to recognize the fragility of the American environment. They set to work despoiling the resources of the New World as quickly as they began destroying its peoples. What had taken nature thousands of centuries to create was largely undone in less than five, beginning in September 1493, when the Admiral of the Ocean Sea returned to America at the head of an armada of seventeen ships. These disgorged on Hispaniola some fifteen hundred would-be empire builders and a Noah's ark of Old World animals and plants including horses, cows, pigs, wheat, barley, and shoots of sugarcane, which was, next to disease, perhaps the most detrimental contribution of the Old World to the New.

Sugarcane merits censure because it harmed both man and the environment. With sugarcane came the plantation system and the initial assault on the tropical rain forests of the New World. Sugarcane was a labor-intensive crop that absorbed huge human resources, beyond what was needed for altering the landscape, to make large-scale production both possible and profitable. Although American Indians were readily enslaved, they just as readily died—in vast numbers from the diseases the Europeans introduced to the New World along with their plants and animals.

Consider, for example, what occurred on the island of Hispaniola, where Columbus established Santo Domingo, the first permanent colony in the New World. In neither Haiti nor the Dominican Republic, which share this island today, are there any descendants of the original Indian inhabitants. Indeed, the native peoples had disappeared by 1600. Although no one knows what their numbers were in 1492, current estimates range from sixty thousand to as many as eight million. Columbus himself remarked that "the Indians of this island . . . are its riches, for it is they who dig and produce the bread and other food for the Christians and get the gold from the mines . . . and perform all the services and labor of men and of draft animals."

If Columbus believed the Indians were the island's riches, he did little to protect Spain's fortune. Bartolomé de las Casas, the Dominican friar and polemicist, whose father and uncle had come with Columbus to Hispaniola in 1493, believed that three million natives had perished after little more than a decade of contact with the Europeans—the result of disease, warfare, forced labor, and enslavement. "Who of those in future centuries will believe this? I myself who am writing this and saw it and know the most about it can hardly believe that such was possible."

When there were no longer sufficient Indians to maintain the New World plantations, Europeans turned to Africa for labor. The exact number of Africans kidnapped and sold into New World slavery will never be known, but estimates range from ten to thirty million. Despite the enormous loss of life, both in the transatlantic passage and in the New World, that slavery entailed—perhaps the life of one slave for each ton of sugar produced—Africans not only made sugar production profitable but they also replaced Indians as the dominant ethnic group in the Caribbean. Ironically, it may have been maize, a New World food taken to Africa by Europeans, that underlaid population growth on that continent and enabled Atlantic slavers to keep the sugar, cotton, and tobacco plantations of the New World supplied with labor.

The real meaning of 1492 can be seen in Montserrat, a small Caribbean island a scant twenty miles from Antigua. When Columbus named it in 1493—after the Jesuit monastery in Spain where he had prayed a novena for a safe return from his second voyage to the New World—Montserrat was typical of Caribbean islands, a lush tropical rain forest providing shelter and sustenance to Arawak Indians.

The indigenous population and vegetation of Montserrat have disappeared. The Indians were replaced, first by Irishmen dumped there as a result of England's domestic policy and then by slaves from Africa; the rain forests were replaced by sugar plantations. Indeed, the ruins of more than one hundred sugar mills still dot the landscape. Although much of Montserrat is rain forest once again, there is a major difference from 1492. Many of the plants on the island today were introduced by its European and African occupants.

The people, of course, are also different today, and this perhaps is the most enduring legacy of Columbus. The population of Montserrat is more than 90 percent black, with the parent stock largely West African in origin. Yet, ask a Montserratian his nationality and he is likely to say, "Mon, I'm Irish!" And why not? The spirit of those early Irish residents pervades all aspects of life on Montserrat. Not without reason is it known as the Emerald Isle of the Caribbean. Many of the place names are Irish as are the dominant surnames of its black residents, many of whom speak English with a touch of brogue. Traditional musical instruments on the island include the fife and drum; one of the folk dances bears a remarkable resemblance to the Irish jig; and island residents celebrate Saint Patrick's Day with exuberant festivities. This then is the true significance of 1492. It was as if a giant blender had been used to concoct an exotic drink, but the ingredients were the plants, animals, and people of two hemispheres, and the product was really a new world.

The continuing influence of Columbus's voyages is an important part of the "Seeds of Change" story. Five hundred years ago, people gave little thought to the environment. Today, acid rain, waste management, global warming, and similar environmental issues command concern the world over. Five hundred years ago tropical rain forests seemed an inexhaustible resource and an impediment to progress. They are now disappearing at the rate of thirty-five acres a minute. Today, rain forests are considered essential to human welfare and a resource to be treasured and husbanded. Not only may rain forests have a major influence on the world's climate, but they shelter plant and animal species unknown to science. The destruction of the rain forests is likened to the destruction of a vast library whose volumes remain unread and unappreciated because the languages in which they are written have yet to be translated.

The Columbus Quincentenary should be a time of contemplation. It is a time to think upon the achievements of those first adventurers who dared to challenge the mythical monsters that had kept Europe isolated by a moat of ignorance, doubt, and anxiety, but it is also a time to reassess and evaluate our options for the future. Ours is an era when decisions have instant ramifications around the globe. Man's continued achievements offer much promise for a healthier, happier future; but technological advances often have environmental implications. The forces of change and despoliation set in motion by Columbus have not abated; if anything, they are accelerating.

Magic Bowls
Leland Ferguson

Archaeology often provides information that complements historical documents. Leland Ferguson, an archaeologist specializing in the archaeology of African Americans in the southeastern United States, presents a study of pottery bowls from the American South and concludes that they show the persistence of African religious ideas among African American slaves. Archaeological and documentary information shows that the dangers and dreadful conditions on slave ships were insufficient to prevent the transmission of African ideas, technology, foods, and arts to the Americas.

In modern Cuba when African American priests make a special charm called *zarabanda,* they begin by "tracing, in white chalk, a cruciform pattern at the bottom of an iron kettle"; and when they make another called *prenda* they also draw "a cross, in chalk or white ashes at the bottom of the kettle." Art historian Robert Farris Thompson has argued that these and other examples of crosses and circles in certain African American rituals are derived from depictions of the cosmos traditional among Bakongo priests from the southwest coast of Africa. The basic form of this cosmogram is a simple cross with one line representing the boundary between the living world and that of the dead, and the other representing the path of power from below to above, as well as the vertical path across the boundary. Marks on the bases of Colono Ware bowls found in river bottoms and slave quarter sites in South Carolina suggest that more than one hundred and fifty years ago African American priests used similar symbols of the cosmos.

While cataloging thousands of Colono Ware sherds, South Carolina archaeologists began noticing marks on the bases of some bowls. Most of these marks were simple crosses or "Xs." In some cases a circle or rectangle enclosed the cross; in others, "arms" extended counterclockwise from the ends of the cross, opposite from the direction of the Nazi swastika. On one there was a circle without a cross, and on a few others we found more complicated marks.

Initially we called these "maker's marks" since the first ones discovered had been incised on the vessel bases before firing and bore a resemblance to maker's marks on European and Oriental pottery. Similar marks, however, were soon found inscribed on interior bottoms, and still others were scratched into the bowls after the vessels were fired. Some archaeologists argued that they were "owner's marks," but there was too little variety in the marks to suggest different owners. Besides,

Leland Ferguson, *Uncommon Ground: Archaeology and Early African America, 1650–1800* (Washington, D.C.: Smithsonian Institution, 1992), 110–16.

most Colono Ware vessels are distinctive enough in shape and coloring to be easily identified. Interpreting the marks as either "maker's" or "owner's" had serious flaws.

Although we could not explain what these marks meant, over a period of several years a strong pattern emerged linking the marks to earthenware bowls collected underwater from lowcountry rivers. What we knew was this:

1. The majority of marks were a cruciform or some variation of a cross or X.
2. All marks were on Colono Ware bowls, none on the Colono Ware cooking jars we commonly found. Also, there were no such marks on imported European bowls, although slaves were using large amounts of European ware as well as Colono Ware.
3. Marks always were located at the very bottom of the bowl, either on the inside or outside. Sometimes they were made before firing and in other cases after firing.
4. Marks were more commonly found on bowls with ring bases than on those with rounded or flattened bases, even though ring-based bowls comprised only a small proportion of the total number of bowls recovered.
5. Although marked pieces have been found around former slave quarters, most were picked up in rivers adjacent to old rice plantations. This was true in spite of the fact that many more Colono Ware sherds had been recovered from terrestrial sites than from those underwater.

Clearly the marks were associated with bowls and with water, but what did they signify? In February 1987 at a Williamsburg symposium on African American culture, I showed slide illustrations of the marked pots from South Carolina and mentioned that while we believed these bowls were in some way associated with the water, we really didn't know how to interpret them. After the presentation, two members of the audience called my attention to the similarity of the marks to Bakongo cosmograms.

The Bakongo are a numerous and powerful people located in the southern portion of modern Zaire (Democratic Republic of Congo, or Congo-Zaire) near the Angolan border. Their homeland is in the area identified in discussions of the Atlantic slave trade as the "Congo-Angolan region." Bakongo culture has been so influential that many non-Bakongo people in Zaire and northern Angola have adopted Bakongo practices, especially in religion. During the time when traders brought slaves to North America, almost half of those arriving in South Carolina came from the Congo-Angolan region, the region of Bakongo influence.

According to Bakongo religion, an almighty God, *Nzambi*, emanates power that may be controlled for either good or evil by living human beings, people who make sacred medicines or *minkisi*. Minkisi control the spirits of the Bakongo cosmos connecting the living with the powers of the dead. Making an African *nkisi* (plural: minkisi) involves packaging a variety of "spirit-embodying materials," which might include cemetery earth, white clay, stones, and other items. Nkisi containers include leaves, shells, bags, wooden images, cloth bundles, and ceramic vessels. "In Kongo mythology, Ne Kongo himself, the progenitor of the kingdom, prepared the primordial medicines in an earthenware pot set on three stones above a fire. Clay pots have therefore always been classical containers of *minkisi*."

Bakongo philosophers explain the earth, the land of the living, as a mountain over a watery barrier separating this world from the land of the dead beneath. Each day the sun rises over the earth and proceeds in a counterclockwise direction, as viewed from the southern hemisphere, across the sky to set in the water. Then, during earthly nighttime, the sun illuminates the underside of the universe, the land of the dead, until it rises again in the northeast. The cycle continues incessantly, representing the continuity of life: birth, death, and rebirth.

Historian Sterling Stuckey points out that circularity, especially counterclockwise circularity, pervades West African ideology from the area of Bakongo culture all the way to Gambia and Senegal on the Windward Coast. The circle, he argues, proved equally important in African American slave culture: "The circle imported [to America] by Africans from the Congo region was so powerful in its elaboration of a religious vision that it contributed disproportionately to the centrality of the circle in slavery." So consistent and profound was the slaves' use of the circle, Stuckey suggests, "that it gave form and meaning to black religion and art."

The watery barrier, which in West and Central African cosmology separates the corporeal and spirit worlds, also found a weighty role in African American ideology. Stuckey quotes Melville Herskovits's assertion of the significance of water spirits and river-cult priests among African American slaves:

> In all those parts of the New World where African religious beliefs have persisted . . . the river cult or, in broader terms, the cult of water spirits, holds an important place. All this testifies to the vitality of this element in African religion, and supports the conclusion . . . as to the possible influence such priests wielded even as slaves.

Considering the ubiquitous West African emphasis on water spirits and circularity, and the dominating influence of Bakongo cosmology and ritual in the Congo-Angolan region, it should not be surprising that early African American religion would bear these same characteristics. The marks on bowls picked up from river bottoms in the Carolina lowcountry strongly resemble Bakongo cosmograms. The association of marks with earthenware vessels, ring bases, and underwater sites also fits the general West African model.

South Carolina's marked bowls were made and used by American descendants of the mythical Ne Kongo who cooked medicines in earthenware pots. Although no marks have been found on Colono Ware cooking jars or pots, some marked bowls show charring from use over a fire. Overall, the traditional African association of medicines or charms with earthenware vessels, and the exclusive archaeological association of marks with handbuilt earthenware bowls, and not with imported European ware, suggests an interpretation of the bowls as receptacles for minkisi or for use in a ritual similar to those involving minkisi.

As Africans came to the Americas they arrived with a belief in water spirits and a profound respect for the cross and circularity as symbols of life and death. Again, we can read these tenets in the archaeological record: two-thirds of the marks are unquestionably cruciform and three out of four marked bowls have been recovered from underwater sites, bowls that embody circularity. Not only are the bowls themselves segments of spheres, and circles the dominating lines of spheres, but the ring bases add even more circles to the vessels, which apparently were made especially to be marked and put in the water. Ring bases are not common on Colono Ware, and the ring bases found on marked bowls often seem to have been quickly pinched-out circles rather than carefully formed rings. Nevertheless, when they are attached to spherical bowls, the ring bases appear as circles attached to circles; when marked they appear as circles enclosing the Bakongo cosmogram.

Overall, the archaeological pattern fits the West African model quite well. The combination of marks, handbuilt earthenware, circles, and underwater context suggest that African American priests performed traditional rituals passed from Africa to the South Carolina lowcountry.

Archaeological Evidence of the Coosa Reaction to European Contact
Marvin T. Smith

Many of the earliest interactions between Native Americans and Europeans are recorded only briefly or not at all in documentary sources. Consequently, archaeologists have an important role to play in reconstructing the events and processes that were part of those interactions. This 1989 article by Marvin Smith, an archaeologist specializing in the period of initial contact between Native Americans and European colonists in North America, discusses the Coosa of Alabama and Georgia, the most powerful chiefdom in that region. Smith discusses the population decline,

Marvin T. Smith, "Indian Responses to European Contact: The Coosa Example." In *First Encounters: Spanish Explorations in the Caribbean and the United States, 1492–1570,* ed. Jerald T. Milanich and Susan Milbrath, Ripley P. Bullen Monographs in Anthropology and History, no. 9 (Gainesville: University of Florida Press, 1989), 135–49.

transformation of government, and changes of technology that attended European entry into this region. The article demonstrates how the specialized methods of archaeology can shed light on human activities that otherwise would remain little known.

According to the accounts of the de Soto and Luna expeditions, Coosa was one of the most important native provinces encountered in eastern North America. It was a powerful and complex chiefdom society with a paramount chief who ruled lesser chiefs and their subjects. Corn, beans, and squash were grown, and meat was supplied by hunting deer, bear, and small mammals and by fishing.

The chief of Coosa was treated like a god. He was carried around on a litter, probably fed special food, and housed in a special dwelling on a mound constructed by his subjects. He commanded a large army and collected tribute from his subjects. In many ways he was typical of other chiefs in the Southeast, although his political authority probably covered more territory than most, extending over a large portion of the Piedmont and Ridge and Valley regions near the southern end of the Appalachian Mountains. Within Coosa there was also a hierarchy of villages, some towns having greater importance than others. Population size, presence of mounds, and other factors reflect differences in importance.

European contact in the province of Coosa occurred on two occasions during the sixteenth century. Hernando de Soto and his army visited Coosa for over a month during 1540, and the Sauz detachment of 100 men from the Tristán de Luna expedition of 1560 were there for several months. Both expeditions left valuable written records of Coosa, naming several towns, detailing political relationships, and providing other information on the area. Subsequent to these relatively brief contact episodes, no Europeans visited the core of the Coosa Province until the late seventeenth century, although the Juan Pardo expedition of 1568 did enter its northern portion in eastern Tennessee.

The core of the Coosa province is the area from the provincial capital, the Little Egypt archaeological site, near the headwaters of the Coosa River drainage in northwestern Georgia down the Coosa drainage to the area around Childersburg, Alabama, the location of the tributary Talisi province mentioned in the de Soto narratives. According to the explorers' narratives, this area was a meaningful political unit, one that corresponds with the archaeologically known Barnett and Kymulga cultures. Within this area, 23 village sites that have produced European trade materials have been found. Six additional Barnett villages are known, but European artifacts have not yet been found at them.

In order to study cultural changes that occurred in Coosa during the sixteenth and later centuries, we must have an accurate way to date the villages in the study area. Unfortunately, the radiocarbon dating technique is not precise or accurate enough for sites of the time span in question. But temporal control is provided by datable European trade materials found at sites. Both the types of artifacts and the frequency of European goods present were used to place the villages in their correct temporal sequence. For example, certain types of glass beads have been excavated in Spanish colonial town sites such as St. Augustine, Florida, or Nueva Cadiz, Venezuela. We know the exact dates that these cities were occupied from the historical records the Spaniards left us. Thus, when we find the same types of glass beads on an Indian site in the interior of the Southeast, we can be reasonably certain that it was occupied at the same time these bead styles were popular in the Spanish towns. Furthermore, there was a steady increase of European artifacts reaching the interior. Therefore, villages that produce an abundance of European artifacts are almost always more recent in time than villages where European artifacts are scarce. Using these trade items and knowledge about them, the Coosa archaeological sites can be divided into a sequence of periods one-third century long beginning with the mid-sixteenth century and continuing through the early eighteenth century. Here we will concentrate on the period 1540–1670, when Spaniards provided the only possible European contact in the area.

Contact with the de Soto expedition in 1540 probably provided the first opportunity for the peoples of Coosa to obtain European artifacts, although it is possible that European goods reached the interior from coastal areas via Indian trade routes anytime subsequent to 1513, when Ponce de León first came to La Florida. The de Soto expedition was motivated primarily by the desire for conquest, and trade was apparently not an important item of business, although gifts to chiefs are mentioned in the accounts of the expedition. We suspect that more trading was carried out than is mentioned in the narratives of the expedition. Glass beads and iron implements are specifically mentioned as gifts, and archaeological finds of swords, a crossbow bolt tip (arrowhead), and other military hardware suggest that the Indians were scavenging European goods.

The Luna expedition included a large number of Mexican Indian farmers and their families as settlers. It is likely that anything and everything was traded by the starving colonists and soldiers to the local Indians for food. Much of the earliest sixteenth-century European goods found on archaeological sites in the interior of the Southeast probably originated with this expedition. Documentary evidence suggests that both de Soto and Luna visited many of the same towns in the same locations, and it is doubtful that it will ever be possible to sort out many of the artifacts left by them.

Finally, the second expedition of Juan Pardo (1568) entered a portion of the province of Coosa in eastern Tennessee north of the core area. Although this expedition did not have any direct contact with the study area, it could have been responsible for the European diseases that reached the region through epidemics.

Following the exploratory expeditions of the sixteenth century, no European set foot in Coosa until sometime late in the seventeenth century. European goods clearly continued to reach the interior, as material recovered from sites increased in quantity and variety over time. Glass bead styles changed, brass ornaments were found more frequently, and more natives gained access to European goods. There is evidence that during the sixteenth century European items were wealth objects hoarded by the aboriginal elite. By the early seventeenth century virtually everyone had access to European goods. Such material must have reached the interior through aboriginal trade networks from areas of coastal European settlement. St. Augustine in Florida, Santa Elena in South Carolina, and coastal missions in Georgia were established in the mid-1560s. Interior Florida missions were established beginning in 1606, with additional missions expanding westward to Tallahassee, Florida, by 1633. Surprisingly, perhaps, the quantity of European goods reaching the interior is greater than the quantity found in mission Indian villages, suggesting that the Spaniards traded goods in remote areas in an attempt to cement political alliances and bring Indians into the mission fold. The fur trade was not to become important in the area until after the founding of Charleston in 1670, although some Spanish deerskin trade with southern Georgia is recorded during the 1640s.

Evidence for Demographic Collapse

Population collapse brought about by the introduction of European diseases is one result of European contact. American Indians had no natural immunity to the diseases that had evolved in the Old World, so when these diseases were introduced into the New World mortality rates were high. Childhood diseases to which Europeans had developed natural immunity, such as measles or various kinds of flu, were significant killers in the New World, and others such as smallpox or bubonic plague were even more serious.

Using historical documents, Henry Dobyns in his book *Their Numbers Become Thinned* demonstrated that population decrease was dramatic in coastal areas where contact with Europeans was frequent. He further suggests that these were pandemics, quickly spreading inland. Work by Ann Ramenofsky in several areas, including the Mississippi Valley, suggests that Dobyns is correct: the diseases did spread inland, although a recent study of New England Indians suggests that epidemics did not reach that area until the seventeenth century. New data to test these findings have been assembled, using better techniques to date population reduction more closely. There are several lines of evidence for demographic collapse in the Coosa area, including decreasing numbers of villages, decreasing village size, burial evidence, and population movements.

Within the Coosa core area, the number of villages occupied decreased dramatically during the early historic period. There are eleven mid-sixteenth-century villages that can be dated by the presence of diagnostic European artifacts and an additional six that appear to date to the mid-sixteenth century on the basis of aboriginal pottery types, although no European artifacts have been found. Then there is a dramatic decrease: only five late sixteenth-century villages, four early seventeenth-century villages, and three mid-seventeenth-century villages are known.

Decrease in village size is more difficult to demonstrate, since some sites are multicomponent (that is, they were often occupied at several different times in prehistory) and the size of the early historic period aboriginal component is not always known. Nevertheless, there seems to be a trend in decreasing village size over time. Using size estimates that appear to be reliable, the average village size for the mid-sixteenth century is approximately 41,000 square meters. Only one village of the late sixteenth century has been identified in the northern portion of the study area, where there had formerly been at least ten, but at 72,000 square meters it is one of the largest sites known, if the survey data are accurate. It is possible that surviving villages had temporarily consolidated following the Spanish expeditions of the mid-sixteenth century. Although it is not possible to determine the total village area occupied during each period since data are not available for some sites, it is clear that the more numerous mid-sixteenth-century villages contain many times the area of any subsequent period.

There is also evidence from burial patterns for disease epidemics. Mass burials (more than two individuals) and multiple burials (two individuals) are common occurrences on sites of the early historic period and are known from sites of the mid-sixteenth and early seventeenth centuries. These burials probably represent the victims of European diseases. A French account of double burials in Arkansas makes it clear that such burials resulted from an epidemic. In 1698, St. Cosmé noted, "Not a month elapsed since they had rid themselves of smallpox, which had carried off most of them. In the village are now nothing but graves, in which they were buried two together, and we estimated that not a hundred men were left."

Not all of these multiple burials may be the result of disease epidemics, however. Recent research by Robert Blakely and David Mathews of Georgia State University indicates that many of the multiple burials at the King site—believed to be a village of Coosa—show evidence of wounds, many from European weapons. It is not certain whether these cuts were the result of conflict with Europeans, such as that chronicled during the de Soto expedition, or if they represent wounds from aboriginal warfare after the introduction of metal weapons and tools. It is also clear that not all of the wounds in these multiple burials were a cause of death—some had clearly healed before the individual's death.

Population movements also suggest disease epidemics, since one documented response to disease episodes is to flee the diseased area.

The Gentleman of Elvas, a member of the de Soto expedition, reported that inhabitants of the town of Talomeco in present South Carolina fled to other towns following an epidemic. This pattern probably also occurred in Coosa, and we have archaeological evidence pointing to it. In the Weiss Reservoir area of northeastern Alabama, a cluster of archaeological sites suddenly appears in a region that had not previously been occupied. Evidently new villages and people appeared, migrants from another region perhaps fleeing epidemics. After the early seventeenth century, there is continued archaeological evidence of a gradual migration of towns farther downriver toward the south. This movement continued until the eighteenth century.

There is also historical evidence of the movement of towns. Using evidence of town names recorded by Spanish explorers, Charles Hudson and his colleagues have identified several of the archaeological sites in Coosa by name. It is thus possible to relocate these named towns again when European records become available in the early eighteenth century. For example, the main town of Coosa in the sixteenth century, identified as the Little Egypt archaeological site, was located near the headwaters of the Coosa River drainage on the Coosawattee River in Murray County, Georgia. By the early eighteenth century, Coosa is located 130 miles to the southwest at the Childersburg archaeological site. Similarly, the town of Apica described by members of the Luna expedition in 1560 has been identified as the Johnstone Farm site near present Rome, Georgia, but by the early eighteenth century it was located not far from the Childersburg site at the Bead Field site.

The region where these two towns migrated was the center of the chiefdom of Talisi in the sixteenth century, and Talisi was still present in this location during the eighteenth century. It is clear that many Coosa towns had moved south and had merged with the Talisi towns by the late seventeenth or early eighteenth centuries. These towns became a portion of the Upper Creeks and were an important part of the Creek Confederacy during the eighteenth century.

It is important to note that some towns named in the sixteenth century are not identifiable in the eighteenth century, suggesting that population amalgamation took place. Apparently small towns banded together to attain a larger population. Such population movements and amalgamation were part of the catalysts for the formation of the Creek Confederacy, probably late in the seventeenth century.

The Demise of Chiefdoms

With the catastrophic decline in population, there was a subsequent collapse of aboriginal culture in the Southeast. While many aspects of culture undoubtedly changed, including social organization and the belief system, we will focus on the demise of the chiefly political organization. There was simply insufficient manpower to continue to construct impressive mounds and buildings and to conduct organized warfare of the type carried out in the Southeast before European contact. Further-more, there were insufficient farmers to produce large agricultural sur-pluses to support the chiefs, their families, armies, and craft specialists, such as those of Coosa.

Anthropologists Christopher Peebles and Susan Kus have proposed archaeological correlates of ranked societies or chiefdoms, including the presence of monumental architecture, hierarchical settlement pat-terns, part-time craft specialization, and elaborate burial ritual signify-ing ascribed status, that is, superior social status conferred on a person simply because of kinship with the chief. Less complex societies have social status achieved only by individual acts, such as heroism in war-fare. It is possible to look at the demise of these criteria to help docu-ment the political collapse of the southeastern chiefdoms.

Mound building was an important activity among the prehistoric people of the study area. The numerous temple mounds found served as platforms for chiefly residences and mortuary temples. Presence of the mounds serves as testimony to the coercive power of the chiefs to conscript labor for large construction projects. The chiefs had the power to force their subjects to perform such labor and controlled the stored food surpluses to support the workers. Based on evidence of European trade goods associated with mound sites, usually as grave goods in mound burials or in village burials around the mound, it is apparent that substantial mound building in Coosa had ceased by the end of the sixteenth century. No evidence has been found that any mounds were begun or even added to after the sixteenth century, although one mound farther down the Alabama River may have had some additions made in the early seventeenth century.

With the end of mound construction, obvious settlement hierar-chies also disappeared. In the sixteenth century, the inner core of the Coosa chiefdom consisted of eight villages along a 20-mile stretch of the Coosawattee River. The Little Egypt site, the capital of Coosa, had three mounds, the Thompson site (probably a secondary administrative center) had one small mound, and six village sites had none.

By the beginning of the seventeenth century no village within the entire study area had a mound, and the four known villages were tightly clustered in a small area. There is no longer an obvious hierarchy of sites according to size or presence or absence of earthworks.

The political elite in Coosa probably supported part-time craft spe-cialization. Such objects as shell gorgets and native copper ornaments apparently were manufactured by specialists who were fed from the chief's granaries. These objects appear in Indian graves no later than the first third of the seventeenth century, and it is entirely possible that none was actually manufactured after the sixteenth century. This sudden end of craft specialties that had been carried out for centuries again sug-gests political collapse. Chiefs simply no longer had control of enough agricultural surplus to support crafts specialists.

Settlement pattern changes also took place. By the first third of the seventeenth century there was a general trend away from compact, nearly square fortified towns, to long, linear arrangements of occupied area. Apparently towns were no longer palisaded but were more dispersed, again suggesting a lack of strong, centralized leadership.

The disappearance of objects of high status can also be documented by comparing the associations of such artifacts with datable European trade goods. Status markers such as embossed native copper and spatulate stone celts, found in prehistoric elite graves, disappear by the first third of the seventeenth century. These objects had previously served as tangible symbols of elite status, just as a king's scepter functioned in medieval Europe.

The demise of these artifacts signaled the demise of the aboriginal status categories. Chiefly organization gave way to less centralized organization. European goods became increasingly common as burial furniture, and the frequency of grave goods increased dramatically until nearly all burials contained artifacts, usually of European manufacture, by the late seventeenth century.

At the same time, there was another breakdown in the burial ritual of the political elite. Formerly, the elite were buried together in a specific locale, such as a burial mound or within their own houses erected atop a mound. As the chiefly system broke down, there was no longer an elite social stratum segregated from the common people in special burial areas. The exact timing of these changes has not been carefully documented, but they seemed to occur by the early seventeenth century.

Acculturation is a type of culture change where one group becomes more like another group during a period of (usually) prolonged contact, most often by a dominant group influencing another, weaker group. It has been argued that although dramatic changes took place in the study area during the early historic period, these changes were not acculturation but deculturation, a loss of cultural elements. In the interior of La Florida there was severe population loss, political collapse, and probably a loss of elements of the belief system. However, with no Europeans present in the interior, there was no opportunity for the natives of the study area to adopt elements of Spanish culture. They had no model to copy. The Indians of the interior Southeast were not becoming hispanicized but were simply losing parts of their own culture. Changes were taking place, but they were not acculturation.

By applying schemes for measuring acculturation in archaeological situations, it can be demonstrated that indeed little acculturation took place. Most new items of European manufacture introduced prior to the late seventeenth century simply acted as substitutes for native categories and represent little real change. Thus glass beads replaced shell beads, brass gorgets replaced shell gorgets, and iron axes replaced stone celts. The Spaniards made it a policy not to trade firearms to the Indians, and this policy seems to have been effectively implemented: only archaeological sites dating to the late seventeenth century, after French and English traders began to appear, produce evidence of firearms. Hunting and warfare patterns were consequently not changed.

The Spaniards also did not trade metal kettles, and the southeastern native ceramic tradition did not decline during the early historic period. By way of contrast, the Dutch and the French in the Northeast had a heavy trade in metal cooking kettles with the local Iroquoian groups. As a result, by the first half of the seventeenth century, the aboriginal ceramic tradition of the Onondaga Iroquois of New York was all but destroyed.

Some new cultivated plants, such as peaches, were introduced into the interior Southeast no later than the early seventeenth century, although no evidence has come from Coosa. But Coosa's inhabitants were horticulturalists prior to contact, and the addition of new crops would seem to have caused little change. Metal working, the medium of native copper, had been practiced prior to contact, so some native-made ornaments of European brass or copper likewise do not reflect any significant level of acculturation.

Dramatic loss of cultural elements took place during the late sixteenth and early seventeenth centuries in the interior of La Florida, but only during the eighteenth century did true acculturation take place. Contact with the de Soto, Luna, and Pardo expeditions resulted in the demise of Coosa as a major aboriginal political unit. Similar changes occurred elsewhere in the Southeast. But it is in Coosa that we have the most dramatic archaeological evidence of the collapse of the chiefdoms that dominated much of the Southeast prior to the sixteenth century.

New Ideas in Old Frameworks
Olive Patricia Dickason

This excerpt from Olive Dickason's The Myth of the Savage *(1984) discusses how Europeans attempted to reconcile Native Americans with Renaissance ideas about the world. Europeans inherited these ideas from earlier writers who had no idea that the Americas and Native Americans existed. The "wild people" of European imagination possessed characteristics that were projected onto American Indians and others encountered during European exploration. While cannibalism was relatively rare around the world, it was prominent in the European vision of "wild people," and it erroneously made its way into many descriptions of American Indians. The European attitudes Dickason discusses shaped European policy and actions, especially in Europe's American colonies.*

Olive Patricia Dickason, *The Myth of the Savage and the Beginnings of French Colonialism in the Americas* (Edmonton: University of Alberta Press, 1984), 17–22.

As European voyages increased so did the "rage to know" about strange people and strange customs; an urge usually satisfied by collecting curiosities. Ferdinand of Hapsburg owned Mexican carvings and feather work that Cortés had brought to Europe; a feather mosaic in the possession of Polish King Sigismond III Vasa may have had the same provenance. Montaigne owned Tupinambá items such as a hammock, a sword club, a wrist guard, and a stamping tube. Although it is far easier to collect objects or information than it is to put them into context, at least one early collector began to put objects into series. Michele Mercati of San Miniato (1541–93), keeper of the botanic garden of Pius V and museum organizer for the Vatican, was among the first to establish that flint arrowheads were man-made. Noting that they had been used by ancient Jews as well as contemporary Amerindians, he speculated that they had also been employed by early inhabitants of Italy.

Mercati's effort was unusual. Generally, during the sixteenth and seventeenth centuries, information and objects were collected fervently but with comparatively little analysis. In the material published during the sixteenth century, the only New World culture to receive much attention was that of the Tupinambá of Brazil, as it was principally in their territory that dyewood was obtained; in the seventeenth century, it was the Huron of Canada, and for a similar reason, the fur trade. Even though it was to their economic advantage to learn about these peoples, Europeans did not systematize the information they collected about the Tupinambá or the Huron until the present century.

The accepted model for describing people of other lands was provided by ancient authorities such as Pliny (A.D. 23/24–79) and Herodotus (fifth century B.C.)—a model constituted largely of sweeping generalizations. In spite of this, a good deal of first-rate ethnographic information was collected during the sixteenth and seventeenth centuries. Much was done by the Spaniards; but their interest was in conquest and administration rather than in learning about New World people as such. Spanish imperial considerations reinforced a penchant for secrecy; this, combined with strong doubts as to the advisability of publicizing pagan customs and beliefs, inhibited the publication of ethnographic material. Some of it did not appear until comparatively recently. This was particularly true for information concerning the peoples of Mexico, Central America, and Peru.

Thus the authority of the ancients continued to maintain its grip even after they had been proved to be incompletely informed, if not completely wrong, about the nature of the world, a situation that was reinforced by the fact that some classical geographical ideas were vindicated. Still, reason, to be effective, had to take into account the findings of experience—an array of strange new facts that did not accord with some cherished beliefs. Writers of the sixteenth and seventeenth centuries apparently never tired of pointing out that Aristotle had erred when he had argued against the habitability of the Torrid Zone, as had Lactantius Firmianus (c.260–c.340) and St. Augustine of Hippo (354–430) when they had maintained that it was absurd to think of man living feet above head in the Antipodes. Reason had its pitfalls — witness the logic of Lactantius's arguments against rain falling upward — so experience should not be ignored. When Cartier, in his report on his second voyage (1535–36) wrote that the ancients had theorized about the habitability of the world without testing their statements by actual experience, he was repeating a point that had been made again and again since the time of Columbus. But it was easier to prove authorities wrong than it was to change patterns of thought, and the ancients were still relied upon even while their errors were reported with undisguised satisfaction.

Where Europeans had been reluctant to believe in the existence of unknown races of men, they willingly (even eagerly) conceded the existence of monsters. During his first voyage to the West Indies, Columbus, while admitting that he did not actually see any monsters, accepted without question a report that on another island he did not visit, "the people are born with tails." Such an easy acquiescence could well have been based on the legendary existence of people with tails — descendants from an era when men and apes mated. He also repeated that on still another island the people were said to have no hair. From his own observations he reported that sirens were not beautiful, as was commonly believed, but had faces like those of men. While he did not consider sirens to be monsters, cannibals were traditionally classed as such, and had inhabited European geographies since classical times. Columbus never did find that favorite variety supposedly inhabiting the Orient, the dog-headed man; but more than half a century later, a stranded English sailor wandering up the North American Atlantic seaboard reported that cannibals "doe most inhabite betweene Norumbega & Bariniah, they have teeth like dogs teeth, and thereby you may know them." Belief in such creatures was not easily shaken; had not even St. Augustine discussed whether the descendants of Adam had produced monstrous races of men? However, the church father had been careful not to equate strangeness of appearance with non-humanity: "let no true believer have any doubt that such an individual is descended from the one man who was first created." Conversely, Vadianus (1484–1551) was not convinced by reports from Africa of men who had nothing human about them except their physical form and ability to speak. He denied the existence of monstrous men: "Homines monstrosos non esse." But folklore would have it otherwise; a popular tale of the late Middle Ages told of Adam warning his daughters against eating certain plants that could make them conceive *semi-homo* monsters with plantlike souls.

Learned physicians of the Middle Ages and Renaissance thought that monsters were generated because of the influence of the stars, which in certain conjunctions prevented the fetus from assuming human form. Others believed that an abnormal quantity of semen was responsible, or perhaps illicit intercourse. Cornelius Gemma (1535–79), professor of medicine of Louvain, pointed to sin in general as the cause, although he indicated that the universal cataclysm and confusion of Babel also had been factors.

The process of eliminating notions of men with one foot, faces in their chests, without mouths or anuses, or with ears so large they could use them for blankets, was to take the better part of three centuries. In fact, the immediate effect of the New World discoveries produced an efflorescence of monsters; new varieties were reported faster than the obviously unverifiable ones died out. For example, years in Cuba did not prevent Governor Diego Velasquez from instructing Cortés to look for men with great flat ears and dogs' faces during his projected expedition to Mexico in 1519. One seventeenth-century historian extolled the bravery of those who crossed the seas and fought monsters. Later in the same century, Pliny's pygmies were reported living in seclusion in mountainous regions of coastal New Spain; and in the Arctic, a tribe of Inuit was said to consist of persons equipped with only one leg and foot, who could truly be called half-men. As late as 1724 Joseph-François Lafitau (1681–1746) included a drawing of an *anecephale* (man with his head in his chest) among illustrations of Amerindians, despite some reservations on the subject. Earlier, another had written that he did not believe there were Amerindians who lived on odors, but such defiance of general belief was rare. Credulity, however, had its limits; some huge bones found in the Dauphiné in 1613 and exhibited in Paris as those of the giant Theutobochus were finally pronounced to be fraudulent, in spite of widespread belief in giants at the time.

Monstrous men receded from the popular imagination as the slow intrusion of other worlds on the European consciousness revealed peoples with cultures diverse enough to satisfy the most developed taste for the bizarre. When Columbus met the Arawak and later the man-eating Carib, he found physical differences to be less than previously imagined, but differences in culture appeared to be much greater. For instance, it was one thing to detect classical affinities in New World nudity, but quite another to accept absence of clothing as a basic condition of everyday life. Spaniards had subdued naked Canary Islanders during the fifteenth century, and varying degrees of nudity had been observed in Africa. Even in Europe, nudity was acceptable under certain circumstances. Indeed, extreme tolerance existed alongside an excessive formalism, in an age when sartorial ostentation was approaching its climax. The much acclaimed pageantry that marked the entry of Henry II into Rouen in 1550 included a tableau featuring fifty naked Brazilians and 150 Norman sailors playing at being Brazilians, all presumably naked (at least, that is how they are depicted in illustrations of the event). The tableau was much praised without reference to the nudity. What particularly surprised Europeans about New World nudity was to see everyone, including those in authority, naked all the time. Columbus, addressed by an eighty-year-old cacique "who seemed respectable enough though he wore no clothes," was surprised when he observed "sound judgment in a man who went naked." Very often, their nudity was the only thing reported of Amerindians, as it was the most obvious characteristic that differentiated them from Europeans.

Cannibalism made an even more profound impact than nudity. The word "cannibal" (cambialle and canibali were among the various spellings) almost immediately became the appellation by which Amerindians were known in Europe. A story that became a favorite toward the end of the sixteenth century told of some Caribs who died as a result of eating a friar; after that, men of the cloth were safe, at least on that island. From the Brazilian coast about Cape Frio, came reports of men who "eate all kinde of people, Frenchmen, Portugals, and Blackamoors." The ritual aspects of cannibalism were missed at first, and it was assumed that the New World men ate each other for food, hunting each other "to eat, like savage beasts." Such a conclusion was perhaps to be expected. In Europe cannibalism was, not infrequently, a result of famine, as indeed it sometimes was in the Americas.

In spite of a general revulsion against cannibalism, and a tendency to look for monsters, the first descriptions of New World men are moderate in tone, although a note of condescension is usually detectable. Even such defenders of Amerindians as Isabella could not resist observing, on being informed by Columbus that the trees of the New World did not have deep roots, "this land where the trees are not firmly rooted, must produce men of little truthfulness and less constance." Many observers, however, seemed to agree with Pigafetta: "They are men and women disposed as we are. Although they eat the flesh of their enemies, it is because of certain customs."

PRIMARY SOURCES

REPRESENTATIONS OF SEVENTEENTH-CENTURY NATIVE AMERICAN VIEWS

Few parts of the Americas used writing at the time of the European entry into the New World, and native writing systems typically were discouraged and nearly eradicated by colonial authorities, who saw them as primitive, diabolical, or potentially seditious. As a result, relatively few accounts of early Native American viewpoints regarding Europeans are known today; those that have been preserved usually were recorded by Europeans and may suffer from mistranslation, confusion, selectivity, and revision. Nonetheless, when examined with care and appropriate source analysis, these accounts provide a window on Native American views regarding Europeans. They reveal a diversity of opinion about European intrusion, religion, and politics.

Response to the French
Anonymous Micmac Elder

Europeans often expected indigenous peoples in their colonies to prefer European culture and lifestyles to their traditional ones, but this often proved not to be the case. This speech made by an anonymous Indian of the Micmac tribe, living on the Gaspé Peninsula of what is now the Canadian province of Quebec, was recorded by Chrestien LeClerq, a Roman Catholic missionary, around 1677. This Micmac elder addressed a gathering of French settlers, asking them to consider whether the French way of life was preferable to that of the Micmac. The elder shows a tolerance of other cultures that was rare among Europeans of that era.

I am greatly astonished that the French have so little cleverness, as they seem to exhibit in the matter of which thou hast just told me on their behalf, in the effort to persuade us to convert our poles, our barks, and our wigwams into those houses of stone and of wood which are tall and lofty, according to their account, as these trees. Very well! But why now, . . . do men of five to six feet in height need houses which are sixty to eighty? For, in fact, as thou knowest very well thyself, Patriarch—do we not find in our own all the conveniences and the advantages that you have with yours, such as reposing, drinking, sleeping, eating, and amusing ourselves with our friends when we wish? This is not all, . . . my brother, hast thou as much ingenuity and cleverness as the Indians, who carry their houses and their wigwams with them so that they may lodge wheresoever they please, independently of any seignior whatsoever? Thou art not as bold nor as stout as we, because when thou goest on a voyage thou canst not carry upon thy shoulders thy buildings and thy edifices. Therefore it is necessary that thou preparest as many lodgings as thou makest changes of residence, or else thou lodgest in a hired house which does not belong to thee. As for us, we find ourselves secure from all these inconveniences, and we can always say, more truly than thou, that we are at home everywhere, because we set up our wigwams with ease wheresoever we go, and without asking permission of anybody. Thou reproachest us, very inappropriately, that our country is a little hell in contrast with France, which thou comparest to a terrestrial paradise, inasmuch as it yields thee, so thou sayest, every kind of provision in abundance. Thou sayest of us also that we are the most miserable and most unhappy of all men, living without religion, without manners, without honour, without social order, and, in a word, without

The World Turned Upside Down: Indian Voices from Early America, ed. Colin C. Calloway (Boston: Bedford Books, 50–52). Originally published as *New Relation of Gaspesia, With the Customs and Religion of the Gaspesian Indians,* ed. and trans. William F. Ganong (Toronto: Champlain Society, 1910), 104–6.

any rules, like the beasts in our woods and our forests, lacking bread, wine, and a thousand other comforts which thou hast in superfluity in Europe. Well, my brother, if thou dost not yet know the real feelings which our Indians have towards thy country and towards all thy nation, it is proper that I inform thee at once. I beg thee now to believe that, all miserable as we seem in thine eyes, we consider ourselves nevertheless much happier than thou in this, that we are very content with the little that we have; and believe also once for all, I pray, that thou deceivest thyself greatly if thou thinkest to persuade us that thy country is better than ours. For if France, as thou sayest, is a little terrestrial paradise, art thou sensible to leave it? And why abandon wives, children, relatives, and friends? Why risk thy life and thy property every year, and why venture thyself with such risk, in any season whatsoever, to the storms and tempests of the sea in order to come to a strange and barbarous country which thou considerest the poorest and least fortunate of the world? Besides, since we are wholly convinced of the contrary, we scarcely take the trouble to go to France, because we fear, with good reason, lest we find little satisfaction there, seeing, in our own experience, that those who are natives thereof leave it every year in order to enrich themselves on our shores. We believe, further, that you are also incomparably poorer than we, and that you are only simple journeymen, valets, servants, and slaves, all masters and grand captains though you may appear, seeing that you glory in our old rags and in our miserable suits of beaver which can no longer be of use to us, and that you find among us, in the fishery for cod which you make in these parts, the wherewithal to comfort your misery and the poverty which oppresses you. As to us, we find all our riches and all our conveniences among ourselves, without trouble and without exposing our lives to the dangers in which you find yourselves constantly through your long voyages. And, whilst feeling compassion for you in the sweetness of our repose, we wonder at the anxieties and cares which you give yourselves night and day in order to load your ship. We see also that all your people live, as a rule, only upon cod which you catch among us. It is everlastingly nothing but cod—cod in the morning, cod at midday, cod at evening, and always cod, until things come to such a pass that if you wish some good morsels, it is at our expense; and you are obliged to have recourse to the Indians, whom you despise so much, and to beg them to go a-hunting that you may be regaled. Now tell me this one little thing, if thou hast any sense: Which of these two is the wisest and happiest—he who labours without ceasing and only obtains, and that with great trouble, enough to live on, or he who rests in comfort and finds all that he needs in the pleasure of hunting and fishing? It is true, . . . that we have not always had the use of bread and of wine which your France produces; but, in fact, before the arrival of the French in these parts, did not the Gaspesians live much longer than now? And if we have not any longer among us any of those old men of a hundred and thirty to forty years, it is only because we are gradually adopting your manner of living, for experience is making it very plain that those of us live longest who, despising your bread, your wine, and your brandy, are content with their natural food of beaver, of moose, of waterfowl, and fish, in accord with the custom of our ancestors and of all the Gaspesian nation. Learn now, my brother, once for all, because I must open to thee my heart: there is no Indian who does not consider himself infinitely more happy and more powerful than the French.

An Indian Dialogue
John Eliot

John Eliot was one of the relatively few Puritan ministers in New England who devoted his efforts to Native Americans. Born in England in 1604, Eliot migrated to the Massachusetts Bay Colony and initially ministered to English Puritans. By 1643 he had learned the Natick dialect of the Algonquian language, and shortly thereafter he founded a mission ("praying town") outside Boston for Indians of the Massachusett tribe. This reading was published in 1671 as part of his Indian Dialogues, *a set of discussions of Christianity as it related to Native Americans. Eliot couched his discussion in the form of a play, and Kinsman, Sontim, Pium, and Pauwau are the characters conversing in this selection. While the dialogue is not a transcription of Massachusett statements (none of which have survived), it nonetheless reflects the variety of attitudes the Native Americans living in Eliot's praying town had toward Christianity.*

KINSMAN: Welcome sontim [friend]. Welcome my friends and kinsmen all. Here is a kinsman and friend of ours come from Natick to visit us. He prayeth for us, and expresseth love to our souls, which you take no thought or care about. He telleth us of light and wisdom which they learn out of the Word of God, which we are strangers unto. He telleth us of hell fire and torments, to be the reward of our sins, which we walk in. He telleth us of repentance for our sins, and of faith to believe in Christ for a pardon, and of salvation in heaven with eternal glory. He telleth us of the danger of living as we do. He telleth us of a better way of living than yet we know. Many such things we have discoursed, which are beyond my understanding. I am well pleased with his love. But I know not what to say to his persuasions, for which cause I have entreated your company, that we may confer together about matters of so great importance, and that we may be mutual helps to each other for our best good.

John Eliot's Indian Dialogues: A Study in Cultural Interaction, ed. Henry W. Bowden and James P. Ronda, Contributions in American History, no. 88 (Westport, Conn.: Greenwood Press, 1980), 85–90. Originally published as *Indian Dialogues for Their Instruction in That Great Service of Christ* (Cambridge, Mass.: N.p., 1671).

SONT: If any man bring us a precious jewel, which will make us rich and happy, everybody will make that man welcome, and if this friend of ours do that, who more welcome? But if by receiving his jewel, we must part with a better jewel for it, then wise men should do well to consider, before they accept his offer. These things you speak of are great things. But if we accept of them, consider what we must part with and forego for ever; viz., all your pleasures and sports, and delights and joys in this world.

ALL: You say true. Ha, ha, he.

PIUM: If foolish youths play in the dirt, and eat dung, and stinking fish and flesh, and rotten corn for company's sake, their sachem makes this law: if you come forth from that filthy place and company, and feed upon this wholesome and good food I have provided, then you shall be honoured and well used all your life time. But if you so love your old company, as that you choose rather to feed on trash, and venture to perish among them, then perish you shall, and thank yourself for your foolish choice. This was our case at first, and is yours to this day. You walk in darkness, defile yourselves with a filthy conversation, you feed your souls with trash and poison, and you choose to do so for your company's sake. Behold, God calls you to come out from among them, and touch no unclean thing, to converse among the wise, and offereth you pardon, life, and salvation in heaven, in glory, among all the elect, saints and angels. Now you are at your choice. Will you forsake those bad courses and companions, and live in glory? Or will you choose your old filthy courses and companions, and perish forever?

SONT: All our forefathers (so far as ever we have heard) have walked and lived as we do, and are we wiser than our fathers?

PIUM: No, we are foolish, weak and sinful and love to be vile. But God is wiser than our fathers, and he hath opened to us this way of wisdom and life, and calleth us to enter, and walk therein. Therefore be wise, and submit your selves to the call of Christ.

SONT: But why do you say that we feed upon trash, stinking meat and poison? Wherein doth our food differ from yours, and wherein do you in that respect excel us?

PIUM: In bodily food we differ not from you. But it is soul food I speak of. We feed our souls with the word of God and prayer. You feed and satiate your souls with lust, lying, stealing, sabbath-breaking, and such like sins. And I appeal to your own conscience, whether these are not trash and filthiness, and what fruit can you expect from such actions, but punishment and wrath?

PAUWAU: Let me add a few words to give check to your high-flown confidence to your new way, and new laws, and to your deep censoriousness of our old ways, the pleasancy and delight whereof everyone, both man, woman, and child, can judge of. And we cannot but dislike to have such pleasant delights taken from us. Tear our hair from our heads, our skin from our flesh, our flesh from our bones, you shall as soon persuade us to suffer you to do by us, as to persuade us to part with our old delights and courses. You tell us of the Englishman's God, and of his laws. We have Gods also, and more than they. And we have laws also by which our forefathers did walk, and why should not we do as they have done? To change our Gods, and laws, and customs, are great things, and not easily to be obtained and accomplished. Let us alone, that we may be quiet in the ways which we like and love, as we let you alone in your changes and new ways.

ALL: You say right. Why trouble they us in our pleasures and delights? Let us alone in our enjoyments.

PIUM: You have spoken many things, which do minister matter to me of much discourse, both concerning God, and our selves, and concerning you, and the offer of God's mercy to you at this time. You say you have many gods, but they are no gods. There is but one God, the great creator of this great world. Did your gods make this world, the heavens, the sun, the moon, the stars, the clouds, the seas, and the whole earth? No, no. God made this whole world. Can any of your gods give rain, or rule the clouds? It is the Devil that blindeth your eyes, and covereth you with darkness. We teach you to know the true God, who can kill us, or keep us alive at his pleasure. Your gods shall all perish with you, for they are no gods.

As for your pleasures and delights, they are all sins against God, which provoke his wrath to plague you forever. We now call you to repent of your evil ways, and to reform your lives to serve the true and living God, to seek for pardon of your sins, and mercy to appease his wrath which is kindled against you. I do now offer you mercy through Jesus Christ. Do not harden your hearts against the Lord. Be therefore persuaded now to forsake your sins and turn unto the Lord. Come unto the light out of your darkness. Awake from your dead sleep, *stand up, and Christ will give you life.* We speak by experience. We were dead and blind as you are. We loved pleasures as you do, but by the grace of Christ we have found light and life, and now call you to partake with us in our mercies.

PAUWAU: We have not only our pleasures, but also prayers and sacrifices. We beat and afflict our selves to pacify our Gods. And when we be sick we use such ways to recover our health, and to obtain all such things as we want, and desire to obtain from our Gods.

PIUM: Your prayers and powwowings are worshipping of the Devil, and not of God, and they are among the greatest of your sins. Your murders, lusts, stealing, lying, etc., they are great sins. Your powwowings are worse sins, because by them you worship the Devil instead of God. When you pauwaus [shamans] use physic by roots, and such other things which God hath made for that purpose, that is no sin. You do well to use physic for your recovery from sickness. But your praying to, and worshipping the Devil, that is your great sin, which now God calls you to forsake. Use only such remedies as God hath appointed, and pray to God. This we call you to do, and this is the way of true wisdom.

KINSMAN: I feel my heart broken and divided. I know not what to do. To part with our former lusts and pleasures is an hard point and I feel my heart very loth and backward to it. Many objections against it. I cannot but confess, that I do not in my inward heart approve of them. I know they are vile and filthy, and I desire to forsake them. They are like burning coals in my bosom. I will shake them out if I can. I am ashamed of my old ways, and loth I am to keep that which I am ashamed to be seen in. The wiser men be, the more they abstain from such lusts, and we account such to be foolish, vile and wicked, that are unbridled and unpersuadable. I would not be myself of the number of them that are vicious and vile above restraint. What I persuade others to leave, I would not do the same myself. We do account it commendable in such as do bridle and restrain themselves from those vices, and what I judge to be commendable in others, would be therein exemplar and a pattern unto such as be young and foolish, and run mad after such beastly courses. In that point I would easily be persuaded, or at least I desire so to be. But the greatest difficulty that I yet find, is this. I am loth to divide myself from my friends and kindred. If I should change my course and not they, then I must leave and forsake their company, which I am very loth to do. I love my sachem, and all the rest of you my good friends. If I should change my life and way, I greatly desire that we might agree to do it together.

SONT: I like well that we should agree upon some amendment of some bad courses that are too oft among us. And I love your love that would have us agree together, and do what we do, in these great matters, by common consent. But to do that is a matter of much discourse, and deep consideration. This meeting was sudden. We have other matters at present to attend. We have been together long enough for this time. We must leave the whole matter to some other time.

PIUM: Two days hence is the sabbath day. God hath commanded all men to *remember the sabbath day to keep it holy.* I request all of you to come together that day, and then I will further teach you (by the assistance of the Lord) touching this matter. And to persuade you to make this beginning to keep the sabbath, besides the commandment of the Lord, we have the reasons annexed by God himself unto it. God himself *rested that day,* to set us an heavenly pattern, and God hath also *blessed that day,* and made it holy, and hath promised that when we shall *meet together in his name, there he will come among us, and bring a blessing with him.* And when the disciples of Christ were met to worship God upon that day, before the day was done, he came among them and blessed them. So if you come together on the sabbath day, my hope and trust is, that we shall find some special token of the presence of Christ Jesus among us.

KINSMAN: I do very well like of this motion, and shall willingly attend. And if you think good, let my house be the place, or if you our beloved sachem think good, we will all come together at your house.

SONT: I like it well. Let it be so. Come to my house, and you shall be welcome.

ALL: Content, we like it well. So let it be.

PIUM: Let the time of meeting be as early as you well can, about nine of the clock.

ALL: So let it be.

THREE DOCUMENTS SHOWING DIFFERENT COLONIAL AGENDAS

European countries differed in the ways they expected to profit from colonies. The English, for example, were interested in establishing new lands where they could reproduce English life through farming and similar occupations. Reduced to a simple generalization, the French were interested in establishing sources of raw materials, especially furs, but they also had an interest in establishing colonies in order to transplant the French way of life. The Spanish, in contrast, were initially more interested in discovering sources of gold and other precious materials to take back to Spain. These colonial agendas, of course, were more complex than the thumbnail characterizations presented here. They are discussed in greater detail in Chapter 24 of *The Global Past.*

The following three documents describe lands newly discovered by European explorers, and they offer telling information about national interests. The focus of each reading is shaped by the concerns of the writer, and they demonstrate nicely the interests of the colonial powers involved.

Description of Puerto Rico
Samuel de Champlain

While best known for his voyages of discovery in northeastern North America, Samuel de Champlain made earlier voyages to the Caribbean. French by birth and sailing under the French flag, he explored this region between 1599 and 1602, and he wrote an early description of Puerto Rico, reproduced here. One of the larger islands in the Caribbean, Puerto Rico was valued highly by all European colonial powers. As a colony of Spain, Puerto Rico had been unsuccessfully invaded by England twice by the time Champlain visited there. While France made no attempt to seize this island, Champlain's description reveals that it possessed many of the qualities that the French sought in their colonies.

The said Island of Porto-rico is pretty agreeable, although it is a little mountainous. It is filled with quantities of fine trees, such as cedars, palms, firs, palmettoes, and another kind of tree which is called sombrade,[1] from which, as it grows, the tops of its branches, falling to the earth, take root immediately, and produce other branches which fall and take root in the same way. And I have seen these trees of such extent that they covered more than a league and a quarter. It bears no fruit, but is very agreeable, having a leaf like that of a laurel and a little more tender.

There are also, in the said island, quantities of good fruits, such as plantes,[2] oranges,[3] lemons of strange size, ground gourds, which are very good, algarobes,[4] pappittes,[5] and a fruit named coraçon, because it is in the form of a heart, of the size of the fist, and of a yellow and red colour; the skin very delicate, and when it is pressed, it gives out an odoriferous humour; and that which is good in this fruit is like thick milk, and has a taste like sugared cream.

There are many other fruits which are not much esteemed, although they are good; there is also a root called "cassave"[6] which the Indians eat instead of bread.

1. Sombrade—from "sombra," Span.—leafy shade. "Ficus americana maxima," the "Clusea rosea" of St. Domingo, or "Figuier maudit marron."

2. Plantes—"Plantano" of the Spaniards, a species of banana, called in the Canaries "plantano."

3. Oranges—oranges and other citrus are Old World plants. If Champlain's identification is accurate, they must have been brought to Puerto Rico by the Spanish.

4. Algarobe—probably the mesquite or some other pod-bearing tree.

5. Pappette—the papaya tree.

6. Cassave—cassava, also known as manioc or yuca.

Samuel de Champlain, *Voyage to West Indies and Mexico*, trans. Alice Winmere, ed. by Norton Shaw ([London]: Hakluyt Society, n.d.; reprint, New York: Burt Shaw, 1964), 10–12.

There grows neither corn nor wine in all this island. In it there are a great quantity of cameleons which, it is said, live on air; this I cannot assure although I have seen them many times. It has the head rather pointed, the body somewhat long for its size, that is to say, of one foot and a half, and has only two legs, which are in front; the tail very pointed, the colours mingled grey and yellowish.

The best merchandise in the island is sugar, ginger, canifiste, honey of canes, tobacco, quantity of hides of oxen, cows, and sheep. The air is very hot, and there are little birds which resemble parrots, called perriquitos, of the size of a sparrow, with a round tail, and which are taught to speak: there are a great number in that isle.

The said island is about seventy leagues in length and forty in breadth, surrounded by good ports and havens, and lies east and west.

Our Entrance into the Country
Alvar Nuñez Cabeza de Vaca

Alvar Nuñez Cabeza de Vaca was a petty Spanish noble who explored parts of North America, Central America, and South America for Spain. His North American exploration, beginning in 1527 and ending eleven years later, is one of the great adventure stories of his era. Starting in Florida, his party was around 600 men. By the end of the trek, the party had passed through the entirety of what is now the southern tier of the United States and southward into western Mexico, and had dwindled to only four survivors. In the interim, Cabeza de Vaca visited and lived among dozens of Indian tribes. This description is from relatively early in his trek, and it describes his entry into the Coosa region (see "Archaeological Evidence of the Coosa Reaction to European Contact") of what is now central Alabama.

The day following [18 April 1528], the Governor resolved to make an incursion to explore the land, and see what it might contain. With him went the Commissary, the Assessor, and myself with forty men, among them six cavalry, of which we could make little use. We took our way towards the north, until the hour of vespers, when we arrived at a very large bay that appeared to stretch far inland. We remained there that night, and the next day we returned to the place where were our ships and people. The Governor ordered that the brigantine should sail along the coast of Florida and search for the harbor that Miruelo, the pilot, said he knew, (though as yet he had failed to find it, and could not tell in

Relation of Alvar Nuñez Cabeza de Vaca, trans. Buckingham Smith (New York: N.p.); Ann Arbor, Mich.: University Microfilms, 1986), 23–25. Originally published in 1542.

what place we were, or where was the port), and that if it were not found, she should steer for Havana and seek the ship of which Alvaro de la Cerda was in command, and, taking provisions, together, they should come to look for us.

After the brigantine left, the same party, with some persons more, returned to enter the land. We kept along the shores of the bay we had found, and, having gone four leagues [about eight miles], we captured four Indians. We showed them maize, to see if they had knowledge of it, for up to that time we had seen no indication of any. They said they could take us where there was some; so they brought us to their town near by, at the head of the bay, and showed us a little corn not yet fit for gathering.

There we saw many cases, such as are used to contain the merchandise of Castilla, in each of them a dead man, and the bodies were covered with painted deer skins. This appeared to the Commissary to be a kind of idolatry, and he burned the cases with the bodies. We also found pieces of linen and of woolen cloth, and bunches of feathers which appeared like those of New Spain [Mexico]. There were likewise traces of gold. Having by signs asked the Indians whence these things came, they motioned to us that very far from there, was a province called Apalachen, where was much gold, and so the same abundance in Palachen [an Indian town visited earlier in the trip] of every thing that we at all cared for.

Taking these Indians for guides, we departed, and traveling ten or twelve leagues we came to a town of fifteen houses. Here a large piece of ground was cultivated in maize then ripe, and we likewise found some already dry. After staying there two days, we returned to where the Comptroller tarried with the men and ships, and related to him and the pilots what we had seen, and the information the natives had given.

The Relation of the Course of the Sunshine
John Davis

Though his name is not widely known outside of the circle of specialists in the history of exploration, John Davis was one of England's foremost navigators of the sixteenth century, voyaging to China, the Arctic, and the Indian Ocean, among other places. His most significant explorations, however, lay in his attempts to find a Northwest Passage that would allow a ship to get from Europe to Asia by sailing around the northern extremity of North America. The account reproduced here is taken from his report of his second voyage seeking the Northwest Passage, published in 1589. The report describes Iceland, which he quaintly spells "Island"; it reflects English concerns in terms of exploiting newly found lands.

The Voyages and Works of John Davis, the Navigator, ed. Albert Hastings Markham ([London]: Hakluyt Society, 1589; reprint, New York: Burt Franklin, n.d.), 33–35.

The relation of the course which the Sunshine, *a barke of fiftie tunnes, and the* Northstarre, *a small pinnesse, being two vessels of the fleet of M. John Davis, held after he had sent them from him, to discover the passage betweene Groenland and Island.*

Written by Henry Morgan, servant to M. William Sanderson of London.

The seventh day of May 1586, we departed out of Dartmouth haven, foure sailes, to wit, the *Mermaid,* the *Sunshine,* the *Mooneshine,* and the *Northstarre.* In the *Sunshine* were sixteene men, whose names were these: Richard Pope, maister; Marke Carter, maisters mate; Henry Morgan, purser; George Draward, John Mandie, Hugh Broken, Philip Jane, Hugh Hempson, Richard Borden, John Filpe, Andrew Madocke, William Wolcome, Robert Wagge (carpenter), John Bruskome, William Ashe, Simon Ellis.

Our course was West northwest, the seventh and eight dayes: and the ninth day in the morning we were on head of the Tarrose of Syllie [the Isles of Scilly, off the southwestern coast of England]. Thus coasting along the South part of Ireland the 11 day, we were on head of the Dorses [Dursey Island, on the Southwestern coast of Ireland]: and our course was South southwest untill six of the clocke the 12 day. The 13 day our course was Northwest. We remained in the company of the *Mermaid* and the *Mooneshine,* untill we came to the latitude of 60 degrees: and there it seemed best to our Generall, M. Davis, to divide his fleet, himselfe sailing to the Northwest and to direct the *Sunshine,* wherein I was, and the pinnesse called the *Northstar,* to seeke a passage Northward betweene Groenland and Island [Greenland and Iceland], to the latitude of 80 degrees, if land did not let us. So the seventh day of June we departed from them: and the ninth of the same we came to a firme land of ice, which we coasted along the ninth, the tenth, and the eleventh dayes of June: and the eleventh day, at six of the clocke at night, we saw land, which was very high, which afterward we knew to be Island: and the twelft day we harbored there, and found many people: the land lyeth East and by North in 66 degrees.

Theyr commodities were greene fish, and Island lings, and stockfish, and a fish which is called catefish: of all which they had great store. They had also kine [cattle], sheepe, and horses, and hay for theyr cattell and for theyr horses. We saw also of theyr dogges. Theyr dwelling houses were made on both sides with stones, and wood laid crosse over them, which was covered over with turfs of earth, and they are flat on the toppes, and many of these stood hard by the shoare. Theyr boats were made with wood, and iron all along the keele like our English boats: and they had nailes for to naile them withall, and fish hooks, and other things for to ketch fish, as we have heere in England.

They had also brasen kettles, and girdles and purses made of leather, and knoppes on them of copper, and hatchets, and other small tooles, as necessarie as we have. They dry theyr fish in the Sun, and when they are dry, they packe them up in the toppe of their houses. If we would go thither to fishing more then we do, we should make it a very good voyage: for we got an hundreth greene fish in one morning. We found heere two English men with a shippe, which came out of England about Easter day of this present yeere 1586, and one of them came aboord of us, and brought us two lambs. The English mans name was M. John Royden of Ipswich, merchant: he was bound for London with his shippe. And this is the summe of that which I observed in Island.

QUESTIONS TO CONSIDER

1. What were some of the ways Old World religions were spread to the New World?

2. What were some of the effects of European contact on Native Americans?

3. How did European attitudes affect their perceptions of Native Americans in the period of early contact?

4. How did Native American attitudes affect their perceptions of Europeans in the period of early contact?

5. How did the colonial agendas of European colonial powers differ?

6. What kind of criticism could be made of John Eliot's Indian dialogue using source analysis? That is, what factors might affect our evaluation of whether the ideas he attributes to Indians actually were held by them?

EUROPE'S GLOBAL REACH

INTRODUCTION

The expansion of Europe's political, social, and cultural influence to the rest of the globe is a major theme of the Early Modern and Modern eras. One consequence of European expansion was the development of new ways of looking at the world. Additionally, revolutions in Europe and the Americas inspired people in the rest of the world to throw off the yoke of colonialism and imperialism. Some revolutionary ideas also emanated from the new scientific discoveries made by Westerners, beginning in the sixteenth century. Because scientific knowledge reached parts of the globe much later in the Modern period, in Part 7 we will focus on the spread of political ideas.

New ways of looking at the world promoted revolutionary perspectives and activities. During the scientific revolution, the sixteenth-century Polish astronomer Nicholas Copernicus argued that the earth was not the center of the universe. The scientists who followed him confirmed that the universe was much more complex than previously conceived by intellectuals, including Copernicus. Nevertheless, the impetus to think anew and to shift the geocentric focus of most Western scientists came from this Polish astronomer.

Out of these scientific explorations came an increased confidence in human powers of observation and reasoning. Philosophers and other thinkers employed rational thought to criticize existing political and social systems, especially in the eighteenth century. Intellectuals promoting this approach named their movement the Enlightenment. They used concepts of natural law to develop a system of thought asserting that human beings possessed certain natural rights.

Certain political leaders employed the idea of natural rights to buttress their independence movements. From the eighteenth through the mid-twentieth centuries, declarations of independence were debated and enacted around the world. Other declarations focused on the rights of man, woman, and the citizen. Ideas that originated with the American Declaration of Independence influenced Europeans, whose ideas in turn inspired Asians and other peoples.

New ways of looking at the world were also developed from the ideas of Charles Darwin. Darwin conducted a series of scientific investigations and formulated a theory of evolution by natural selection. This theory fundamentally changed the way most people thought about the origin of human beings. Social Darwinists, people who extended Darwin's ideas to society, focused on the process of natural selection and developed ideas such as survival of the fittest to argue for the inherent superiority and domination of one social group by another. Such arguments, for example, were employed by imperialists to justify their domination of subject peoples.

Nationalism, the emphasis on national identity above all else, was used along with social Darwinism to support the control of one people by another. Nationalism also offered political leaders an ideological and emotional glue to hold together people who otherwise might drift apart.

As governments used nationalism to hold countries together, so they employed other means of holding empires together. Beginning in the nineteenth century, industrialization provided the means to establish bigger and more efficient empires over far-flung areas. Using social Darwinist and racist ideas, imperialists developed rationales for their subjugation of others. Indigenous peoples, however, not only resisted such domination but also justified their resistance by using ideas from the Enlightenment. Vietnamese nationalists, for example, drafted a declaration of independence, calling for their liberation from French rule. That document, written in 1945, did not become fully realized until 1975. Thus, Europe's global reach provided the means to establish and overthrow its own global empires.

SCHOLARLY WORK

The Greatest Revolution
Richard Leakey and Roger Lewin

In this selection written in 1977, an anthropologist and a science writer discuss two of the most revolutionary perspectives coming from science in the last few centuries: Nicholas Copernicus's realization that the earth was not at the center of the universe and Charles Darwin's theory of evolution. Leakey and Lewin spend most of their essay discussing Charles Darwin and the theory he developed. The concept of evolution by means of natural selection transformed the ways people thought about their origins. Darwin used evidence gathered from a long ocean voyage and scientific

Richard Leakey and Roger Lewin, *Origins* (New York: E. P. Dutton, 1977), 21–33.

expedition to formulate his controversial theory. This new way of viewing the origins and development of life is still held in high scientific regard.

On hearing, one June afternoon in 1860, the suggestion that mankind was descended from the apes, the wife of the Bishop of Worcester is said to have exclaimed, "My dear, descended from the apes! Let us hope it is not true, but if it is, let us pray that it will not become generally known." As it turns out, she need not have been quite so worried: we are *not* descended from the apes, though we do share a common ancestor with them. Even though the distinction may have been too subtle to offer her much comfort, it is nevertheless important.

The question, indeed, was no less than the second of two major intellectual revolutions through which humanity has had to come to terms with its place in the natural world. The first occurred more than four hundred years ago, when the Polish mathematician Nicolaus Copernicus shattered the notion that the earth is the center of the universe. The second began to erupt when Charles Darwin showed that mankind was part of nature rather than apart from it.

Goethe once declared that of all the discoveries and opinions proclaimed, surely nothing has made such a deep impression on the human mind as the science of Copernicus. Although one would be hard put to choose between the two discoveries, it would have been interesting to hear Goethe's opinion had he lived to witness the impact of the Darwinian revolution. Certainly the science based on Darwin's notion of a steady progression of more and more complex organisms as a result of natural selection has a legitimate claim to being the greatest intellectual and philosophical revolution in human history.

For almost two millennia the Judeo-Christian story of the Creation was taken for granted throughout the Western world. With no good reason to doubt it, the teaching of the increasingly powerful Christian churches that God created man in his own image was a comfortable one. There was a certain curiosity, though, about just when this miraculous event had occurred. James Ussher (1581–1656), Archbishop of Armagh, came up with an answer in 1650, when he announced, as a result of his calculations based on the numerology of the Old Testament, that the Creation had taken place in 4004 B.C. Ussher's calculations were later given even greater precision by Dr. John Lightfoot, Master of St. Catherine's College, Cambridge, England, who declared the precise day to be 23 October, and the time exactly nine o'clock in the morning. Along with an impressive though dubious chronology, Lightfoot's dating showed a tender concern for himself and his colleagues, as it coincided with the beginning of the academic year!

The Ussher/Lightfoot calculation thus gave the earth a past of a modest six thousand years. Although the extraordinary longevity of many of the Old Testament characters ought to have presented a few problems if it had been seriously contemplated, the six thousand-year period was generally accepted until evidence to the contrary started to turn up. Amateur geologists, many of whom were also clergymen, began to be puzzled by the stratified nature of many rocks, implying a process of formation that was believed not to be operating in contemporary times, but which was somewhat difficult to reconcile with received accounts of the Creation. And, to make matters worse, there were fossils too, and these were clearly the remains of animals no longer in existence.

During the eighteenth century, as evidence of this kind became overwhelming, an explanation was sought that would still be consonant with the teachings of the Bible. The result was the Diluvial Theory, which accounted for fossils by stating that they were the remains of animals which had perished in the Noachian Flood.

Soon, however, the Diluvial Theory came under pressure, as it became clear that a single event like the Flood could not explain the apparent progression of fossils in different layers of rocks, those of each layer more primitive than in the one above it. The final blow came with the discovery of "pre-Flood" fossils that were clearly related to animals living after the Deluge.

Meanwhile, the view of human origins remained essentially the same as had been laid down in the Old Testament: that humanity had appeared all at once, in the fully modern shape of Adam and Eve. As the steady trickle of ancient stone and flint tools, at first discounted as works of nature or as thunderbolts, went on being unearthed, questions began to stir in some enlightened minds. The first recorded suggestion of a great antiquity for man came in 1797, when John Frere in a paper delivered to the Royal Society in London described flint tools discovered under twelve feet of earth at Hoxne, near Diss in Suffolk. Frere, who, incidentally, was Mary Leakey's great great great grandfather, opined that the tools "were fabricated and used by a people who had not the use of metals. . . . The situation [depth] at which these weapons were found may tempt us to refer them to a very remote period indeed, even beyond that of the present world." Frere's insight — and courage — apparently went unheeded, until the mid-nineteenth century, when it was adduced to demonstrate Britain's accomplishments in archeology!

Meanwhile, orthodox Christianity [Christian denominations believing that the earth was created in 4004 B.C.] was saved from the embarrassing inadequacies of the Diluvial Theory by the French geologist, naturalist, and member of the Académie des Sciences, Baron Georges Cuvier (1769–1832). To explain the progressive sequences of fossils found in rock sediments, Cuvier proposed a series of catastrophes, each of which had totally wiped out animal and plant populations (thus producing the fossils), followed by a period of calm during which God restocked the earth with new (and improved) species. The Noachian Flood was just one of these.

The Catastrophe Theory was a great balm to many troubled minds. Adam Sedgwick, a geologist at Cambridge University and a teacher of Charles Darwin, expounded the theory thus: "At succeeding periods new tribes of beings were called into existence, not merely as progeny of those that had appeared before them, but as new and living proof of creative interference; and though formed on the same plan, and bearing the same marks of wise contrivance, oftentimes unlike those creatures which preceded them, as if they had been matured in a different portion of the universe and cast upon the earth by the collision of another planet."

In formulating the Catastrophe Theory, Cuvier routinely took for granted an extreme rapidity of changes in times past as compared with the present, but conceded that perhaps a little more than six thousand years was required. So, following the example of his countryman, Comte Georges de Buffon (1707–1778), he added eighty thousand years on to the age of the earth. According to calculations of members of the Académie, made after Cuvier's death, there had been twenty-seven successive acts of creation, the products of each but the last being obliterated in subsequent catastrophes, thus providing a geological "clock." An Englishman, William Smith (1769–1839), raised the number of strata to thirty-two.

It is evident that a major problem throughout this period of debate concerning the origin of fossils was that of attributing a correct age to the earth and the strata from which fossils were retrieved. The first real pioneer in the effort to solve the problem was a Scotsman, James Hutton (1726–1797), who concluded from a study of the available geological evidence that the forces that had shaped the world in the past, built mountains and created continents, were still at work in the modern world. He saw the life of the earth as a continuum, rather than as a past and a present neatly divided by a line that marked the creation of man by God. Hutton, though not the first to suspect that the world was far more ancient than had been generally supposed, was the first writer to set forth a coherent argument for such a view—his *Theory of the Earth*. Published in 1795, when it was met with scorn and ridicule, it proposed a thesis that came to be known as Uniformitarianism. Hutton died just two years later, in 1797—a year that saw the birth, to well-to-do parents in Scotland, of Charles Lyell. And it was Lyell who revived and established Uniformitarianism as a theory without which the achievement of Charles Darwin would have been impossible.

In 1830 Lyell published the first volume of his monumental *Principles of Geology* and thus became the father of modern geology. In part his work was one of synthesis, documenting in meticulous detail the evidence leading to the inescapable conclusion that *Homo sapiens* inhabited a planet of great antiquity.

The message of his *Principles* was not received without opposition, however. Adam Sedgwick in England, and Cuvier in France, as convinced Catastrophists, aligned themselves against it. Meanwhile, ironically, some of the most impressive evidence supporting the antiquity of mankind was being unearthed at Abbeville, in the northwest of France. There, Jacques Boucher de Crèvecœur de Perthes was excavating stone implements together with the fossilized bones of extinct animals, a contemporaneity which any theory involving the Deluge could not explain.

In the intellectual schism that opened during the eighteenth century between the Creationists and those who believed in some kind of evolution, Erasmus Darwin (1731–1802), Charles's grandfather, was a pioneer and principal spokesman on the side of the evolutionists. Physician, philosopher, poet, and celebrated personality, in his writings between 1784 and 1802 Erasmus Darwin posed two questions: first, whether all living creatures are ultimately descended from a single common ancestor; and second, how species could be transformed. To answer the first question he assembled evidence from embryology, comparative anatomy, systematics, and geographical distribution, assimilating the fossil data on the way, for a single source of all life, "one living filament," an evolving web of life that included mankind. This after all was in keeping with the eighteenth-century classification of all animals and plants into families, genera and species by the Swedish botanist Carolus Linnaeus (1707–1778), who classed *Homo sapiens* as a close relative of the Old World monkeys and the apes — although scientists and theologians alike had exerted great efforts to extricate mankind from this unseemly association!

The second question — concerning the forces through which evolution is achieved — was trickier to deal with. It is, however, fair to say that Erasmus Darwin's treatment of the problem contained at least the seeds of almost all the important principles of evolutionary theory. He saw that competition and selection were possible agents of change; that overpopulation was an important factor in sharpening competition; that plants should not be left out of evolutionary theory; that competition between males for females has important structural implications in their evolution; and that fertility and susceptibility to disease were areas of selection. He did not state definitively, however, that the principal agent of evolution is passive adaptation through natural selection, but seemed to admit the possibility that animals may evolve through active adaptation to their environment, including the inheritance of acquired characteristics.

It remained for Jean Baptiste de Lamarck (1744–1829) to take up Erasmus Darwin's mention of inheritance of acquired characteristics and expand it into a fully-fledged theory of evolution. In the process, Lamarck unwittingly exposed the absurdity of supposing that the giraffe's long neck, for example, was simply the result of generations of neck stretching, with the result that Lamarckism, as his theory was dubbed, brought the

entire cause of evolution into some disrepute. In 1813, three men—
William C. Wells (an expatriate American), James C. Pritchard, and
William Lawrence—presented independent rebuttals of Lamarckism to
the Royal Society in London. All three of these papers upheld the view
of natural selection foreshadowed by Erasmus Darwin, as the engine of
evolution. According to Pritchard, "All acquired conditions of the body
end with the life of the individual in whom they are produced." But for
this salutary law the universe would be filled with monstrous shapes.

Inevitably, these propositions were soon the target of sharp attack,
particularly from the Church and associated establishments. Nevertheless, the papers of Wells, Pritchard, and Lawrence were read with great
interest by contemporary naturalists, and Charles Darwin himself must
later have been aware of them. Meanwhile, Charles Naudin, a Frenchman,
had been impressed with the structural changes that could be induced
in domesticated crops and animals through selective breeding, and reasoned that perhaps a similar process might be operating in nature, but
passively.

Yet another of Charles Darwin's intellectual antecedents was Edward
Blyth, who as a young man had been much impressed by Lyell's ideas. In
1835 and 1837 he contributed articles to the *Magazine of Natural History,*
a magazine with which Darwin was familiar. "Among animals which produce their food by means of their agility, strength or delicacy of sense,"
Blyth wrote, "the one best organized must always obtain the greatest
quantity; and must, therefore, become physically the strongest and be
thus enabled, by routing its opponents, to transmit its superior qualities
to a greater number of its offspring."

Such ideas, with the principles of Lyell in the background, came to
the very edge of Darwinism. But it remained for the man himself to assemble all the data and to construct an unassailable theory. For Charles
Darwin, like Lyell, was an effective synthesizer of existing information;
his theory was not entirely new, but he presented it to the world at a time
when the intellectual climate was at its most favorable. Moreover, Darwin
collected a vast amount of data of his own to buttress the theory against
the inevitably skeptical reception.

Charles Darwin was born in 1809 in the pleasant English country
town of Shrewsbury. His father, Robert Waring Darwin, was a medical
doctor and a devoutly religious man. Not unnaturally Charles was steered
towards the medical profession, and he went to Edinburgh University to
read medicine. Soon, however, he realized that the profession was not
for him, and so—again guided by his father's influence—he went to
Cambridge to read divinity. As Charles remarked of his father, "He was
very properly vehement against my turning into an idle sporting man."

At Cambridge, as at Edinburgh, Charles was no academic prodigy.
Along with his interest in such "idle sports" as shooting, he had a passion

for natural history. At both universities his friends were mainly botanists and geologists — among them Adam Sedgwick and the botanist J. S. Henslow, a professor at Cambridge.

It was Henslow who later was responsible for obtaining for Darwin a post on H.M.S. *Beagle,* the ship aboard which Darwin was to amass the evidence that would form the bedrock of his theory. When Charles's father heard of the expedition, he at first forbade his son to join it, but relented following the intervention of Charles's uncle, Josiah Wedgwood. So, two days after Christmas in 1831 Charles Darwin, equipped with a Cambridge degree in theology, Euclid and the classics, but with no qualifications in science, set out as naturalist on the *Beagle* on a five-year voyage around the world. Darwin was following the tradition of the gifted amateur, learning his skills from professionals around him. Thus, equipped with what his uncle Josiah called "an enlarged curiosity," this quiet, reticent man set out on the voyage that was to launch possibly the greatest revolution in humanity's concept of itself.

The journey took Darwin first to South America, where he visited many places along the coast, then via the Galapagos Islands to New Zealand and Australia, and home again, calling in at South African ports on the way. The *Beagle* arrived back at Falmouth, England on 2 October 1836. Throughout the voyage, Darwin went through periods of illness, including two weeks of seasickness at the beginning. But wherever the ship halted, Darwin collected samples in profusion: rocks and fossils, birds, insects, and bigger animals too, putting his skills as a taxidermist to good effect.

For Darwin, probably the most significant part of the entire voyage, and arguably even of his whole life, was the four weeks he spent exploring the Galapagos Islands, a lonely Pacific archipelago several hundred miles due west of Ecuador. There he noticed that each island appeared to have its own type of finch. More than that, different ecological niches on a single island were often inhabited by different finches. And yet they clearly all came from a common stock. Specimens of each were added to his collection, which by the time of his return to England was the most comprehensive ever collected by one man.

What he had seen on his long voyage had convinced Darwin that species were not immutable, that they were capable of transformation. The question that remained was — how? Meanwhile, he had a prodigious amount of work to do, and set about it with enthusiasm. Within six months of his return he had sorted out his specimens with the help of Sir Richard Owen, who was known as the British Cuvier, and had had them described by appropriate experts for the official *Zoology of the Voyage of the Beagle,* which was under Darwin's general editorship. He also wrote his own fascinating general account of the voyage, the classic *Journal of Researches.* There followed three more books, *The Structure and Distribution of Coral Reefs* (1842), *Volcanic Islands* (1844), and *Geological Ob-*

servations of South America (1846). His published output on these topics is in marked contrast to his reluctance to broach on paper the subject of evolution. Some of that reluctance may be traced to a blunder he made while he was secretary of the Geological Society (1838–1841). A set of mysterious rock formations at Glenroy, Scotland, which Darwin identified as ancient marine beaches cut off from the sea by subsidence, turned out to have been carved by glaciers. The mistake had wounded Darwin's pride. He was not going to be wrong in print again.

Within fifteen months of beginning to set down notes for *The Transmutation of Species* in 1837, he was more than ever convinced that species did change, and he now believed that selection was the key. He had seen how selective breeding with crops and stock brought about basic changes in the organisms; but, as he put it, "How selection could be applied to organisms living in a state of nature remained for some time a mystery to me." A flash of insight that was to illuminate the whole problem for him came on 3 October 1838, while he was reading "for amusement" the book on population by Thomas Malthus (1766–1834), asserting that populations tend to increase geometrically unless constrained. Here, it came to him, was the answer: changes that favored an individual would allow it to prosper as compared with others not possessing these new properties; populations of animals with such advantageous mutations thrived, while those with less advantageous traits declined.

It was not until 1842 that Darwin allowed himself "the satisfaction of writing a very brief abstract" (it was thirty-five pages long) of his theory. A more extended version, amounting to some 230 pages, followed two years later. Then, in 1846, Darwin turned away from the theory of evolution and devoted himself to a study of barnacles, the product of which was four monographs.

Midway through 1856, urged on by his friends Charles Lyell and Joseph Hooker. Darwin began his magnum opus, to be entitled simply *Natural Selection.* Two years later Darwin had completed ten chapters and was well into the eleventh, on the subject of pigeons. But on 8 June 1858 he received a letter that shattered his plans. It was from the naturalist-explorer Alfred Russel Wallace, who knew of Darwin's interest in evolution. In February of that same year, during an expedition to the island of Ternate in the Moluccas, between New Guinea and Borneo, Wallace had been in bed with a fever. As he lay there, tossing and restless, he had been thinking about the problem of *how* species might be transmuted. He too had read Malthus, and he now experienced a sudden flash of insight sparked by that same theory. This was the news conveyed by the short note that arrived on Darwin's desk some four months later. Accompanying it was a twelve-page summary of Wallace's ideas on evolution. They paralleled Darwin's exactly. The fears that Lyell and Hooker had expressed two years earlier, that someone else would arrive at the theory of natural selection before Darwin published his, had now been realized.

Darwin, aghast, turned to his friends for advice. They suggested a joint presentation on the subject to the Linnaean Society. Wallace agreed, and just over a month later this is precisely what they did. Curiously, the short papers they produced ignited no controversy. The world seemed not to notice. But because of Wallace's parallel experience, Darwin was now forced to produce the long-delayed book. He did so within fifteen months. A mere pamphlet as compared with the mammoth work he had planned, *On the Origin of Species by Means of Natural Selection* ran to 502 pages. It was published on 24 November 1859. The first printing, 1,250 copies, sold out the same day.

What Darwin had accomplished was to demonstrate how, through an exceedingly gradual (passive) adaptation to the environment and through changes from generation to generation, a species may diversify or simply become better attuned to its world, producing, ultimately, a creature which is different in form from its ancestor. Thus, as the ages passed some species would remain the same while still others would emerge; and the arbiter for their survival or extinction Darwin called natural selection. Those creatures best fitted to their environment in competition with others survived, while others did not. The picture was one of a steady progression of biological complexity, the most sophisticated product of which is *Homo sapiens.* Such, at any rate, was the inescapable conclusion, though Darwin confined himself to the modest comment that "much light will be thrown on the origin of Man and his history." But he must have known that his book would meet a stormy reception, and it did. Charles Lyell and Joseph Hooker were, of course, behind Darwin, and so was Thomas Henry Huxley — the best geologist, the best botanist, and the best zoologist in Britain. But there were hostile reactions from Philip Gosse, the devoutly religious father of the novelist Edmund Gosse, from Adam Sedgwick, and from Sir Richard Owen. And so the debate began.

Before publication Darwin had written to Wallace, "I think I shall avoid the whole subject [of the origin of Man], as so surrounded by prejudices, though I fully admit that it is the highest and most interesting problem for the naturalist." In contrast with the energetic young man who had returned from the voyage of the *Beagle,* the Darwin of 1859 suffered from chronic lassitude and avoided social contact whenever he could. His condition has been described by some as the result of Chagas' disease, a parasitic ailment which he may have contracted during the voyage, and by others as a psychoneurotic device permitting him to retreat from society and concentrate on his work. At any rate, it was more than six months before the crucial confrontation between Evolutionists and Creationists took place. The occasion was the annual meeting of the British Association for the Advancement of Science, held in Oxford. Darwin was absent. The protagonists in the famous debate of 1860 were Bishop Samuel Wilberforce (who was a mouthpiece for Richard Owen) and Thomas Huxley. The verbal battle between the two followed the presentation of a paper by a Dr. Draper, an American, on "Intellectual Development, Considered with Reference to the Views of Mr. Darwin." In the lecture hall, crowded with some seven hundred students, the atmosphere was tense. The audience must have sensed that a watershed between the age of Creationism and the age of Evolutionism had been reached.

Wilberforce, an outstanding orator, now rose and began an eloquent attack on Darwin's thesis. He had been thoroughly primed by Owen. But in the end, his eagerness to score a point was his undoing. Turning to Huxley, he asked with barbed sarcasm. "And you, sir, are you related to the ape on your grandfather's or your grandmother's side?" At this Huxley murmured to himself, "The Lord hath delivered him into mine hands." He then rose, brilliantly expounded the scientific questions at issue, and only then returned to Wilberforce's clever gibe. "A man has no reason," he said, "to be ashamed of having an ape for a grandfather or a grandmother. If I had the choice of an ancestor, whether it should be an ape, or one who having scholastic education should use his logic to mislead an untutored public, and should treat not with argument but with ridicule the facts and reasoning adduced in support of a grave and serious philosophical question, I would not hesitate for a moment to prefer the ape." Gales of laughter greeted this riposte, and the humiliated Wilberforce had to concede defeat.

Evolution had won, at least for the moment. For the first time in history it was possible to discuss the animal origin of *Homo sapiens* and its implication for human communities in an atmosphere that was not predominantly hostile.

PRIMARY SOURCES

NATURAL AND SOCIAL SCIENCES

Astronomy was one of the pathbreaking sciences in the sixteenth and seventeenth centuries. Astronomers changed the way human beings thought about the universe and themselves, and they offered a view of a cosmos run by universal laws, such as gravitation. The new scientific method became a tool to discover new knowledge, and by the nineteenth century biologists were presenting new ways of seeing how human beings evolved from earlier hominids, once again altering fundamental perceptions long held by humanity. By the end of the century, psychology developed into a discipline dedicated to unraveling the mysteries of the human mind. The following selections present these ideas in the words of those who participated in — even instigated — their discovery: Galileo Galilei, Charles Darwin, and Sigmund Freud.

The Two New Sciences
Galileo Galilei

In this selection from 1638, Galileo explores several ideas he derived from his experiments with mechanics and motion. He presents his ideas by means of a dialogue in which several people discuss them, exposing the ideas to a reasoned criticism. These participants in the conversation were likely friends of Galileo or representative of people who had ideas that Galileo held earlier in his life. Salviati and the Academician usually present Galileo's views.

SALVIATI: Frequent experience of your famous arsenal, my Venetian friends, seems to me to open a large field to speculative minds for philosophizing, and particularly in that area which is called mechanics, inasmuch as every sort of instrument and machine is continually put in operation there. And among its great number of artisans there must be some who, through observations handed down by their predecessors as well as those which they attentively and continually make for themselves, are truly expert and whose reasoning is of the finest.

SAGREDO: You are quite right. And since I am by nature curious, I frequent the place for my own diversion and to watch the activity of those whom we call "key men" [*Proti*] by reason of a certain preeminence that they have over the rest of the workmen. Talking with them has helped me many times in the investigation of the reason for effects that are not only remarkable, but also abstruse, and almost unthinkable. Indeed, I have sometimes been thrown into confusion and have despaired of understanding how some things can happen that are shown to be true by my own eyes, things remote from any conception of mine. Nevertheless, what we were told a little while ago by that venerable workman is something commonly said and believed, despite which I hold it to be completely idle, as are many other things that come from the lips of persons of little learning, put forth, I believe, just to show they can say something concerning that which they don't understand.

Galileo Galilei: Two New Sciences, trans. Stillman Drake (Madison: University of Wisconsin Press, 1974), 11–15.

SALV.: You mean, perhaps, that last remark that he offered when we were trying to comprehend the reason why they make the sustaining apparatus, supports, blocks, and other strengthening devices so much larger around that huge galley that is about to be launched than around smaller vessels. He replied that this is done in order to avoid the peril of its splitting under the weight of its own vast bulk, a trouble to which smaller boats are not subject.

SAGR.: I mean that, and particularly the finishing touch that he added, which I have always considered to be an idle notion of the common people. This is that in these and similar frameworks one cannot reason from the small to the large, because many mechanical devices succeed on a small scale that cannot exist in great size. Now, all reasonings about mechanics have their foundations in geometry, in which I do not see that largeness and smallness make large circles, triangles, cylinders, cones, or any other figures [or] solids subject to properties different from those of small ones; hence if the large scaffolding is built with every member proportional to its counterpart in the smaller one, and if the smaller is sound and stable under the use for which it is designed, I fail to see why the larger should not also be proof against adverse and destructive shocks that it may encounter.

SALV.: The common notion is indeed an idle one, so much so that with equal truth its contrary may be asserted; one may say that many machines can be made to work more perfectly on a large scale than on a small one. For example, take a clock that is both to show the hours and to strike; one of a certain size will run more accurately than any smaller one. The common idea is adopted on better grounds by some persons of good understanding when, to explain the occurrence in large machines of effects not in agreement with pure and abstract geometrical demonstrations, they assign the cause of this to the imperfection of matter, which is subject to many variations and defects.

   Here I do not know whether I can declare, without risking reproach for arrogance, that even recourse to imperfections of matter, capable of contaminating the purest mathematical demonstrations, still does not suffice to excuse the misbehavior of machines in the concrete as compared with their abstract ideal counterparts. Nevertheless I do say just that, and I affirm that abstracting all imperfections of matter, and assuming it to be quite perfect and inalterable and free from all accidental change, still the mere fact that it is material makes the larger framework, fabricated from the same material and in the same proportions as the smaller, correspond in every way to it except in strength and resistance against violent shocks [*invasioni*]; and the larger the structure is, the weaker in proportion it will be. And since I am assuming matter to be inalterable—that is, always the same—it is evident that for this [condition] as for any other eternal and necessary property, purely mathematical demonstrations can be produced that are no less rigorous than any others.

Therefore, Sagredo, give up this opinion you have held, perhaps along with many other people who have studied mechanics, that machines and structures composed of the same materials and having exactly the same proportions among their parts must be equally (or rather, proportionally) disposed to resist (or yield to) external forces and blows [*impeti*]. For it can be demonstrated geometrically that the larger ones are always proportionately less resistant than the smaller. And finally, not only artificial machines and structures, but natural ones as well, have limits necessarily placed on them beyond which neither art nor nature can go while maintaining always the same proportions and the same material.

SAGR.: Already I feel my brain reeling, and like a cloud suddenly cleft by lightning, it is troubled. First a sudden and unfamiliar light beckons to me from afar, and then immediately my mind becomes confused, and hides its strange and undigested fancies.

From what you have said, it seems to me, must follow the impossibility of constructing two similar and unequal structures of the same material that would have proportionate resistance. But if that is so, it will be impossible even to find two sticks of the same wood that differ in size and are nevertheless similar in strength and stability.

SALV.: So it is, Sagredo. And the better to make sure that we both have the same idea, I say that if we shape a wooden rod to a length and thickness that will fit into a wall at right angles, horizontally, and the rod is of the greatest length that can support itself, so that if it were a hairbreadth longer, it would break of its own weight, then that rod will be absolutely unique [in shape and size]. For example, if its length is one hundred times its thickness, then no different rod of the same material can be found which has, like this, a length one hundred times its thickness, and is just able to sustain its own weight and no more; for longer bars will break, and shorter ones will be able to sustain something more than their own weights. And what I have said about the state of self-support, assume to be said about any other constituents [*constituzione*]; thus if a scantling can bear the weight of ten like scantlings, a [geometrically] similar beam will by no means be able to bear the weight of ten like beams.

Here you and Simplicio must note how conclusions that are true may seem improbable at a first glance, and yet when only some small thing is pointed out, they cast off their concealing cloaks and, thus naked and simple, gladly show off their secrets. For who does not see that a horse falling from a height of three or four braccia will break its bones, while a dog falling from the same height, or a cat from eight or ten, or even more, will suffer no harm? Thus a cricket might fall without damage from a tower, or an ant from the moon. Small children remain unhurt in falls that would break the legs, or the heads, of their elders. And just as smaller animals are proportionately stronger or more robust than larger ones, so smaller plants will sustain themselves better. I think you both know that if an oak were two hundred feet high, it could not support branches spread out similarly to those of an oak of average size. Only by a miracle could nature form a horse the size of twenty horses, or a giant ten times the height of a man—unless she greatly altered the proportions of the members, especially those of the skeleton, thickening the bones far beyond their ordinary symmetry.

Similarly, to believe that in artificial machines the large and small are equally practicable and durable is a manifest error. Thus, for example, small spires, little columns, and other solid shapes can be safely extended or heightened without risk of breaking them, whereas very large ones will go to pieces at any adverse accident, or for no more cause than that of their own weight.

Here I must tell you of a case really worth hearing about, as are all events beyond expectation, especially when some precaution taken to prevent trouble turns out to be a powerful cause thereof. A very large column of marble was laid down, and its two ends were rested on sections of a beam. After some time had elapsed, it occurred to a mechanic that in order to insure against its breaking of its own weight in the middle, it would be wise to place a third similar support there as well. This suggestion seemed opportune to most people, but the result showed quite the contrary. Not many months passed before the column was found cracked and broken, directly over the new support at the center.

SIMP.: A truly remarkable event, and most unexpected, if indeed this was due to the addition of the new support in the middle.

SALV.: It surely did result from that, and to recognize the cause of the effect removes the marvel of it. For the two pieces of the column being placed flat on the ground, it was seen that the beam-section on which one end had been supported had rotted and settled over a long period of time, while the support at the middle remained solid and strong. This had caused one half of the column to remain suspended in the air; and, abandoned by the support at the other end, its excessive weight made it do what it would not have done had it been supported only on the two original [beams], for if one of them had settled, the column would simply have gone along with it. And doubtless no such accident would have happened to a small column of the same stone, if its length bore to its thickness the same ratio as that of the length to the thickness of the large column.

SAGR.: Thus far I am convinced of the truth of the effect, but stop short of the reason why any material, in becoming larger, should not by that very accumulation [of size] multiply its resistance and its strength. I am the more puzzled by seeing other cases in which there is a much greater increase in hardiness and resistance to rupture than there is in size of material. For example, if two nails are driven into a wall, and one is twice as thick as the other, it will hold not only twice the weight, but three or four times as much.

SALV.: Say eight times, and you will not be far from the truth. But this effect is not contrary to that other, although superficially it seems to be.

SAGR.: Then smooth out for us these rough spots, Salviati, and clear up these obscurities, if you have any way of doing so, for indeed I am beginning to think that this subject of resistance is a field full of beautiful and useful considerations. And if you are willing that it be made the subject of our discussions today, that will be most welcome to me, and I believe to Simplicio.

SALV.: I cannot refuse to be of service, provided that memory serves me in bringing back what I once learned from our Academician [Galileo] who made many speculations about this subject, all geometrically demonstrated, according to his custom, in such a way that not without reason this could be called a new science. For though some of the conclusions have been noted by others, and first of all by Aristotle, those are not the prettiest; and what is more important, they were not proved by necessary demonstrations from their primary and unquestionable foundations.

The Origin of Species
Charles Darwin

In this introduction and overview to his Origin of Species *(1859), Charles Darwin outlines his reasons for writing that book. As he discusses the scope of each chapter, Darwin presents a summary of the argument for natural selection as the means by which creatures evolve. In addition, Darwin confronts those who would be confounded by his theory on religious grounds and those who disbelieve in the mutability of species. Darwin closes with a visionary sweep of the evolution of species on a planet bound by the laws of gravity, linking himself to Isaac Newton, a scientific visionary of an earlier time.*

Charles Darwin, *The Origin of Species* (New York: Random House, 1993), 18–23.

When on board H.M.S. *Beagle,* as naturalist, I was much struck with certain facts in the distribution of the organic beings inhabiting South America, and in the geological relations of the present to the past inhabitants of that continent. These facts, as will be seen in the latter chapters of this volume, seemed to throw some light on the origin of species — that mystery of mysteries, as it has been called by one of our greatest philosophers. On my return home, it occurred to me, in 1837, that something might perhaps be made out on this question by patiently accumulating and reflecting on all sorts of facts which could possibly have any bearing on it. After five years' work I allowed myself to speculate on the subject, and drew up some short notes; these I enlarged in 1844 into a sketch of the conclusions, which then seemed to me probable: from that period to the present day I have steadily pursued the same object. I hope that I may be excused for entering on these personal details, as I give them to show that I have not been hasty in coming to a decision.

My work is now (1859) nearly finished; but as it will take me many more years to complete it, and as my health is far from strong, I have been urged to publish this Abstract. I have more especially been induced to do this, as Mr. Wallace, who is now studying the natural history of the Malay archipelago, has arrived at almost exactly the same general conclusions that I have on the origin of species. In 1858 he sent me a memoir on this subject, with a request that I would forward it to Sir Charles Lyell, who sent it to the Linnean Society, and it is published in the third volume of the Journal of that society. Sir C. Lyell and Dr. Hooker, who both knew of my work — the latter having read my sketch of 1844 — honoured me by thinking it advisable to publish, with Mr. Wallace's excellent memoir, some brief extracts from my manuscripts.

This Abstract, which I now publish, must necessarily be imperfect. I cannot here give references and authorities for my several statements; and I must trust to the reader reposing some confidence in my accuracy. No doubt errors will have crept in, though I hope I have always been cautious in trusting to good authorities alone. I can here give only the general conclusions at which I have arrived, with a few facts in illustration, but which, I hope, in most cases will suffice. No one can feel more sensible than I do of the necessity of hereafter publishing in detail all the facts, with references, on which my conclusions have been grounded; and I hope in a future work to do this. For I am well aware that scarcely a single point is discussed in this volume on which facts cannot be adduced, often apparently leading to conclusions directly opposite to those at which I have arrived. A fair result can be obtained only by fully stating and balancing the facts and arguments on both sides of each question; and this is here impossible.

I much regret that want of space prevents my having the satisfaction of acknowledging the generous assistance which I have received from very many naturalists, some of them personally unknown to me. I cannot, however, let this opportunity pass without expressing my deep obligations to Dr. Hooker, who, for the last fifteen years, has aided me in every possible way by his large stores of knowledge and his excellent judgment.

In considering the Origin of Species, it is quite conceivable that a naturalist, reflecting on the mutual affinities of organic beings, on their embryological relations, their geographical distribution, geological succession, and other such facts, might come to the conclusion that species had not been independently created, but had descended, like varieties, from other species. Nevertheless, such a conclusion, even if well founded, would be unsatisfactory, until it could be shown how the innumerable species inhabiting this world have been modified, so as to acquire that perfection of structure and coadaptation which justly excites our admiration. Naturalists continually refer to external conditions, such as climate, food, &c., as the only possible cause of variation. In one limited sense, as we shall hereafter see, this may be true; but it is preposterous to attribute to mere external conditions, the structure, for instance, of the woodpecker, with its feet, tail, beak, and tongue, so admirably adapted to catch insects under the bark of trees. In the case of the mistletoe, which draws its nourishment from certain trees, which has seeds that must be transported by certain birds, and which has flowers with separate sexes absolutely requiring the agency of certain insects to bring pollen from one flower to the other, it is equally preposterous to account for the structure of this parasite, with its relations to several distinct organic beings, by the effects of external conditions, or of habit, or of the volition of the plant itself.

It is, therefore, of the highest importance to gain a clear insight into the means of modification and coadaptation. At the commencement of my observations it seemed to me probable that a careful study of domesticated animals and of cultivated plants would offer the best chance of making out this obscure problem. Nor have I been disappointed; in this and in all other perplexing cases I have invariably found that our knowledge, imperfect though it be, of variation under domestication, afforded the best and safest clue. I may venture to express my conviction of the high value of such studies, although they have been very commonly neglected by naturalists.

From these considerations, I shall devote the first chapter of this Abstract to Variation under Domestication. We shall thus see that a large amount of hereditary modification is at least possible; and, what is equally or more important, we shall see how great is the power of man in accumulating by his Selection successive slight variations. I will then pass on to the variability of species in a state of nature; but I shall, unfortunately, be compelled to treat this subject far too briefly, as it can be treated properly only by giving long catalogues of facts. We shall, however, be enabled to discuss what circumstances are most favourable to variation. In the next chapter the Struggle for Existence amongst all organic beings throughout the world, which inevitably follows from the high geometrical ratio of their increase, will be considered. This is the doctrine of Malthus, applied to the whole animal and vegetable kingdoms. As many more individuals of each species are born than can possibly survive; and as, consequently, there is a frequently recurring struggle for existence, it follows that any being, if it vary however slightly in any manner profitable to itself, under the complex and sometimes varying conditions of life, will have a better chance of surviving, and thus be *naturally selected.* From the strong principle of inheritance, any selected variety will tend to propagate its new and modified form.

This fundamental subject of Natural Selection will be treated at some length in the fourth chapter; and we shall then see how Natural Selection almost inevitably causes much Extinction of the less improved forms of life, and leads to what I have called Divergence of Character. In the next chapter I shall discuss the complex and little known laws of variation. In the five succeeding chapters, the most apparent and gravest difficulties in accepting the theory will be given; namely, first, the difficulties of transitions, or how a simple being or a simple organ can be changed and perfected into a highly developed being or into an elaborately constructed organ; secondly, the subject of Instinct, or the mental powers of animals; thirdly, Hybridism, or the infertility of species and the fertility of varieties when intercrossed; and fourthly, the imperfection of the Geological Record. In the next chapter I shall consider the geological succession of organic beings throughout time; in the twelfth and thirteenth, their geographical distribution throughout space; in the fourteenth, their classification or mutual affinities, both when mature and in an embryonic condition. In the last chapter I shall give a brief recapitulation of the whole work, and a few concluding remarks.

No one ought to feel surprise at much remaining as yet unexplained in regard to the origin of species and varieties, if he makes due allowance for our profound ignorance in regard to the mutual relations of the many beings which live around us. Who can explain why one species ranges widely and is very numerous, and why another allied species has a narrow range and is rare? Yet these relations are of the highest importance, for they determine the present welfare and, as I believe, the future success and modification of every inhabitant of this world. Still less do we know of the mutual relations of the innumerable inhabitants of the world during the many past geological epochs in its history. Although much remains obscure, and will long remain obscure, I can entertain no doubt, after the most deliberate study and dispassionate judgment of which I am capable, that the view which most naturalists until recently entertained, and which I formerly entertained—namely, that each species has been independently created—is erroneous. I am fully convinced that species are not immutable; but that those belonging to what are called the same genera are lineal descendants of some other and generally extinct species, in the same manner as the acknowledged varieties of any one species are the descendants of that species. Furthermore, I am convinced that Natural Selection has been the most important, but not the exclusive, means of modification.

The Premisses and Technique of Interpretation [of Dreams]
Sigmund Freud

Psychology and psychotherapy owe an immense debt to the work of Sigmund Freud. In this selection, written in 1889, Freud discussed how dreams might be analyzed to yield important clues about the dreamer. Freud developed his theory of dream interpretation while disagreeing with most of his contemporaries, who believed that dreams had nothing to do with psychological activity. Wish fulfillment was the meaning of dreams for Freud, who offered a language with which to translate various symbols in one's dreams.

Ladies and Gentlemen, — What we need, then, is a new path, a method which will enable us to make a start in the investigation of dreams. I will put a suggestion to you which presents itself. Let us take it as a premiss from this point onwards that *dreams are not somatic but psychical phenomena*. You know what that means, but what justifies our making the assumption? Nothing: but there is nothing either to prevent our making it. Here is the position: if dreams are somatic phenomena they are no concern of ours, they can only interest us on the assumption that they are mental phenomena. We will therefore work on the assumption that they really are, to see what comes of it. The outcome of our work will decide whether we are to hold to this assumption and whether we may then go on to treat it in turn as a proved finding. But what is it actually that we want to arrive at? What is our work aiming at? We want something that is sought for in all scientific work — to understand the phenomena, to establish a correlation between them and, in the latter end, if it is possible, to enlarge our power over them.

We proceed with our work, accordingly, on the supposition that dreams are psychical phenomena. In that case they are products and utterances of the dreamer's, but utterances which tell us nothing, which we do not understand. Well, what do you do if I make an unintelligible utterance to you? You question me, is that not so? Why should we not do

Sigmund Freud, *The Complete Introductory Lectures on Psychoanalysis,* trans. James Strachey (New York: W. W. Norton & Co., 1966), 100–104. Translation originally published in *Introductory Lectures on Psycho-Analysis* (New York: Liveright Publishing, 1965), 122–28.

the same thing to the dreamer—*question him as to what his dream means?*

As you will remember, we found ourselves in this situation once before. It was while we were investigating certain parapraxes—a case of a slip of the tongue. Someone had said: "Then facts came to *Vorschwein*" and we thereupon asked him—no, it was luckily not we but some other people who had no connection at all with psycho-analysis—these other people, then, asked him what he meant by this unintelligible remark. And he replied at once that he had intended to say "these facts were *Schweinereien* [disgusting]," but had forced this intention back in favour of the milder version "then facts came to *Vorschein* [light]." I pointed out to you at the time that this piece of information was the model for every psycho-analytic investigation, and you will understand now that psycho-analysis follows the technique of getting the people under examination so far as possible themselves to produce the solution of their riddles. Thus, too, it is the dreamer himself who should tell us what his dream means.

But, as we know, things are not so simple with dreams. With parapraxes[1] it worked all right in a number of cases; but then others came along in which the person who was questioned would say nothing, and even indignantly rejected the answer we proposed to him. With dreams cases of the first sort are entirely lacking; the dreamer always says he knows nothing. He cannot reject our interpretation as we have none to offer him. Are we to give up our attempt then? Since he knows nothing and we know nothing and a third person could know even less, there seems to be no prospect of finding out. If you feel inclined, then, give up the attempt! But if you feel otherwise, you can accompany me further. For I can assure you that it is quite possible, and highly probable indeed, that the dreamer *does* know what his dream means: *only he does not know that he knows it and for that reason thinks he does not know it.*

You will point out to me that I am once more introducing an assumption, the second already in this short argument, and that in doing so I am enormously reducing my procedure's claim to credibility: "Subject to the premiss that dreams are psychical phenomena, and subject to the further premiss that there are mental things in a man which he knows without knowing that he knows them . . ." and so on. If so, one has only to consider the internal improbability of each of these two premisses, and one can quietly divert one's interest from any conclusions that may be based on them.

I have not brought you here, Ladies and Gentlemen, to delude you or to conceal things from you. In my prospectus, it is true, I announced

---

1. Parapraxes are actions in which one's conscious intentions are not carried out, such as a slip of the tongue.

a course of "Elementary Lectures to Serve as an Introduction to Psycho-Analysis," but what I had in mind was nothing in the nature of a presentation *in usum Delphini*,[2] which would give you a smooth account with all the difficulties carefully concealed, with the gaps filled in and the doubts glossed over, so that you might believe with an easy mind that you had learnt something new. No, for the very reason of your being beginners, I wanted to show you our science as it is, with its unevennesses and roughnesses, its demands and hesitations. For I know that it is the same in all sciences and cannot possibly be otherwise, especially in their beginnings. I know also that ordinarily instruction is at pains to start out by concealing such difficulties and incompletenesses from the learner. But that will not do for psycho-analysis. So I have in fact laid down two premises, one within the other; and if anyone finds the whole thing too laborious and too insecure, or if anyone is accustomed to higher certainties and more elegant deductions, he need go no further with us. I think, however, that he should leave psychological problems entirely alone, for it is to be feared that in this quarter he will find impassable the precise and secure paths which he is prepared to follow. And, for a science which has something to offer, there is no necessity to sue for a hearing and for followers. Its findings are bound to canvass on its behalf and it can wait until these have compelled attention to it.

But for those who would like to persist in the subject, I can point out that my two assumptions are not on a par. The first, that dreams are psychical phenomena, is the premiss which we seek to prove by the outcome of our work; the second one has already been proved in another field, and I am merely venturing to bring it over from there to our own problems.

Where, then, in what field, can it be that proof has been found that there is knowledge of which the person concerned nevertheless knows nothing, as we are proposing to assume of dreamers? After all, this would be a strange, surprising fact and one which would alter our view of mental life and which would have no need to hide itself: a fact, incidentally, which cancels itself in its very naming and which nevertheless claims to be something real — a contradiction in terms. Well, it does not hide itself. It is not its fault if people know nothing about it or do not pay enough attention to it. Any more than we are to blame because judgement is passed on all these psychological problems by people who have kept at a distance from all the observations and experiences which are decisive on the matter.

The proof was found in the field of hypnotic phenomena. When, in 1889, I took part in the extraordinarily impressive demonstrations by Liébeault and Bernheim at Nancy, I witnessed the following experiment

2. "For the use of the Dauphin" — an edition of the Classics prepared for his son by order of Louis XIV: "bowdlerized."

among others. If a man was put into a state of somnambulism, was made to experience all kinds of things in a hallucinatory manner, and was then woken up, he appeared at first to know nothing of what had happened during his hypnotic sleep. Bernheim then asked him straight out to report what had happened to him under hypnosis. The man maintained that he could remember nothing. But Bernheim held out against this, brought urgent pressure to bear on him, insisted that he knew it and must remember it. And, lo and behold! the man grew uncertain, began to reflect, and recalled in a shadowy way one of the experiences that had been suggested to him, and then another piece, and the memory became clearer and clearer and more and more complete, and finally came to light without a break. Since, however, he knew afterwards what had happened and had learnt nothing about it from anyone else in the interval, we are justified in concluding that he had known it earlier as well. It was merely inaccessible to him; he did not know that he knew it and thought he did not know it. That is to say, the position was exactly the same as what we suspected in our dreamer.

I hope you will be surprised that this fact has been established and will ask me: "Why did you omit to bring this proof forward earlier, in connection with the parapraxes, when we came to the point of attributing to a man who had made a slip of the tongue an intention to say things of which he knew nothing and which he denied? If a person thinks he knows nothing of experiences the memory of which he nevertheless has within him, it is no longer so improbable that he knows nothing of other mental processes within him. This argument would certainly have impressed us, and helped us to understand parapraxes." Of course I could have brought it forward then, but I reserved it for another place, where it was more needed. The parapraxes explained themselves in part, and in part left us with a suggestion that, in order to preserve the continuity of the phenomena concerned, it would be wise to assume the existence of mental processes of which the subject knows nothing. In the case of dreams we are compelled to bring in explanations from elsewhere and moreover I expect that in their case you will find it easier to accept my carrying over of the explanations from hypnosis. The state in which a parapraxis occurs is bound to strike you as being the normal one; it has no similarity with the hypnotic state. On the other hand there is an obvious kinship between the hypnotic state and the state of sleep, which is a necessary condition of dreaming. Hypnosis, indeed, is described as an artificial sleep. We tell the person we are hypnotizing to sleep, and the suggestions we make are comparable to the dreams of natural sleep. The psychical situations in the two cases are really analogous. In natural sleep we withdraw our interest from the whole external world; and in hypnotic sleep we also withdraw it from the whole world, but with the single exception of the person who has hypnotized us and with whom we remain in rapport. Incidentally, the sleep of a nursing mother, who remains in rapport with her child and can be woken only by him, is a normal counterpart of hypnotic sleep. So it scarcely seems a very bold venture to transpose a situation from hypnosis to natural sleep. The assumption that in a dreamer too a knowledge about his dreams is present, though it is inaccessible to him so that he himself does not believe it, is not something entirely out of the blue. It should be noticed, moreover, that a third line of approach to the study of dreams is opened at this point: from the stimuli which disturb sleep, from day-dreams, and now in addition from the suggested dreams of the hypnotic state.

THE ENLIGHTENMENT AND REVOLUTIONS

Since the eighteenth century, many revolutions have been at least partly driven by Enlightenment ideas. Some revolutionaries believed that people have unalienable rights, including life, liberty, and the pursuit of happiness. Others insisted that men are born and remain free, while a few claimed these things for women. From these ideas and accumulated sufferings came movements struggling for freedom and equality of all.

The next six readings reveal some of the ways that these Enlightenment ideas became part of the political landscape in the eighteenth, nineteenth, and twentieth centuries. The excerpt from Immanuel Kant sets the scene by stressing how Enlightenment thinking is liberating, then the next four documents present attempts to turn these liberating ideas into political reality. Finally, an essay by Edmund Burke discusses how the architects of the French Revolution failed to exercise adequate restraint, thus failing to implement Enlightenment ideas.

What is Enlightenment?
Immanuel Kant

Immanuel Kant, an influential German philosopher of the eighteenth century, considered himself a proponent of the Enlightenment. Always concerned about moral behavior, Kant saw thinking for oneself as both a right and an obligation, yet he maintained that few people considered issues for themselves and drew their independent conclusions, finding it more comforting to accept direction from authority. This excerpt written in 1788 explains how Kant saw Enlightenment thinking as a force that liberated individuals from the direction of others, encouraging them to draw rational, independent conclusions.

Immanuel Kant, *Critique of Practical Reason,* trans. Lewis White Beck, 3d ed. (New York: Macmillan, 1956); reprinted in *Readings in World Civilizations,* by Kevin Reilly, vol. 2, *The Development of the Modern World* (New York: St. Martin's Press, 1995), 116–17.

Enlightenment is man's release from his self-incurred tutelage. Tutelage is man's inability to make use of his understanding without direction from another. Self-incurred is this tutelage when its cause lies not in lack of reason but in lack of resolution and courage to use it without direction from another. *Sapere aude!* "Have courage to use your own reason!" — that is the motto of enlightenment.

Laziness and cowardice are the reasons why so great a portion of mankind, after nature has long since discharged them from external direction, nevertheless remains under lifelong tutelage, and why it is so easy for others to set themselves up as their guardians. It is so easy not to be of age. If I have a book which understands for me, a pastor who has a conscience for me, a physician who decides my diet, and so forth, I need not trouble myself. I need not think, if I can only pay — others will readily undertake the irksome work for me.

That the step to competence is held to be very dangerous by the far greater portion of mankind (and by the entire fair sex) — quite apart from its being arduous — is seen to by those guardians who have so kindly assumed superintendence over them. After the guardians have first made their domestic cattle dumb and have made sure that these placid creatures will not dare take a single step without the harness of the cart to which they are confined, the guardians then show them the danger which threatens if they try to go alone. Actually, however, this danger is not so great, for by falling a few times they would finally learn to walk alone. But an example of this failure makes them timid and ordinarily frightens them away from all further trials.

For any single individual to work himself out of the life under tutelage which has become almost his nature is very difficult. He has come to be fond of this state, and he is for the present really incapable of making use of his reason, for no one has ever let him try it out. Statutes and formulas, those mechanical tools of the rational employment or rather mis-employment of his natural gifts, are the fetters of an everlasting tutelage. Whoever throws them off makes only an uncertain leap over the narrowest ditch because he is not accustomed to that kind of free motion. Therefore, there are only few who have succeeded by their own exercise of mind both in freeing themselves from incompetence and in achieving a steady pace.

But that the public should enlighten itself is more possible; indeed, if only freedom is granted, enlightenment is almost sure to follow. For there will always be some independent thinkers, even among the established guardians of the great masses, who, after throwing off the yoke of tutelage from their own shoulders, will disseminate the spirit of the rational appreciation of both their own worth and every man's vocation for thinking for himself. But be it noted that the public, which has first been brought under this yoke by their guardians, forces the guardians themselves to remain bound when it is incited to do so by some of the guardians who are themselves capable of some enlightenment — so harmful is it to implant prejudices, for they later take vengeance on their cultivators or on their descendants. Thus the public can only slowly attain enlightenment. Perhaps a fall of personal despotism or of avaricious or tyrannical oppression may be accomplished by revolution, but never a true reform in ways of thinking. Rather, new prejudices will serve as well as old ones to harness the great unthinking masses.

For this enlightenment, however, nothing is required but freedom, and indeed the most harmless among all the things to which this term can properly be applied. It is the freedom to make public use of one's reason at every point. But I hear on all sides, "Do not argue!" The officer says: "Do not argue but drill!" The tax-collector: "Do not argue but pay!" The cleric: "Do not argue but believe!" Everywhere freedom is restricted.

The American Declaration of Independence
Thomas Jefferson

While the American Declaration of Independence was drafted in committee, Thomas Jefferson was its primary author. Jefferson and his colleagues in the Continental Congress grounded this seminal document in the ideas of the Enlightenment, especially in the ideas of natural law and natural rights. The declaration, approved by the Congress in July 1776, also sets forth the reasons why the colonists decided to declare themselves free from what they considered British tyranny.

In Congress, July 4, 1776 the Unanimous Declaration of the Thirteen United States of America

When in the course of human events, it becomes necessary for one people to dissolve the political bands which have connected them with another, and to assume among the powers of the earth, the separate and equal station to which the Laws of Nature and of Nature's God entitle them, a decent respect to the opinions of mankind requires that they should declare the causes which impel them to the separation.

We hold these truths to be self-evident, that all men are created equal, that they are endowed by their Creator with certain unalienable rights, that among these are life, liberty and the pursuit of happiness. That to secure these rights, governments are instituted among men, deriving their just powers from the consent of the governed. That whenever any form of government becomes destructive of these ends, it is the right of the people to alter or to abolish it, and to institute new government, laying its foundation on such principles and organizing its powers in such form, as to them shall seem most likely to effect their safety and happiness. Prudence, indeed, will dictate that governments long established should not be changed for light and transient causes; and accordingly all experience hath shown, that mankind are more disposed to suffer, while evils are sufferable, than to right themselves by abolishing the forms to which they are accustomed. But when a long train of abuses and usurpations, pursuing invariably the same object evinces a design to reduce them under absolute despotism, it is their right, it is their duty, to throw off such government, and to provide new guards for their future security. Such has been the patient sufferance of these Colonies; and such is now the necessity which constrains them to alter their former systems of government. The history of the present King of Great Britain is a history of repeated injuries and usurpations, all having in direct object the establishment of an absolute tyranny over these States. To prove this, let facts be submitted to a candid world.

He has refused his assent to laws, the most wholesome and necessary for the public good.

He has forbidden his Governors to pass laws of immediate and pressing importance, unless suspended in their operation till his assent should be obtained; and when so suspended, he has utterly neglected to attend to them.

He has refused to pass other laws for the accommodation of large districts of people, unless those people would relinquish the right of representation in the Legislature, a right inestimable to them and formidable to tyrants only.

He has called together legislative bodies at places unusual, uncomfortable, and distant from the depository of their public records, for the sole purpose of fatiguing them into compliance with his measures.

He has dissolved representative houses repeatedly, for opposing with manly firmness his invasions on the rights of the people.

He has refused for a long time, after such dissolutions, to cause others to be elected; whereby the legislative powers, incapable of annihilation, have returned to the people at large for their exercise; the State remaining in the meantime exposed to all the dangers of invasion from without and convulsions within.

He has endeavoured to prevent the population of these states; for that purpose obstructing the laws of naturalization of foreigners; refusing to pass others to encourage their migration hither, and raising the conditions of new appropriations of lands.

He has obstructed the administration of justice, by refusing his assent to laws for establishing judiciary powers.

He has made judges dependent on his will alone, for the tenure of their offices, and the amount and payment of their salaries.

He has erected a multitude of new offices, and sent hither swarms of officers to harass our people, and eat out their substance.

He has kept among us, in times of peace, standing armies without the consent of our legislatures.

He has affected to render the military independent of and superior to the civil power.

He has combined with others to subject us to a jurisdiction foreign to our constitution, and unacknowledged by our laws; giving his assent to their acts of pretended legislation:

For quartering large bodies of armed troops among us:

For protecting them, by a mock trial, from punishment for any murders which they should commit on the inhabitants of these States:

For cutting off our trade with all parts of the world:

For imposing taxes on us without our consent:

For depriving us in many cases, of the benefits of trial by jury:

For transporting us beyond seas to be tried for pretended offences:

For abolishing the free system of English laws in a neighbouring Province, establishing therein an arbitrary government, and enlarging its boundaries so as to render it at once an example and fit instrument for introducing the same absolute rule into these Colonies:

For taking away our Charters, abolishing our most valuable laws, and altering fundamentally the forms of our governments:

For suspending our own Legislatures, and declaring themselves invested with power to legislate for us in all cases whatsoever.

He has abdicated government here, by declaring us out of his protection and waging war against us.

He has plundered our seas, ravaged our coasts, burnt our towns, and destroyed the lives of our people.

He is at this time transporting large armies of foreign mercenaries to complete the works of death, desolation and tyranny, already begun with circumstances of cruelty and perfidy scarcely paralleled in the most barbarous ages, and totally unworthy the head of a civilized nation.

He has constrained our fellow citizens taken captive on the high seas to bear arms against their country, to become the executioners of their friends and brethren, or to fall themselves by their hands.

He has excited domestic insurrections amongst us, and has endeavoured to bring on the inhabitants of our frontiers, the merciless Indian savages, whose known rule of warfare, is an undistinguished destruction of all ages, sexes, and conditions.

In every state of these oppressions we have petitioned for redress in the most humble terms: our repeated petitions have been answered only by repeated injury. A prince whose character is thus marked by every act which may define a tyrant is unfit to be the ruler of a free people.

Nor have we been wanting in attention to our British brethren. We have warned them from time to time of attempts by their legislature to extend an unwarrantable jurisdiction over us. We have reminded them of the circumstances of our emigration and settlement here. We have appealed to their native justice and magnanimity, and we have conjured them by the ties of our common kindred to disavow these usurpations, which would inevitably interrupt our connections and correspondence. They too have been deaf to the voice of justice and of consanguinity. We must, therefore, acquiesce in the necessity, which denounces our separation, and hold them, as we hold the rest of mankind, enemies in war, in peace friends.

We, therefore, the Representatives of the United States of America, in General Congress assembled, appealing to the Supreme Judge of the world for the rectitude of our intentions, do, in the name, and by authority of the good people of these Colonies, solemnly publish and declare, That these United Colonies are, and of right ought to be Free and Independent States; that they are absolved from all allegiance to the British Crown, and that all political connection between them and the State of Great Britain, is and ought to be totally dissolved; and that as Free and Independent States, they have full power to levy war, conclude peace, contract alliances, establish commerce, and to do all other acts and things which Independent States may of right do. And for the support of this declaration, with a firm reliance on the protection of Divine Providence, we mutually pledge to each other our lives, our fortunes, and our sacred honor.

The [French] Declaration of the Rights of Man and the Citizen
French National Assembly

The French National Assembly meeting in August of 1789 started to draft a declaration of general principles to guide its actions and those of any future governments. Like the principles that were the basis of the American Declaration of Independence, many of their ideas came from Enlightenment thinkers. Some of the French politicians who drafted the Declaration of the Rights of Man and the Citizen even consulted with Thomas Jefferson, who was the American ambassador to France.

The representatives of the French people, organized as a national assembly, considering that ignorance, neglect, and scorn of the rights of man are the sole causes of public misfortunes and of corruption of governments, have resolved to display in a solemn declaration the natural, inalienable, and sacred rights of man, so that this declaration, constantly in the presence of all members of society, will continually remind them of their rights and their duties, so that the acts of the legislative power and those of the executive power, being subject at any time to compari-

The French Revolution, ed. Paul Beik (New York: Harper & Row, 1970), 95–97; reprinted in *A Short History of the French Revolution*, by Jeremy D. Popkin (Englewood Cliffs, N.J.: Prentice Hall, 1995), 152–54.

son with the purpose of any political institution, will be better respected; so that the demands of the citizens, based henceforth on simple and incontestable principles, will always contribute to the maintenance of the constitution and the happiness of all.

Consequently, the National Assembly recognizes and declares, in the presence and under the auspices of the Supreme Being, the following rights of man and citizen.

Article 1. Men are born and remain free and equal in rights; social distinctions can be established only for the common benefit.

2. The aim of every political association is the conservation of the natural and imprescriptible rights of man; these rights are liberty, property, security, and resistance to oppression.

3. The source of all sovereignty is located in essence in the nation; no body, no individual can exercise authority which does not emanate from it expressly.

4. Liberty consists in being able to do anything that does not harm another person. Thus the exercise of the natural rights of each man has no limits except those which assure to the other members of society the enjoyment of these same rights; these limits can be determined only by law.

5. The law has the right to forbid only those actions harmful to society. All that is not forbidden by the law cannot be hindered, and no one can be forced to do what it does not order.

6. The law is the expression of the general will; all citizens have the right to concur personally or through their representatives in its formation; it must be the same for all, whether it protects or punishes. All citizens being equal in its eyes are equally admissible to all honors, positions, and public employments, according to their capabilities and without other distinctions than those of their virtues and talents.

7. No man can be accused, arrested, or detained except in cases determined by the law, and according to the forms which it has prescribed. Those who solicit, draw up, execute, or have executed arbitrary orders must be punished; but any citizen summoned or seized by virtue of the law must obey instantly; he renders himself culpable by resisting.

8. The law must establish only penalties that are strictly and clearly necessary, and no one can be punished except in virtue of a law established and published prior to the offense and legally applied.

9. Every man being presumed innocent until he has been declared guilty, if it is judged indispensable to arrest him, all severity that is not necessary for making sure of his person must be severely repressed by the law.

10. No one may be disturbed because of his opinions, even religious, provided that their public demonstration does not disturb the public order established by law.

11. The free communication of thoughts and opinions is one of the most precious rights of man: every citizen can therefore freely speak, write, and print: he is answerable for abuses of this liberty in cases determined by the law.

12. The guaranteeing of the rights of man and citizen necessitates a public force; this force is therefore instituted for the advantage of all, and not for the private use of those to whom it is entrusted.

13. For the maintenance of the public force, and for the expenses of administration, a tax supported in common is indispensable; it must be assessed on all citizens in proportion to their capacities to pay.

14. Citizens have the right to determine for themselves or through their representatives the need for taxation of the public, to consent to it freely, to investigate its use, and to determine its rate, basis, collection, and duration.

15. Society has the right to demand an accounting of his administration from every public agent.

16. Any society in which guarantees of rights are not assured nor the separation of powers determined has no constitution.

17. Property being an inviolable and sacred right, no one may be deprived of it unless public necessity, legally determined, clearly requires such action, and then only on condition of a just and prior indemnity.

Declaration of the Rights of
Woman and the Female Citizen

Olympe de Gouges

Olympe de Gouges believed that French women did not enjoy the rights and benefits accorded to men. To remedy the situation, she drafted a declaration that pertained to women in 1791 and addressed it to Marie Antoinette, the Queen of France. The tone of de Gouges' preamble is confrontational as she establishes the proposition that men unjustly oppress women. Furthermore, she uses examples from nature and Enlightenment thought to assert that women have rights and should be citizens of France.

For the National Assembly to decree in its last sessions, or in those of the next legislature:

Preamble

Mothers, daughters, sisters [and] representatives of the nation demand to be constituted into a national assembly. Believing that ignorance, omission, or scorn for the rights of woman are the only causes of public

Women in Revolutionary Paris, 1789–1795, trans. Darlene Gay Levy et al. (Urbana: University of Illinois Press, 1979), 89–96.

misfortunes and of the corruption of governments, [the women] have resolved to set forth in a solemn declaration the natural, inalienable, and sacred rights of woman in order that this declaration, constantly exposed before all the members of the society, will ceaselessly remind them of their rights and duties; in order that the authoritative acts of women and the authoritative acts of men may be at any moment compared with and respectful of the purpose of all political institutions; and in order that citizens' demands, henceforth based on simple and incontestable principles, will always support the constitution, good morals, and the happiness of all.

Consequently, the sex that is as superior in beauty as it is in courage during the sufferings of maternity recognizes and declares in the presence and under the auspices of the Supreme Being, the following Rights of Woman and of Female Citizens.

Article I

Woman is born free and lives equal to man in her rights. Social distinctions can be based only on the common utility.

Article II

The purpose of any political association is the conservation of the natural and imprescriptible rights of woman and man; these rights are liberty, property, security, and especially resistance to oppression.

Article III

The principle of all sovereignty rests essentially with the nation, which is nothing but the union of woman and man; no body and no individual can exercise any authority which does not come expressly from it [the nation].

Article IV

Liberty and justice consist of restoring all that belongs to others; thus, the only limits on the exercise of the natural rights of woman are perpetual male tyranny; these limits are to be reformed by the laws of nature and reason.

Article V

Laws of nature and reason proscribe all acts harmful to society; everything which is not prohibited by these wise and divine laws cannot be prevented, and no one can be constrained to do what they do not command.

Article VI

The law must be the expression of the general will; all female and male citizens must contribute either personally or through their representatives to its formation; it must be the same for all: male and female citizens, being equal in the eyes of the law, must be equally admitted to all honors, positions, and public employment according to their capacity and without other distinctions besides those of their virtues and talents.

Article VII

No woman is an exception; she is accused, arrested, and detained in cases determined by law. Women, like men, obey this rigorous law.

Article VIII

The law must establish only those penalties that are strictly and obviously necessary, and no one can be punished except by virtue of a law established and promulgated prior to the crime and legally applicable to women.

Article IX

Once any woman is declared guilty, complete rigor is [to be] exercised by the law.

Article X

No one is to be disquieted for his very basic opinions; woman has the right to mount the scaffold; she must equally have the right to mount the rostrum, provided that her demonstrations do not disturb the legally established public order.

Article XI

The free communication of thoughts and opinions is one of the most precious rights of woman, since that liberty assures the recognition of children by their fathers. Any female citizen thus may say freely, I am the mother of a child which belongs to you, without being forced by a barbarous prejudice to hide the truth; [an exception may be made] to respond to the abuse of this liberty in cases determined by the law.

Article XII

The guarantee of the rights of woman and the female citizen implies a major benefit; this guarantee must be instituted for the advantage of all, and not for the particular benefit of those to whom it is entrusted.

Article XIII

For the support of the public force and the expenses of administration, the contributions of woman and man are equal; she shares all the duties [*corvées*] and all the painful tasks; therefore, she must have the same share in the distribution of positions, employment, offices, honors, and jobs [*industrie*].

Article XIV

Female and male citizens have the right to verify, either by themselves or through their representatives, the necessity of the public contribution. This can only apply to women if they are granted an equal share, not only of wealth, but also of public administration, and in the determination of the proportion, the base, the collection, and the duration of the tax.

Article XV

The collectivity of women, joined for tax purposes to the aggregate of men, has the right to demand an accounting of his administration from any public agent.

Article XVI

No society has a constitution without the guarantee of rights and the separation of powers; the constitution is null if the majority of individuals comprising the nation have not cooperated in drafting it.

Article XVII

Property belongs to both sexes whether united or separate; for each it is an inviolable and sacred right; no one can be deprived of it, since it is the true patrimony of nature, unless the legally determined public need obviously dictates it, and then only with a just and prior indemnity.

Postscript

Woman, wake up; the tocsin of reason is being heard throughout the whole universe; discover your rights. The powerful empire of nature is no longer surrounded by prejudice, fanaticism, superstition, and lies. The flame of truth has dispersed all the clouds of folly and usurpation. Enslaved man has multiplied his strength and needs recourse to yours to break his chains. Having become free, he has become unjust to his companion. Oh, women, women! When will you cease to be blind? What advantage have you received from the Revolution? A more pronounced scorn, a more marked disdain. In the centuries of corruption you ruled only over the weakness of men. The reclamation of your patrimony, based on the wise decrees of nature—what have you to dread from such a fine undertaking? The *bon mot* of the legislator of the marriage of Cana? Do you fear that our French legislators, correctors of that morality, long ensnared by political practices now out of date, will only say again to you: women, what is there in common between you and us? Everything, you will have to answer. If they persist in their weakness in putting this non sequitur in contradiction to their principles, courageously oppose the force of reason to the empty pretentions of superiority; unite yourselves beneath the standards of philosophy; deploy all the energy of your character, and you will soon see these haughty men, not groveling at your feet as servile adorers, but proud to share with you the treasures of the Supreme Being. Regardless of what barriers confront you, it is in your power to free yourselves; you have only to want to. Let us pass now to the shocking tableau of what you have been in society; and since national education is in question at this moment, let us see whether our wise legislators will think judiciously about the education of women.

Women have done more harm than good. Constraint and dissimulation have been their lot. What force had robbed them of, ruse returned to them; they had recourse to all the resources of their charms, and the most irreproachable person did not resist them. Poison and the sword were both subject to them; they commanded in crime as in fortune. The French government, especially, depended throughout the centuries on the nocturnal administration of women; the cabinet kept no secret from their indiscretion; ambassadorial post, command, ministry, presidency, pontificate, college of cardinals; finally, anything which characterizes the folly of men, profane and sacred, all have been subject to the cupidity and ambition of this sex, formerly contemptible and respected, and since the revolution, respectable and scorned.

In this sort of contradictory situation, what remarks could I not make! I have but a moment to make them, but this moment will fix the attention of the remotest posterity. Under the Old Regime, all was vicious, all was guilty; but could not the amelioration of conditions be perceived even in the substance of vices? A woman only had to be beautiful or amiable; when she possessed these two advantages, she saw a hundred fortunes at her feet. If she did not profit from them, she had a bizarre character or a rare philosophy which made her scorn wealth; then she was deemed to be like a crazy woman; the most indecent made herself respected with gold; commerce in women was a kind of industry in the first class [of society], which, henceforth, will have no more credit. If it still had it, the revolution would be lost, and under the new relationships we would always be corrupted; however, reason can always be deceived [into believing] that any other road to fortune is closed to the woman whom a man buys, like the slave on the African coasts. The difference is great; that is known. The slave is commanded by the master; but if the master gives her liberty without recompense, and at an age when the slave has lost all her charms, what will become of this unfortunate woman? The victim of scorn, even the doors of charity are closed to her; she is poor and old, they say; why did she not know how to make her fortune? Reason finds other examples that are even more touching. A young, inexperienced woman, seduced by a man whom she loves, will abandon her parents to follow him; the ingrate will leave her after a few years, and the older she has become with him, the more inhuman is his inconstancy; if she has children, he will likewise abandon them. If he is rich, he will consider himself excused from sharing his fortune with his noble victims. If some involvement binds him to his duties, he will deny them, trusting that the laws will support him. If he is married, any other obligation loses its rights. Then what laws remain to extirpate vice all the way to its root? The law of dividing wealth and public administration between men and women. It can easily be seen that one who is born into a rich family gains very much from such equal sharing. But the one born into a poor family with merit and virtue—what is her lot? Poverty and opprobrium. If she does not precisely excel in music or painting, she cannot be admitted to any public function when she has all the capacity for it. I do not want to give only a sketch of things; I will go more deeply into this in the new edition of all my political writings, with notes, which I propose to give to the public in a few days.

I take up my text again on the subject of morals. Marriage is the tomb of trust and love. The married woman can with impunity give bastards to her husband, and also give them the wealth which does not belong to them. The woman who is unmarried has only one feeble right; ancient and inhuman laws refuse to her for her children the right to the name and the wealth of their father; no new laws have been made in this matter. If it is considered a paradox and an impossibility on my part to try to give my sex an honorable and just consistency, I leave it to men to attain glory for dealing with this matter; but while we wait, the way can be prepared through national education, the restoration of morals, and conjugal conventions.

Form for a Social Contract Between Man and Woman

We, _____ and _____, moved by our own will, unite ourselves for the duration of our lives, and for the duration of our mutual inclinations, under the following conditions: We intend and wish to make our wealth communal, meanwhile reserving to ourselves the right to divide it in favor of our children and of those toward whom we might have a particular inclination, mutually recognizing that our property belongs directly to our children, from whatever bed they come, and that all of them without distinction have the right to bear the name of the fathers and mothers who have acknowledged them, and we are charged to subscribe to the law which punishes the renunciation of one's own blood. We likewise obligate ourselves, in case of separation, to divide our wealth and to set aside in advance the portion the law indicates for our children, and in the event of a perfect union, the one who dies will divest himself of half his property in his children's favor, and if one dies childless, the survivor will inherit by right, unless the dying person has disposed of half the common property in favor of one whom he judged deserving.

That is approximately the formula for the marriage act I propose for execution. Upon reading this strange document, I see rising up against me the hypocrites, the prudes, the clergy, and the whole infernal sequence. But how it [my proposal] offers to the wise the moral means of achieving the perfection of a happy government! I am going to give in a few words the physical proof of it. The rich, childless Epicurean finds it very good to go to his poor neighbor to augment his family. When there is a law authorizing a poor man's wife to have a rich one adopt their children, the bonds of society will be strengthened and morals will be purer. This law will perhaps save the community's wealth and hold back the disorder which drives so many victims to the almshouses of shame, to a low station, and into degenerate human principles where nature has groaned for so long. May the detractors of wise philosophy then cease to cry out against primitive morals, or may they lose their point in the source of their citations.[1]

Moreover, I would like a law which would assist widows and young girls deceived by the false promises of a man to whom they were attached; I would like, I say, this law to force an inconstant man to hold to his obligations or at least [to pay] an indemnity equal to his wealth. Again, I would like this law to be rigorous against women, at least those who have the effrontery to have recourse to a law which they themselves had violated by their misconduct, if proof of that were given. At the same time, as I showed in *Le Bonheur primitif de l'homme,* in 1788, that prostitutes should be placed in designated quarters.[2] It is not prostitutes who contribute the most to the depravity of morals, it is the women of society. In regenerating the latter, the former are changed. This link of fraternal union will first bring disorder, but in consequence it will produce at the end a perfect harmony.

I offer a foolproof way to elevate the soul of women; it is to join them to all the activities of man; if man persists in finding this way impractical, let him share his fortune with woman, not at his caprice, but by the wisdom of laws. Prejudice falls, morals are purified, and nature regains all her rights. Add to this the marriage of priests and the strengthening of the king on his throne, and the French government cannot fail.

It would be very necessary to say a few words on the troubles which are said to be caused by the decree in favor of colored men in our islands. There is where nature shudders with horror; there is where reason and humanity have still not touched callous souls; there, especially, is where division and discord stir up their inhabitants. It is not difficult to divine the instigators of these incendiary fermentations; they are even in the midst of the National Assembly; they ignite the fire in Europe which must inflame America. Colonists make a claim to reign as despots over the men whose fathers and brothers they are; and, disowning the rights of nature, they trace the source of [their rule] to the scantiest tint of their blood. These inhuman colonists say: our blood flows in their veins, but we will shed it all if necessary to glut our greed or our blind ambition. It

---

1. Abraham had some very legitimate children by Agar, the servant of his wife.

2. See Olympe de Gouges, *Le Bonheur primitif de l'homme, ou les Rêveries patriotiques* (Amsterdam and Paris, 1789).

is in these places nearest to nature where the father scorns the son; deaf to the cries of blood, they stifle all its attraction; what can be hoped from the resistance opposed to them? To constrain [blood] violently is to render it terrible; to leave [blood] still enchained is to direct all calamities towards America. A divine hand seems to spread liberty abroad throughout the realms of man; only the law has the right to curb this liberty if it degenerates into license, but it must be equal for all; liberty must hold the National Assembly to its decree dictated by prudence and justice. May it act the same way for the state of France and render her as attentive to new abuses as she was to the ancient ones which each day become more dreadful. My opinion would be to reconcile the executive and legislative power, for it seems to me that the one is everything and the other is nothing—whence comes, unfortunately perhaps, the loss of the French Empire. I think that these two powers, like man and woman, should be united but equal in force and virtue to make a good household. . . .

The Vietnamese Declaration of Independence
Ho Chi Minh

On September 2, 1945, Ho Chi Minh and other members of the Vietminh, a patriotic Vietnamese organization, declared the independence of the Vietnamese people from French rule. Passages from the American and French declarations are quoted in the Vietnamese declaration. The purpose in quoting these earlier declarations was to show that all peoples are free and equal. In addition to establishing the ideas of fundamental truths and rights, the Vietnamese document catalogues the tyrannical practices of the French imperialists in Vietnam, much as the American colonists had presented the tyrannical acts of George III. The drafters argued that apart from general principles, the Vietnamese had earned the right to independence because they had fought against the Japanese for their freedom.

"All men are created equal. They are endowed by their Creator with certain inalienable rights, among these are Life, Liberty, and the pursuit of Happiness."

This immortal statement was made in the Declaration of Independence of the United States of America in 1776. In a broader sense, this means: All the peoples on the earth are equal from birth, all the peoples have a right to live, to be happy and free.

Ho Chi Minh, *Selected Works*, vol. 3 (Hanoi: 1960–62), 17–21; reprinted in *Vietnam: History, Documents, and Opinions on a Major World Crisis*, ed. Marvin E. Gettleman (New York: Fawcett Publications, 1965), 57–59.

The Declaration of the French Revolution made in 1791 on the Rights of Man and the Citizen also states: "All men are born free and with equal rights, and must always remain free and have equal rights." Those are undeniable truths.

Nevertheless, for more than eighty years, the French imperialists, abusing the standard of Liberty, Equality, and Fraternity, have violated our Fatherland and oppressed our fellow-citizens. They have acted contrary to the ideals of humanity and justice. In the field of politics, they have deprived our people of every democratic liberty.

They have enforced inhuman laws; they have set up three distinct political regimes in the North, the Center and the South of Vietnam in order to wreck our national unity and prevent our people from being united.

They have built more prisons than schools. They have mercilessly slain our patriots; they have drowned our uprisings in rivers of blood. They have fettered public opinion; they have practiced obscurantism against our people. To weaken our race they have forced us to use opium and alcohol.

In the fields of economics, they have fleeced us to the backbone, impoverished our people, and devastated our land.

They have robbed us of our rice fields, our mines, our forests, and our raw materials. They have monopolized the issuing of bank-notes and the export trade.

They have invented numerous unjustifiable taxes and reduced our people, especially our peasantry, to a state of extreme poverty.

They have hampered the prospering of our national bourgeoisie; they have mercilessly exploited our workers.

In the autumn of 1940, when the Japanese Fascists violated Indochina's territory to establish new bases in their fight against the Allies, the French imperialists went down on their bended knees and handed over our country to them.

Thus, from that date, our people were subjected to the double yoke of the French and the Japanese. Their sufferings and miseries increased. The result was that from the end of last year to the beginning of this year, from Quang Tri province to the North of Vietnam, more than two million of our fellow-citizens died from starvation. On March 9, the French troops were disarmed by the Japanese. The French colonialists either fled or surrendered, showing that not only were they incapable of "protecting" us, but that, in the span of five years, they had twice sold our country to the Japanese.

On several occasions before March 9, the Vietminh League urged the French to ally themselves with it against the Japanese. Instead of agreeing to this proposal, the French colonialists so intensified their terrorist activities against the Vietminh members that before fleeing they massacred a great number of our political prisoners detained at Yen Bay and Caobang.

Notwithstanding all this, our fellow-citizens have always manifested toward the French a tolerant and humane attitude. Even after the Japanese putsch of March 1945, the Vietminh League helped many Frenchmen to cross the frontier, rescued some of them from Japanese jails, and protected French lives and property.

From the autumn of 1940, our country had in fact ceased to be a French colony and had become a Japanese possession.

After the Japanese had surrendered to the Allies, our whole people rose to regain our national sovereignty and to found the Democratic Republic of Vietnam.

The truth is that we have wrested our independence from the Japanese and not from the French.

The French have fled, the Japanese have capitulated, Emperor Bao Dai has abdicated. Our people have broken the chains which for nearly a century have fettered them and have won independence for the Fatherland. Our people at the same time have overthrown the monarchic regime that has reigned supreme for dozens of centuries. In its place has been established the present Democratic Republic.

For these reasons, we, members of the Provisional Government, representing the whole Vietnamese people, declare that from now on we break off all relations of a colonial character with France; we repeal all the international obligation that France has so far subscribed to on behalf of Vietnam and we abolish all the special rights the French have unlawfully acquired in our Fatherland.

The whole Vietnamese people, animated by a common purpose, are determined to fight to the bitter end against any attempt by the French colonialists to reconquer their country.

We are convinced that the Allied nations which at Tehran and San Francisco have acknowledged the principles of self-determination and equality of nations, will not refuse to acknowledge the independence of Vietnam.

A people who have courageously opposed French domination for more than eighty years, a people who have fought side by side with the Allies against the Fascists during these last years, such a people must be free and independent.

For these reasons, we, members of the Provisional Government of the Democratic Republic of Vietnam, solemnly declare to the world that Vietnam has the right to be a free and independent country—and in fact it is so already. The entire Vietnamese people are determined to mobilize all their physical and mental strength, to sacrifice their lives and property in order to safeguard their independence and liberty.

The Errors of the French Revolution
Edmund Burke

In this selection written in 1790, the English political philosopher Edmund Burke chides the French for seeking to destroy all traces of the old order and building a new one from scratch. Burke believed that change ought to come slowly and should be based on foundations laid in the past. Because of their haste and sweeping changes, Burke believed the French had created a tyrannical system that had many of the worst elements of the old order. Burke felt that by sweeping away the past, the French had discarded good along with bad and had built a new order that abused liberty and unleashed dissoluteness in manners. Unless properly leashed and disciplined, human nature would burst forth in bloody frenzies.

Instead of Destroying the Old State the French Should Have Built on the Foundation Their Ancestors Had Left Them

You might, if you pleased, have profited of our example and have given to your recovered freedom a correspondent dignity. Your privileges, though discontinued, were not lost to memory. Your constitution, it is true, whilst you were out of possession, suffered waste and dilapidation; but you possessed in some parts the walls and, in all, the foundations of a noble and venerable castle. You might have repaired those walls; you might have built on those old foundations. Your constitution was suspended before it was perfected, but you had the elements of a constitution very nearly as good as could be wished. In your old states[1] you possessed that variety of parts corresponding with the various descriptions of which your community was happily composed; you had all that combination and all that opposition of interests; you had that action and counteraction which, in the natural and in the political world, from the reciprocal struggle of discordant powers, draws out the harmony of the universe. These opposed and conflicting interests which you considered as so great a blemish in your old and in our present constitution interpose a salutary check to all precipitate resolutions. They render deliberation a matter, not of choice, but of necessity; they make all change a subject of *compromise*, which naturally begets moderation; they produce *temperaments* preventing the sore evil of harsh, crude, unqualified reformations and rendering all the headlong exertions of arbitrary

---

1. The States-General, which had not met prior to 1789 since 1614. The three estates were: (1) the clergy; (2) the nobles; (3) the commoners.

Edmund Burke: Reflections on the Revolution in France, ed. Thomas Mahoney (New York: Liberal Arts Press, 1955), 39–45.

power, in the few or in the many, forever impracticable. Through that diversity of members and interests, general liberty had as many securities as there were separate views in the several orders, whilst, by pressing down the whole by the weight of a real monarchy, the separate parts would have been prevented from warping, and starting from their allotted places.

You had all these advantages in your ancient states, but you chose to act as if you had never been molded into civil society and had everything to begin anew. You began ill, because you began by despising everything that belonged to you. You set up your trade without a capital. If the last generations of your country appeared without much luster in your eyes, you might have passed them by and derived your claims from a more early race of ancestors. Under a pious predilection for those ancestors, your imaginations would have realized in them a standard of virtue and wisdom beyond the vulgar practice of the hour; and you would have risen with the example to whose imitation you aspired. Respecting your forefathers, you would have been taught to respect yourselves. You would not have chosen to consider the French as a people of yesterday, as a nation of low-born servile wretches until the emancipating year of 1789. In order to furnish, at the expense of your honor, an excuse to your apologists here for several enormities of yours, you would not have been content to be represented as a gang of Maroon slaves[2] suddenly broke loose from the house of bondage, and therefore to be pardoned for your abuse of the liberty to which you were not accustomed and ill fitted. Would it not, my worthy friend, have been wiser to have you thought, what I, for one, always thought you, a generous and gallant nation, long misled to your disadvantage by your high and romantic sentiments of fidelity, honor, and loyalty; that events had been unfavorable to you, but that you were not enslaved through any illiberal or servile disposition; that in your most devoted submission you were actuated by a principle of public spirit, and that it was your country you worshiped in the person of your king? Had you made it to be understood that in the delusion of this amiable error you had gone further than your wise ancestors, that you were resolved to resume your ancient privileges, whilst you preserved the spirit of your ancient and your recent loyalty and honor; or if, diffident of yourselves and not clearly discerning the almost obliterated constitution of your ancestors, you had looked to your neighbors in this land who had kept alive the ancient principles and models of the old common law of Europe meliorated and adapted to its present state — by following wise examples you would have given new examples of wisdom to the world. You would have rendered the cause of liberty venerable in the eyes of every worthy mind in every nation. You would have shamed despotism from the earth by showing that

2. Fugitive slaves in the West Indies.

freedom was not only reconcilable, but, as when well disciplined it is, auxiliary to law. You would have had an unoppressive but a productive revenue. You would have had a flourishing commerce to feed it. You would have had a free constitution, a potent monarchy, a disciplined army, a reformed and venerated clergy, a mitigated but spirited nobility to lead your virtue, not to overlay it; you would have had a liberal order of commons to emulate and to recruit that nobility; you would have had a protected, satisfied, laborious, and obedient people, taught to seek and to recognize the happiness that is to be found by virtue in all conditions; in which consists the true moral equality of mankind, and not in that monstrous fiction which, by inspiring false ideas and vain expectations into men destined to travel in the obscure walk of laborious life, serves only to aggravate and embitter that real inequality which it never can remove, and which the order of civil life establishes as much for the benefit of those whom it must leave in a humble state as those whom it is able to exalt to a condition more splendid, but not more happy. You had a smooth and easy career of felicity and glory laid open to you, beyond anything recorded in the history of the world, but you have shown that difficulty is good for man.

The Consequences of This False Policy

Compute your gains: see what is got by those extravagant and presumptuous speculations which have taught your leaders to despise all their predecessors, and all their contemporaries, and even to despise themselves until the moment in which they become truly despicable. By following those false lights, France has bought undisguised calamities at a higher price than any nation has purchased the most unequivocal blessings! France has bought poverty by crime! France has not sacrificed her virtue to her interest, but she has abandoned her interest, that she might prostitute her virtue. All other nations have begun the fabric of a new government, or the reformation of an old, by establishing originally or by enforcing with greater exactness some rites or other of religion. All other people have laid the foundations of civil freedom in severer manners and a system of a more austere and masculine morality. France, when she let loose the reins of regal authority, doubled the license of a ferocious dissoluteness in manners and of an insolent irreligion in opinions and practice, and has extended through all ranks of life, as if she were communicating some privilege or laying open some secluded benefit, all the unhappy corruptions that usually were the disease of wealth and power. This is one of the new principles of equality in France.

France, by the perfidy of her leaders, has utterly disgraced the tone of lenient council in the cabinets of princes, and disarmed it of its most potent topics. She has sanctified the dark, suspicious maxims of tyrannous distrust, and taught kings to tremble at (what will hereafter be called) the delusive plausibility of moral politicians. Sovereigns will consider those who advise them to place an unlimited confidence in their people as subverters of their thrones, as traitors who aim at their destruction by leading their easy good-nature, under specious pretenses, to admit combinations of bold and faithless men into a participation of their power. This alone (if there were nothing else) is an irreparable calamity to you and to mankind. Remember that your parliament of Paris told your king that, in calling the states together, he had nothing to fear but the prodigal excess of their zeal in providing for the support of the throne. It is right that these men should hide their heads. It is right that they should bear their part in the ruin which their counsel has brought on their sovereign and their country. Such sanguine declarations tend to lull authority asleep; to encourage it rashly to engage in perilous adventures of untried policy; to neglect those provisions, preparations, and precautions which distinguish benevolence from imbecility, and without which no man can answer for the salutary effect of any abstract plan of government or of freedom. For want of these, they have seen the medicine of the state corrupted into its poison. They have seen the French rebel against a mild and lawful monarch with more fury, outrage, and insult than ever any people has been known to rise against the most illegal usurper or the most sanguinary tyrant. Their resistance was made to concession, their revolt was from protection, their blow was aimed at a hand holding out graces, favors, and immunities.

This was unnatural. The rest is in order. They have found their punishment in their success: laws overturned; tribunals subverted; industry without vigor; commerce expiring; the revenue unpaid, yet the people impoverished; a church pillaged, and a state not relieved; civil and military anarchy made the constitution of the kingdom; everything human and divine sacrificed to the idol of public credit, and national bankruptcy the consequence; and, to crown all, the paper securities of new, precarious, tottering power, the discredited paper securities of impoverished fraud and beggared rapine, held out as a currency for the support of an empire in lieu of the two great recognized species [i.e. gold and silver] that represent the lasting, conventional credit of mankind, which disappeared and hid themselves in the earth from whence they came, when the principle of property, whose creatures and representatives they are, was systematically subverted.

Were all these dreadful things necessary? Were they the inevitable results of the desperate struggle of determined patriots, compelled to wade through blood and tumult to the quiet shore of a tranquil and prosperous liberty? No! nothing like it. The fresh ruins of France, which shock our feelings wherever we can turn our eyes, are not the devastation of civil war; they are the sad but instructive monuments of rash and ignorant counsel in time of profound peace. They are the display of inconsiderate and presumptuous, because unresisted and irresistible, authority. The persons who have thus squandered away the precious treasure of their crimes, the persons who have made this prodigal and wild waste of public evils (the last stake reserved for the ultimate ransom of the state) have met in their progress with little or rather with no opposition at all. Their whole march was more like a triumphal procession than the progress of a war. Their pioneers have gone before them and demolished and laid everything level at their feet. Not one drop of *their* blood have they shed in the cause of the country they have ruined. They have made no sacrifices to their projects of greater consequence than their shoebuckles, whilst they were imprisoning their king, murdering their fellow citizens, and bathing in tears and plunging in poverty and distress thousands of worthy men and worthy families. Their cruelty has not even been the base result of fear. It has been the effect of their sense of perfect safety, in authorizing treasons, robberies, rapes, assassinations, slaughters, and burnings throughout their harassed land. But the cause of all was plain from the beginning.

NATIONALISM, IMPERIALISM, AND INDEPENDENCE STRUGGLES

The Industrial Revolution created for North America, Europe, and Japan the means to pursue imperialist policies and create global empires. Manufacturers who produced large quantities of textiles, for example, needed markets where they could be sold. Supplies of raw materials were also demanded by industrialists. Weapons could be mass produced for armies that conquered and helped rule colonies. Industrialization both promoted and permitted the growth of empire.

Various theories and ideas were created to justify the fact of imperialist domination. Racist assertions were used to argue that one race should dominate or guide people of "inferior" races. Social Darwinists argued that the strong had to rule the weak, no matter what race to which the weak belonged.

Nationalism was also employed to cement groups that resisted colonial rule. Peoples who spoke the same language and who shared common traditions were urged to unite against the colonial ruler who was of a different nationality. Nationalism was a powerful tool used to build and to resist colonial empires.

Confession of Faith
Cecil Rhodes

In this testament written in the late 1870s, Cecil Rhodes, Britain's strongest promoter of empire, outlined his views on empire and British domination of the world. Rhodes mixed nationalism and racism to propose that

John Flint, *Cecil Rhodes* (Boston: Little, Brown & Co., 1974), 248–50.

the world would be better off under British rule. He believed that British education was the best, that British institutions were the best, and that the British people were the best. Rhodes proposed the creation of a secular "religion" of imperialism, an ideology directed toward and dedicated to world domination by the Anglo-Saxons. Thus, Rhodes illustrated the rising tide of secularism in the nineteenth century.

It often strikes a man to inquire what is the chief good in life; to one the thought comes that it is a happy marriage, to another great wealth, and as each seizes on his idea, for that he more or less works for the rest of his existence. To myself thinking over the same question the wish came to render myself useful to my country. I then asked myself how could I and after reviewing the various methods I have felt that at the present day we are actually limiting our children and perhaps bringing into the world half the human beings we might owing to the lack of country for them to inhabit that if we had retained America there would at this moment be millions more of English living. I contend that we are the finest race in the world and that the more of the world we inhabit the better it is for the human race. Just fancy those parts that are at present inhabited by the most despicable specimens of human beings what an alteration there would be if they were brought under Anglo-Saxon influence, look again at the extra employment a new country added to our dominions gives. I contend that every acre added to our territory means in the future birth to some more of the English race who otherwise would not be brought into existence. Added to this the absorption of the greater portion of the world under our rule simply means the end of all wars, at this moment had we not lost America I believe we could have stopped the Russian-Turkish war by merely refusing money and supplies. Having these ideas what scheme could we think of to forward this object. I look into history and I read the story of the Jesuits I see what they were able to do in a bad cause and I might say under bad leaders.

In the present day I become a member in the Masonic order I see the wealth and power they possess the influence they hold and I think over their ceremonies and I wonder that a large body of men can devote themselves to what at times appear the most ridiculous and absurd rites without an object and without an end.

The idea gleaming and dancing before ones eyes like a will-of-the-wisp at last frames itself into a plan. Why should we not form a secret society with but one object the furtherance of the British Empire and the bringing of the whole uncivilised world under British rule for the recovery of the United States for the making the Anglo-Saxon race but one Empire. What a dream, but yet it is probable, it is possible. I once heard it argued by a fellow in my own college, I am sorry to own it by an Englishman, that it was a good thing for us that we have lost the United States. There are some subjects on which there can be no arguments, and to an Englishman this is one of them, but even from an American's point of view just picture what they have lost, look at their government, are not the frauds that yearly come before the public view a disgrace to any country and especially their's which is the finest in the world. Would they have occurred had they remained under English rule great as they have become how infinitely greater they would have been with the softening and elevating influences of English rule, think of those countless 000's of Englishmen that during the last 100 years would have crossed the Atlantic and settled and populated the United States. Would they have not made without any prejudice a finer country of it than the low class Irish and German emigrants? All this we have lost and that country loses owing to whom? Owing to two or three ignorant pig-headed statesmen of the last century, at their door lies the blame. Do you ever feel mad? do you ever feel murderous? I think I do with those men. I bring facts to prove my assertion. Does an English father when his sons wish to emigrate ever think of suggesting emigration to a country under another flag, never — it would seem a disgrace to suggest such a thing I think that we all think that poverty is better under our own flag than wealth under a foreign one.

Put your mind into another train of thought. Fancy Australia discovered and colonised under the French flag, what would it mean merely several millions of English unborn that at present exist we learn from the past and to form our future. We learn from having lost to cling to what we possess. We know the size of the world we know the total extent. Africa is still lying ready for us it is our duty to take it. It is our duty to seize every opportunity of acquiring more territory and we should keep this one idea steadily before our eyes that more territory simply means more of the Anglo-Saxon race more of the best the most human, most honourable race the world possesses.

To forward such a scheme what a splendid help a secret society would be a society not openly acknowledged but who would work in secret for such an object.

I contend that there are at the present moment numbers of the ablest men in the world who would devote their whole lives to it. I often think what a loss to the English nation in some respects the abolition of the Rotten Borough System has been. What thought strikes a man entering the house of commons, the assembly that rules the whole world? I think it is the mediocrity of the men but what is the cause. It is simply — an assembly of wealth of men whose lives have been spent in the accumulation of money and whose time has been too much engaged to be able to spare any for the study of past history. And yet in the hands of such men rest our destinies. Do men like the great Pitt, and Burke and Sheridan not now exist. I contend they do. . . . They live and die unused unemployed. What has been the main cause of the success of the Romish Church? The fact that every enthusiast, call it if you like every madman finds employment in it. Let us form the same kind of society a Church for the extension of the British Empire. A society which should have its members in every part of the British Empire working with one object and one idea we should have its members placed at our universities and our schools and should watch the English youth passing through their hands just one perhaps in every thousand would have the mind and feelings for such an object, he should be tried in every way, he should be tested whether he is endurant, possessed of eloquence, disregardful of the petty details of life, and if found to be such, then elected and bound by oath to serve for the rest of his life in his Country. He should then be supported if without means by the Society and sent to that part of the Empire where it was felt he was needed.

Take another case, let us fancy a man who finds himself his own master with ample means on attaining his majority whether he puts the question directly to himself or not, still like the old story of virtue and vice in the Memorabilia a fight goes on in him as to what he should do. Take if he plunges into dissipation there is nothing too reckless he does not attempt but after a time his life palls on him, he mentally says this is not good enough, he changes his life, he reforms, he travels, he thinks now I have found the chief good in life, the novelty wears off, and he tires, to change again, he goes into the far interior after the wild game he thinks at last I've found that in life of which I cannot tire, again he is disappointed. He returns he thinks is there nothing I can do in life? Here I am with means, with a good house, with everything that is to be envied and yet I am not happy I am tired of life, . . . to such a man the Society should go, should test, and should finally show him the greatness of the scheme and list him as a member.

Take one more case of the younger son with high thoughts, high aspirations, endowed by nature with all the faculties to make a great man, and with the sole wish in life to serve his Country but he lacks two things the means and the opportunity, ever troubled by a sort of inward deity urging him on to high and noble deeds, he is compelled to pass his time in some occupation which furnishes him with mere existence, he lives unhappily and dies miserably. Such men as these the Society should search out and use for the furtherance of their object.

(In every Colonial legislature the Society should attempt to have its members prepared at all times to vote or speak and advocate the closer union of England and the colonies, to crush all disloyalty and every movement for the severance of our Empire. The Society should inspire and even own portions of the press for the press rules the mind of the people. The Society should always be searching for members who might by their position in the world by their energies or character forward the object but the ballot and test for admittance should be severe.)

Once make it common and it fails. Take a man of great wealth who is bereft of his children perhaps having his mind soured by some bitter disappointment who shuts himself up separate from his neighbours and makes up his mind to a miserable existence. To such men as these the society should go gradually disclose the greatness of their scheme and entreat him to throw in his life and property with them for this object. I think that there are thousands now existing who would eagerly grasp at the opportunity. Such are the heads of my scheme.

For fear that death might cut me off before the time for attempting its development I leave all my worldly goods in trust to S. G. Shippard and the Secretary for the Colonies at the time of my death to try to form such a Society with such an object.

The Need for Emigration and Expansion
Hashimoto Kingoro

Writing in the late 1930s, Hashimoto Kingoro in the following essay attempted to justify Japanese expansion on the Asian mainland. He argues that Western countries prevented Japanese immigration and that Japanese goods were shut out of Western-controlled markets. Therefore, only with the expansion of Japan's empire would Japanese prosperity from emigration and trade increase. Hashimoto states that the Westerners' justifications for their expansion should be employed by the Japanese as well. While he makes a case for Japanese expansion, Hashimoto grounds his argument in imperialist traditions long established by Westerners. Hashimoto's views reflect the ultranationalist philosophy shared by many of his fellow Japanese scholars in the 1930s.

We have already said that there are only three ways left to Japan to escape from the pressure of surplus population. We are like a great crowd of people packed into a small and narrow room, and there are only three doors through which we might escape, namely emigration, advance into world markets, and expansion of territory. The first door, emigration, has been barred to us by the anti-Japanese immigration policies of other countries. The second door, advance into world markets, is being pushed shut by tariff barriers and the abrogation of commercial treaties. What should Japan do when two of the three doors have been closed against her?

It is quite natural that Japan should rush upon the last remaining door.

It may sound dangerous when we speak of territorial expansion, but the territorial expansion of which we speak does not in any sense of the

Sources of Japanese Tradition, ed. Ryusaku Tsunoda, William Theodore de Bary, and Donald Keene (New York: Columbia University Press, 1958), 796–98; reprinted in *Japan, 1931–1945*, ed. Ivan Morris (Boston: D. C. Heath & Co., 1963), 64–65.

word involve the occupation of the possessions of other countries, the planting of the Japanese flag thereon, and the declaration of their annexation to Japan. It is just that since the Powers have suppressed the circulation of Japanese materials and merchandise abroad, we are looking for some place overseas where Japanese capital, Japanese skills and Japanese labor can have free play, free from the oppression of the white race.

We would be satisfied with just this much. What moral right do the world powers who have themselves closed to us the two doors of emigration and advance into world markets have to criticize Japan's attempt to rush out of the third and last door?

If they do not approve of this, they should open the doors which they have closed against us and permit the free movement overseas of Japanese emigrants and merchandise. . . .

At the time of the Manchurian incident, the entire world joined in criticism of Japan. They said that Japan was an untrustworthy nation. They said that she had recklessly brought cannon and machine guns into Manchuria, which was the territory of another country, flown airplanes over it, and finally occupied it. But the military action taken by Japan was not in the least a selfish one. Moreover, we do not recall ever having taken so much as an inch of territory belonging to another nation. The result of this incident was the establishment of the splendid new nation of Manchuria. The Powers are still discussing whether or not to recognize this new nation, but regardless of whether or not other nations recognize her, the Manchurian empire has already been established, and now, seven years after its creation, the empire is further consolidating its foundations with the aid of its friend, Japan.

And if it is still protested that our actions in Manchuria were excessively violent, we may wish to ask the white race just which country it was that sent warships and troops to India, South Africa, and Australia and slaughtered innocent natives, bound their hands and feet with iron chains, lashed their backs with iron whips, proclaimed these territories as their own, and still continues to hold them to this very day?

They will invariably reply, these were all lands inhabited by untamed savages. These people did not know how to develop the abundant resources of their land for the benefit of mankind. Therefore it was the wish of God, who created heaven and earth for mankind, for us to develop these undeveloped lands and to promote the happiness of mankind in their stead. God wills it.

This is quite a convenient argument for them. Let us take it at face value. Then there is another question that we must ask them.

Suppose that there is still on this earth land endowed with abundant natural resources that have not been developed at all by the white race. Would it not then be God's will and the will of Providence that Japan go there and develop those resources for the benefit of mankind?

And there still remain many such lands on this earth.

Satyagraha — *Soul-Force*
Mohandas (Mahatma) Gandhi

Mohandas Gandhi, who spent much of his life under British rule, adapted an ancient Indian philosophical principle to political purposes. He argued that satyagraha *(usually translated as "soul-force" but literally meaning "truth and persistence") could produce passive resistance that would effectively oppose British rule. Throughout his life Gandhi opposed physical force (the use of weapons and physical combat), instead advocating soul-force, which is the use of one's spirit to overcome tyranny. In this essay (1938), which is part of a larger work advocating Indian independence, Gandhi outlines the principles of passive resistance, building on Indian traditions of using nonviolence to combat unjust policies. He employs the technique of the dialogue to present and answer questions about his movement.*

READER: Is there any historical evidence as to the success of what you have called soul-force or truth-force? No instance seems to have happened of any nation having risen through soul-force. I still think that evil-doers will not cease doing evil without physical punishment.

EDITOR: The poet Tulsidas has said: "Of religion, pity, or love, is the root, as egotism of the body. Therefore, we should not abandon pity so long as we are alive." This appears to me to be a scientific truth. I believe in it as much as I believe in two and two being four. The force of love is the same as the force of the soul or truth. We have evidence of its working at every step. The universe would disappear without the existence of that force. But you ask for historical evidence. It is, therefore, necessary to know what history means. The Gujarati equivalent means: "It so happened." If that is the meaning of history, it is possible to give copious evidence. But, if it means the doings of kings and emperors, there can be no evidence of soul-force or passive resistance in such history. You cannot expect silver ore in a tin mine.

History, as we know it, is a record of the wars of the world, and so there is a proverb among Englishmen that a nation which has no history, that is, no wars, is a happy nation. How kings played, how they became enemies of one another, how they murdered one another, is found accurately recorded in history, and if this were all that had happened in the world, it would have been ended long ago. If the story of the universe had commenced with wars, not a man would have been found alive today. Those people who have been warred against have disappeared as, for instance, the natives of Australia of whom hardly a man was left alive by the intruders. Mark, please, that these natives did not

The Moral and Political Works of Mahatma Gandhi, ed. Raghavan Iver (Oxford: Oxford University Press, 1986), 244–51.

use soul-force in self-defence, and it does not require much foresight to know that the Australians will share the same fate as their victims. "Those that take the sword shall perish by the sword." With us the proverb is that professional swimmers will find a watery grave.

The fact that there are so many men still alive in the world shows that it is based not on the force of arms but on the force of truth or love. Therefore, the greatest and most unimpeachable evidence of the success of this force is to be found in the fact that, in spite of the wars of the world, it still lives on.

Thousands, indeed tens of thousands, depend for their existence on a very active working of this force. Little quarrels of millions of families in their daily lives disappear before the exercise of this force. Hundreds of nations live in peace. History does not and cannot take note of this fact. History is really a record of every interruption of the even working of the force of love or of the soul. Two brothers quarrel; one of them repents and re-awakens the love that was lying dormant in him; the two again begin to live in peace; nobody takes note of this. But if the two brothers, through the intervention of solicitors or some other reason take up arms or go to law — which is another form of the exhibition of brute force, — their doings would be immediately noticed in the Press, they would be the talk of their neighbours and would probably go down to history. And what is true of families and communities is true of nations. There is no reason to believe that there is one law for families and another for nations. History, then, is a record of an interruption of the course of nature. Soul-force, being natural, is not noted in history.

READER: According to what you say, it is plain that instances of this kind of passive resistance are not to be found in history. It is necessary to understand this passive resistance more fully. It will be better, therefore, if you enlarge upon it.

EDITOR: *Satyagraha* is referred to in English as passive resistance. Passive resistance is a method of securing rights by personal suffering; it is the reverse of resistance by arms. When I refuse to do a thing that is repugnant to my conscience, I use soul-force. For instance, the Government of the day has passed a law which is applicable to me. I do not like it. If by using violence I force the Government to repeal the law, I am employing what may be termed body-force. If I do not obey the law and accept the penalty for its breach, I use soul-force. It involves sacrifice of self.

Everybody admits that sacrifice of self is infinitely superior to sacrifice of others. Moreover, if this kind of force is used in a cause that is unjust, only the person using it suffers. He does not make others suffer for his mistakes. Men have before now done many things which were subsequently found to have been wrong. No man can claim that he is absolutely in the right or that a particular thing is wrong because he thinks so, but it is wrong for him so long as that is his deliberate judgment. It is therefore meet that he should not do that which he knows to be wrong, and suffer the consequence whatever it may be. This is the key to the use of soul-force.

READER: You would then disregard laws — this is rank disloyalty. We have always been considered a law-abiding nation. You seem to be going even beyond the extremists. They say that we must obey the laws that have been passed, but that if the laws be bad, we must drive out the law-givers even by force.

EDITOR: Whether I go beyond them or whether I do not is a matter of no consequence to either of us. We simply want to find out what is right and to act accordingly. The real meaning of the statement that we are a law-abiding nation is that we are passive resisters. When we do not like certain laws, we do not break the heads of law-givers but we suffer and do not submit to the laws. That we should obey laws whether good or bad is a new-fangled notion. There was no such thing in former days. The people disregarded those laws they did not like and suffered the penalties for their breach. It is contrary to our manhood if we obey laws repugnant to our conscience. Such teaching is opposed to religion and means slavery. If the Government were to ask us to go about without any clothing, should we do so? If I were a passive resister, I would say to them that I would have nothing to do with their law. But we have so forgotten ourselves and become so compliant that we do not mind any degrading law.

A man who has realized his manhood, who fears only God, will fear no one else. Man-made laws are not necessarily binding on him. Even the Government does not expect any such thing from us. They do not say: "You must do such and such a thing," but they say: "If you do not do it, we will punish you." We are sunk so low that we fancy that it is our duty and our religion to do what the law lays down. If man will only realize that it is unmanly to obey laws that are unjust, no man's tyranny will enslave him. This is the key to self-rule or home rule.

It is a superstition and ungodly thing to believe that an act of a majority binds a minority. Many examples can be given in which acts of majorities will be found to have been wrong and those of minorities to have been right. All reforms owe their origin to the initiation of minorities in opposition to majorities. If among a band of robbers a knowledge of robbing is obligatory, is a pious man to accept the obligation? So long as the superstition that men should obey unjust laws exists, so long will their slavery exist. And a passive resister alone can remove such a superstition.

To use brute-force, to use gunpowder, is contrary to passive resistance, for it means that we want our opponent to do by force that which we desire but he does not. And if such a use of force is justifiable, surely he is entitled to do likewise by us. And so we should never come to an agreement. We may simply fancy, like the blind horse moving in a circle round a mill, that we are making progress. Those who believe that they are not bound to obey laws which are repugnant to their conscience have only the remedy of passive resistance open to them. Any other must lead to disaster.

READER: From what you say I deduce that passive resistance is a splendid weapon of the weak, but that when they are strong they may take up arms.

EDITOR: This is gross ignorance. Passive resistance, that is, soul-force, is matchless. It is superior to the force of arms. How, then, can it be considered only a weapon of the weak? Physical-force men are strangers to the courage that is requisite in a passive resister. Do you believe that a coward can ever disobey a law that he dislikes? Extremists are considered to be advocates of brute force. Why do they, then, talk about obeying laws? I do not blame them. They can say nothing else. When they succeed in driving out the English and they themselves become governors, they will want you and me to obey their laws. And that is a fitting thing for their constitution. But a passive resister will say he will not obey a law that is against his conscience, even though he may be blown to pieces at the mouth of a cannon.

What do you think? Wherein is courage required — in blowing others to pieces from behind a cannon, or with a smiling face to approach a cannon and be blown to pieces? Who is the true warrior — he who keeps death always as a bosom-friend, or he who controls the death of others? Believe me that a man devoid of courage and manhood can never be a passive resister.

This, however, I will admit: that even a man weak in body is capable of offering this resistance. One man can offer it just as well as millions. Both men and women can indulge in it. It does not require the training of an army; it needs no jiu-jitsu. Control over the mind is alone necessary, and when that is attained, man is free like the king of the forest and his very glance withers the enemy.

Passive resistance is an all-sided sword, it can be used anyhow; it blesses him who uses it and him against whom it is used. Without drawing a drop of blood it produces far-reaching results. It never rusts and cannot be stolen. Competition between passive resisters does not exhaust. The sword of passive resistance does not require a scabbard. It is strange indeed that you should consider such a weapon to be a weapon merely of the weak.

READER: You have said that passive resistance is a speciality of India. Have cannons never been used in India?

EDITOR: Evidently, in your opinion, India means its few princes. To me it means its teeming millions on whom depends the existence of its princes and our own.

Kings will always use their kingly weapons. To use force is bred in them. They want to command, but those who have to obey commands do not want guns: and these are in a majority throughout the world. They have to learn either body-force or soul-force. Where they learn the former, both the rulers and the ruled become like so many madmen; but where they learn soul-force, the commands of the rulers do not go beyond the point of their swords, for true men disregard unjust commands. Peasants have never been subdued by the sword, and never will be. They do not know the use of the sword, and they are not frightened by the use of it by others. That nation is great which rests its head upon death as its pillow. Those who defy death are free from all fear. For those who are labouring under the delusive charms of brute-force, this picture is not overdrawn. The fact is that, in India, the nation at large has generally used passive resistance in all departments of life. We cease to co-operate with our rulers when they displease us. This is passive resistance.

I remember an instance when, in a small principality, the villagers were offended by some command issued by the prince. The former immediately began vacating the village. The prince became nervous, apologized to his subjects and withdrew his command. Many such instances can be found in India. Real Home Rule is possible only where passive resistance is the guiding force of the people. Any other rule is foreign rule.

READER: Then you will say that it is not at all necessary for us to train the body?

EDITOR: I will certainly not say any such thing. It is difficult to become a passive resister unless the body is trained. As a rule, the mind, residing in a body that has become weakened by pampering, is also weak, and where there is no strength of mind there can be no strength of soul. We shall have to improve our physique by getting rid of infant marriages and luxurious living. If I were to ask a man with a shattered body to face a cannon's mouth, I should make a laughing-stock of myself.

READER: From what you say, then, it would appear that it is not a small thing to become a passive resister, and, if that is so, I should like you to explain how a man may become one.

EDITOR: To become a passive resister is easy enough but it is also equally difficult. I have known a lad of fourteen years become a passive resister; I have known also sick people do likewise; and I have also known physically strong and otherwise happy people unable to take up passive resistance. After a great deal of experience it seems to me that those who want to become passive resisters for the service of the country have to observe perfect chastity, adopt poverty, follow truth, and cultivate fearlessness.

Chastity is one of the greatest disciplines without which the mind cannot attain requisite firmness. A man who is unchaste loses stamina, becomes emasculated and cowardly. He whose mind is given over to animal passions is not capable of any great effort. This can be proved by innumerable instances. What, then, is a married person to do is the question that arises naturally; and yet it need not. When a husband and wife gratify the passions, it is no less an animal indulgence on that account. Such an indulgence, except for perpetuating the race, is strictly prohibited. But a passive resister has to avoid even that very limited indulgence because he can have no desire for progeny. A married man, therefore, can observe perfect chastity. This subject is not capable of being treated at greater length. Several questions arise: How is one to carry one's wife with one, what are her rights, and other similar questions. Yet those who wish to take part in a great work are bound to solve these puzzles.

Just as there is necessity for chastity, so is there for poverty. Pecuniary ambition and passive resistance cannot well go together. Those who have money are not expected to throw it away, but they *are* expected to be indifferent about it. They must be prepared to lose every penny rather than give up passive resistance.

Passive resistance has been described in the course of our discussion as truth-force. Truth, therefore, has necessarily to be followed and that at any cost. In this connection, academic questions such as whether a man may not lie in order to save a life, etc., arise, but these questions occur only to those who wish to justify lying. Those who want to follow truth every time are not placed in such a quandary; and if they are, they are still saved from a false position.

Passive resistance cannot proceed a step without fearlessness. Those alone can follow the path of passive resistance who are free from fear, whether as to their possessions, false honour, their relatives, the government, bodily injuries or death.

These observances are not to be abandoned in the belief that they are difficult. Nature has implanted in the human breast ability to cope with any difficulty or suffering that may come to man unprovoked. These qualities are worth having, even for those who do not wish to serve the country. Let there be no mistake, as those who want to train themselves in the use of arms are also obliged to have these qualities more or less. Everybody does not become a warrior for the wish. A would-be warrior will have to observe chastity and to be satisfied with poverty as his lot. A warrior without fearlessness cannot be conceived of. It may be thought that he would not need to be exactly truthful, but that quality follows real fearlessness. When a man abandons truth, he does so owing to fear in some shape or form. The above four attributes, then, need not frighten anyone. It may be as well here to note that a physical-force man has to have many other useless qualities which a passive resister never needs. And you will find that whatever extra effort a swordsman needs is due to lack of fearlessness. If he is an embodiment of the latter, the sword will drop from his hand that very moment. He does not need its support. One who is free from hatred requires no sword. A man with a stick suddenly came face to face with a lion and instinctively raised his weapon in self-defence. The man saw that he had only prated about fearlessness when there was none in him. That moment he dropped the stick and found himself free from all fear.

The Nigerian Youth Movement
Obafemi Awolowo

In this selection from his 1960 autobiography, Chief Obafemi Awolowo of Nigeria recalls the creation of the Nigerian Youth Movement, a nationalist organization dedicated to resisting British rule. The British government's discriminatory policies angered Nigerians and provoked them into forming the Lagos Youth Movement. This group's vision expanded as nationalism spread across Nigeria in the 1930s, until it finally became known as the Nigerian Youth Movement and helped bring about Nigerian independence after World War II.

In 1934, the Nigerian Government inaugurated the Yaba Higher College. This institution, which was not affiliated to any British university, was to award its own Nigerian diplomas in a number of faculties, including medicine, arts, agriculture, economics and engineering. This institution was assailed by Nigerian nationalists. In the first place, it was inferior in status to a British university; and under no circumstance would an institution of higher learning which bore the stamp of inferiority be tolerated by Nigerians. In the second place, the diplomas to be awarded by the institution were also inferior, since the holders of these diplomas were only expected, in various government departments and institutions, to occupy posts which were permanently subordinate to those filled by the holders of British university degrees (mostly expatriates) in the same faculties and professions. Africanisation of the civil service had been in the air for some time, and it was believed that the Yaba Higher College was an infernal device by British imperialism to foil this legitimate aspiration. This view was further strengthened by the fact that, only five years previously, the Nigerian government had planned to introduce a Nigerian School Certificate in place and to the exclusion of the then Cambridge and Oxford School Certificates. The plan was dropped as a

Awo: The Autobiography of Chief Obafemi Awolo (Cambridge: Cambridge University Press, 1960), 115–16.

result of the undivided opposition to it by all the political leaders in Lagos, irrespective of their party leanings, Mr. P. J. C. Thomas, Mr. Eric Moore, Dr. Akinola Maja, Sir Adeyemo Alakija, Henry Carr, "H.M." himself and other stalwarts in the public life of Lagos, spearheaded the agitation. In the third place, the diplomas to be awarded by the college would only enjoy an inferior recognition in Nigeria and would not command any respect, much less recognition, outside the country. In the fourth place, though the diplomas were in all respects to be inferior to university degrees, the time required to do a course was longer than was the case for a university degree in the same subject. There was, therefore, widespread resentment in political circles in Lagos, and in some circles in Southern Nigeria. It was in order to canalise this resentment, and to present a united front to the Nigerian government in representing the feelings of the people, that the Lagos Youth Movement was founded by Dr. J. C. Vaughan, Mr. Ernest Ikoli, Oba Samuel Akisanya, and others. I remember the memorandum submitted by the Lagos Youth Movement, the Movement's rejoinder to the government's reply, and Oba Samuel Akisanya's open letter to Duse Mohammed Ali Effendi, who in his paper *Comet* had criticised the leaders of the Movement and had described them as "half-baked critics." All these remonstrances were analytical, constructive, scathing and crushing. In them, the Movement elaborated its reasons for opposing the establishment of the college as it was then constituted, and made suggestions for its improvement. The Nigerian government, however, persisted in going on with its scheme as originally conceived. The Lagos Youth Movement, on the other hand, continued in existence to initiate and conduct agitations against other unjust manifestations of British rule in Nigeria. In 1936, as a result of clamour from different parts of the country, the name "Lagos Youth Movement" was changed to "Nigerian Youth Movement."

A History of the Chinese Revolution
Sun Yat-sen

In 1911–1912 Sun Yat-sen played a key role in the overthrow of the Qing Empire. Although monarchical rule had ended, the Chinese republic that Sun helped create eventually failed. Sun wrote a political statement to explain the republic's failure and outline his plans for rebuilding the nation in the future. Sun believed a new order had to be built on nationalism, democracy, and public welfare. Sun combined Western thought with Chinese traditions to fashion his opinions about how to create a new China. Failure led Sun to believe that nation building was a slow process demanding rule by the military before a constitutional system could be created.

Prescriptions for Saving China: Selected Writings of Sun Yat-sen, ed. Julie Lee Wei, Ramon H. Myers, and Donald G. Gillin; trans. Julie Lee Wei, E-su Zen, and Linda Chao (Stanford, Calif.: Hoover Institution Press, 1994), 252–55.

The Principles of the Revolution

The term *revolution* originates with Confucius. Since the days of Emperors Tang and Wu, China has seen numerous revolutions; not until the seventeenth and eighteenth centuries was Europe swept by those same storms. To revolution we owe not only the democracies but even the constitutional monarchies. The principles that I have held in carrying out the Chinese Revolution are partly rooted in our nation's intellectual legacy, partly derived from European thought and events, and partly the product of my own insights and innovations. I will describe these separately, as follows.

The Principle of Nationalism

From observing the course of China's history, we know that the Chinese people are of an independent spirit and have the capacity for independence. Whenever China encountered other nations, it either coexisted peacefully with them or else assimilated them. To be sure, during times of political disorder and military laxity, it has been temporarily subjugated and controlled by other nations, but it has always managed to overcome those nations by force of arms. . . . From this we knew that, although the Manchus controlled China, the Chinese people would ultimately be able to expel them. For nationalism is a legacy left by our forefathers, and, from the very beginning, there has been no need to import it. My Principle of Nationalism takes our ancestral legacy and develops it to greater brilliance. Moreover, I have remedied its defects. Toward the Manchus, I do not seek revenge, urging rather that we coexist with them within China on terms of equality. This is how the Principle of Nationalism deals with the various nationalities within our borders. Toward the other peoples of the world, I have urged that we preserve our independence, develop our traditional culture, and at the same time absorb and further develop the culture of the world to greater brilliance, in the hope of advancing in step with other nations and of eventually achieving world unity. This is how the Principle of Nationalism will be used to deal with the various nations of the world.

The Principle of the People's Rights

In ancient China, Emperor Tang humbly abdicated the throne to Yü. From the revolution of Emperor Tang and Emperor Wu, various sayings have come down through the ages, such as, "Heaven sees as my people see, heaven hears as my people hear"; and "I have heard that a fellow Zhou was executed; I have not heard that a subject killed his king"; and "The people are nobler than the emperor." From this we know that we cannot say China did not have the concept of the people's rights. However, though there was the concept, it was never institutionalized. In order to create a system in which the people are the foundation of the nation, we must look to Europe and America. Some nations of Europe and America are constitutional democracies; others are constitutional monarchies.

Even the constitutional monarchies, let alone the constitutional democracies, have resulted from the expansion of the rights of the people and the shrinking of the power of the kings. But in the case of the constitutional monarchies, the vestigial power of the rulers has not been completely eradicated. I myself have taken part in revolution because I consider democracy indispensable for China.

There are three reasons for this: (1) Since the people are known to be the foundation of the nation, where can there, theoretically speaking, be room for a ruler in a nation where everyone is equal to everyone else? (2) When the Manchus occupied China, the Chinese people became a subject people, and so enduring is the pain of our nation's extinction that 260 years is as a day. Thus, constitutional monarchy may be temporarily viable in other nations, where the animosity between the people and their rulers is not so intense, but it is out of the question in China. I speak from historical fact. (3) The reason China's past revolutions have resulted in prolonged chaos and confusion is that everyone wanted to be emperor, so that the fighting went on endlessly. In a democratic system, all such conflict will automatically disappear (speaking from the viewpoint of future reconstruction). In keeping with these three points, my Principle of the People's Rights has democracy as its primary element and as its second element the idea that a democratic dictatorship cannot work and a constitution is necessary for good government. Since its inception with Montesquieu, European constitutionalism has in essence consisted of the division of powers into the legislative, judicial, and executive, a scheme that has been adopted by all the constitutional nations of Europe and America. In the course of my inquiries, during my travels in Europe and America, into the pros and cons of their political and legal systems, I realized that certain shortcomings in their electoral systems had to be corrected. On the other hand, the examination and censorial institutions of China, handed down through the ages, possess genuine merit and are quite sufficient to compensate for the inadequacies of the European and American legal and political systems. Therefore, I proposed that the legislative, judicial, and executive powers be complemented by branches charged with the powers of examination and censorship, all combining into a five-power constitution. Furthermore, I advocate a system of direct popular rights that will realize the concept of popular sovereignty. Thus, my Principle of the People's Rights is now complete.

The Principle of the People's Livelihood

The invention of machines has introduced the unequal distribution of wealth in Europe and America. Wherever that violent force has struck, the flames of economic revolution have been even fiercer than those of political revolution. This is something that few in our country heeded thirty years ago. During my visits to Europe and America, I observed the precarious state of their economies and the beleaguered and helpless state of the gentlemen of their cities. I thought that, although wealth in our country is not distributed as unequally as in Europe and America, the difference is one of degree, not originally of kind. Furthermore, that phenomenon will grow daily more serious when the economic influence of Europe and America reaches our country, so we must take precautions beforehand. Upon which I inquired into the various social and economic theories, comparing their pros and cons, and felt that nationalizing industry is an especially deep, sound, and practicable concept. We must formulate plans to deal with a trend that has become a matter of such deep, practical concern in Europe and America. Consequently, I have decided to combine the Principle of the People's Livelihood with the Principle of Nationalism and the Principle of the People's Rights and implement them simultaneously, so that we can at one stroke accomplish our political goals and choke economic revolution at its very source.

To sum up, the content of my revolutionary principles, generally speaking, consists of the Three Principles of the People and the five-power constitution. Anyone who is aware of world trends and of the situation in China will know that my principles are really both necessary and practicable.

QUESTIONS TO CONSIDER

1. Do you agree that Copernicus and Darwin developed ideas that transformed the ways peoples thought about themselves and their environment? Why or why not? What other ideas from Galileo and Freud have altered our outlook?

2. Immanuel Kant draws a connection between enlightened thinking and freedom. From your readings, how can you support his conclusion? Would Edmund Burke agree with Kant? Why or why not?

3. How did imperialists use racist and nationalistic ideas to build or strengthen empires? Use examples from your readings to support your answer. How does nationalism undermine imperialism?

P A R T　　　E I G H T

GLOBAL WAR
AND REVOLUTION

INTRODUCTION

The twentieth-century totalitarian state was in part a response to the upheaval brought by war and revolution. World War I was a war of attrition in which governments committed massive amounts of material and huge numbers of human lives in an effort to bring victory or stave off defeat. To ensure the survival of their states in this deadly environment, political leaders amassed unheard of power and assumed greater control over society and the economy. State intervention in the nation's economy became a standard practice in the war years.

In the 1920s, many countries appeared to forget the war. The Great Depression left millions of workers idle and ripped the social fabric of numerous nations. Looking for solutions, many political leaders looked back at the successes of World War I and sought to apply them to the crisis of the Depression. In Germany, for example, the Nazi Party came to power in 1933 and began fashioning a totalitarian state ruled by Adolf Hitler.

The Russian and Chinese revolutions brought to power politicians committed to the idea of dictatorship. They started to build totalitarian governments, controlling most aspects of their subjects' lives. Many people who had never worked in agriculture or industry were mandated to toil for the state.

One characteristic shared by countries at war and totalitarian states was the employment of women in jobs where they previously had rarely been employed. During World War I, women found work in factories, especially in munitions works. In the Soviet Union and China, large numbers of women were encouraged or forced to work outside the home. While in nontotalitarian states women often left their factory jobs after war ended and men began to return to work, totalitarian regimes usually kept women at work.

A major development in the twentieth century was the use of forced labor. Totalitarian regimes, especially Nazi Germany, the Soviet Union,

97

and the People's Republic of China, used criminals and political prisoners as laborers. During the 1930s, gulag labor was used to build major Soviet projects, such as the White Sea Canal. Prisoner-of-war labor was commonly used during World War II, especially by the Japanese and Germans. Large numbers of prisoners died in these operations. The Nazis had furthermore planned to exterminate their camp laborers when they finished their tasks.

Readings in this part of this volume address the building of a totalitarian state and the use of traditionally nonlaboring groups in the workplace. Some selections examine the role of women in the expanding workforce, while others focus on prison labor.

SCHOLARLY WORKS

Ludendorff:
The German Concept of Total War
Hans Speier

World War I (1914–1918) was a prolonged conflict that demanded a massive commitment of materials and people by the combatant states. Germany organized its society and economy in an attempt to win the war, mobilizing millions of men and women. In this essay (1960), historian Hans Speier examines Erich Ludendorff's ideas about total war. In the war's aftermath, Ludendorff, a famous German general of World War I, wrote about his wartime experiences, arguing that a total mobilization was necessary for waging a war such as World War I.

Ludendorff outlined the basis for the totalitarian regimes that developed between 1918 and 1939. The National Socialists in Germany developed many of Ludendorff's ideas, expanding them to fashion an immensely powerful totalitarian state in the 1930s and 1940s.

I

Erich Ludendorff's contribution to the development of military thought is that of a general who lost a war. He began to write almost immediately after the defeat of the German armies in 1918. Although his books are born of a rich strategical and organizational experience, they are full of conceit and resentment, and are apologetic in character. They attempt to prove that, in a military sense, Germany did not lose the first World War. Considering the vital importance of this opinion, known under the

---

Hans Speier, "Ludendorff: The German Concept of Total War," in *Makers of Modern Strategy*, by Edward M. Earle (Princeton: Princeton University Press, 1960), 306–21.

slogan of "the stab in the back" in German domestic politics in the time of the Weimar republic, one is justified in regarding Ludendorff's literary activity as political pamphleteering. Certainly, his writings are not distinguished by detachment or subtlety. It was Ludendorff's fame as a great general rather than the intrinsic merit of his works which accounted for his amazing literary success in republican Germany.

Ludendorff wrote on three main subjects, of which only one is of immediate interest to this study. He specialized in reminiscing, debunking, and forecasting. In reminiscing about the military events of the first World War, he tried to enhance his historical stature as a general and he polemicized against those who belittled his generalship. Amplifying his prejudices against Freemasons, Jews, Jesuits, and Christianity at large, and advocating under the influence of his wife a martial religion of his own, he tried to expose those sinister forces which he held responsible for Germany's defeat in the first World War. He was convinced that both his political enemies and his National Socialist competitors after the war were also under the influence of those forces. Finally, in putting forth his ideas on total war, Ludendorff outlined the conditions which in his opinion would have enabled him to operate more effectively as a general in the first World War.

Ludendorff's theory of total war is not based on a study of military developments between the two world wars. Nor is it derived from a careful consideration of the interrelations between politics, warfare, technology, economics, and popular morale. In fact, there are few military writers to whose historical works Friedrich Schlegel's statement that "history is retrospective prophecy" can be applied with more justice. And in appraising Ludendorff's writings on total war one is sometimes tempted to modify Schlegel's aphorism by saying that the general's prophecies were history projected into the future.

For the historian of military thought Ludendorff's criticism of Clausewitz' ideas on war is particularly arresting. The carelessness of this criticism makes it easy to note Ludendorff's intellectual inferiority to the master of German military thought, but the point of interest is the political motive of the criticism rather than its content. Not as a military scientist and historian, but as a politician, did Ludendorff, the advocate of total war, renounce Clausewitz, the theoretician of "absolute war." After stating his unqualified demand of complete authority of the supreme military leader in all *political* matters as well, Ludendorff adds, "I can hear how politicians will get excited about such an opinion, as they will about the idea in general that politics is to serve the conduct of war, as though Clausewitz had not taught that war is but the continuation of politics with different means. Let the politicians get excited and let them regard my opinions as those of a hopeless 'militarist.' This does not change any of the demands of reality, which require precisely what I demand for the conduct of war and thus for the preservation of the life of the people."

In such phrases, which abound in his work, Ludendorff discarded the principles of Prussian statecraft and militarism as they existed in the latter half of the nineteenth century, and suggested a return to the days of his hero, Frederick the Great. . . .

II

Ludendorff's idea of total war can be stated in the form of five basic propositions. War is total; first, because the theater of war extends over the whole territory of the belligerent nations. In addition to this diffusion of risks, total war also involves the active participation of the whole population in the war effort. Not armies but nations wage total war. Thus, the effective prosecution of total war necessitates the adaptation of the economic system to the purposes of war. Thirdly, the participation of large masses in war makes it imperative to devote special efforts, by means of propaganda, to the strengthening of morale at home and to the weakening of the political cohesion of the enemy nation. Fourth, the preparation of total war must begin before the outbreak of overt fighting. Military, economic, and psychological warfare influence the so-called peacetime pursuits in modern societies. Finally, in order to achieve an integrated and efficient war effort, total war must be directed by one supreme authority, that of the commander in chief.

Ludendorff's relatively simple idea of total war is not devoid of a few interesting details. The geographical extension of the theaters of total war is a consequence of the technical progress of the means of destruction and of the increasing functional interdependence of modern nations. Not only are the fighting zones widened by the technical improvement of long range weapons of all kinds, but the regions behind the actual fighting zones are also affected "by hunger blockade and propaganda." The nation at war can thus be compared to the people in a besieged fortress. As the besiegers try to force a fortress to surrender not only by directing strictly military means against its military defenders, but also by starving its civil inhabitants, so total warfare implements the military assault upon the armed forces of a nation by the use of nonmilitary weapons directed against the noncombatant parts of the enemy population. The distinction between combatants and noncombatants loses its former significance.

In order to secure the necessary military supplies and foodstuffs for the sustenance of the besieged nation, Ludendorff advocated economic self-sufficiency. His ideas on war economics, however, are little else than textbook generalities. He dealt with the organizational aspect of war economics rather than with the strategic possibilities of improving the raw material, food, and labor supply of the nation at war through conquest.

Surprisingly enough, the most original contribution General Ludendorff made to the theory of total war does not lie in the field of military warfare, but in the realm of what is often inadequately called "psychological warfare." Ludendorff is almost excessively concerned with the problem of the "cohesion" of the people. It is in this regard that he differs most strikingly from National Socialist writers on total war. He despised, and regarded as ineffective, any attempt to achieve social unity by force and drill. Such methods he called "mechanical" or "external." "An external unity of the people, achieved by compulsion—a unity in which the soul of the people has no share by common and conscious racial and religious experience—is not a unity which people and army need in war, but a mechanical phantom dangerous to the government and the state." Similarly, he spoke with unconcealed derision of such measures as the Fascists and National Socialists had taken in the field of the premilitary training of youth. He compared this training with that of dogs and doubted that mass drill, which "deprives youth of personalities," prepared young men satisfactorily for military service.

His model of a closely knit social unity is therefore not the old Prussia, nor is it the new Germany of Hitler. Ludendorff thought of Japan when he spoke of unity and cohesion. "Entirely different [from mechanical unity] is the unity of the Japanese people; it is a spiritual one, essentially resting upon Shinto religion, which compels the Japanese to serve their Emperor in order thus to preserve the road to the life of their ancestors. For the Japanese, service for the Emperor and thus for the state is prescribed by his experience of God. Shintoism, stemming from the racial heritage of the Japanese, corresponds to the needs of the people and the state. . . . In the unity of racial heritage and faith and in the philosophy of life erected upon them resides the strength of the Japanese people."

Ludendorff's own racial religion was to provide the Germans with a faith corresponding to Shintoism in Japan. However fantastic this may sound, Ludendorff must be credited with understanding the fact that something more profound than merely a clever propaganda policy is needed in order to produce a state of popular morale which enables people in modern industrial society to endure the hardships of total war. Like Ernst Juenger, Ludendorff realized dimly that "a mobilization may organize the technical abilities of a man without penetrating to the core of his faith," and that the spirit of sacrifice cannot be injected into the body politic by a clever doctor. Ludendorff realized that the source of concord in society lies in deep rooted traditions rather than in an efficient organization of the police. In fact, he did not advocate violence against dissenters in his book on *Total War,* and when he spoke in his memoirs of the fact that the government may use force against those who jeopardize the common war effort he did so in an almost apologetic fashion.

On the whole, Ludendorff's ideas on the role of propaganda were sounder than Hitler's. In the realm of propaganda techniques as well, Ludendorff's opinions revealed surprising expertness. He deplored the German government's concealment of the defeat in the battle of the Marne from the German people and advocated a policy of frankness in order not to give "free reign to the 'discontented' and the rumor-mongers." Similarly, Ludendorff wrote in his memoirs that every German, whether man or woman, should have been told every day what a lost war meant for the fatherland. Pictures and films should have broadcast the same story. The presentation of the dangers would have had a different effect than the thinking about profits, or talking and writing about a peace by negotiation. Goebbels, in the propaganda strategy of gloom upon which he embarked a few months after the invasion of Russia, seems to have taken a few leaves from Ludendorff's book. Whenever possible, Goebbels also follows that advice of Ludendorff which several National Socialist authors on propaganda have repeated: "A good propaganda must anticipate the development of the real events." Finally, Ludendorff regarded the circulation of rumors, in which the National Socialists were to become past masters, "the best means of propaganda" against the enemy.

Ludendorff's theory of total war culminates in the role assigned to the supreme military commander. In addition to conducting the military operations he is to direct the foreign and economic policies of the nation and also its propaganda policy. "The military staff must be adequately composed: it must contain the best brains in the fields of land, air, and sea warfare, propaganda, war technology, economics, politics and also those who know the people's life. They have to inform the Chief-of-Staff, and if required, the Commander-in-Chief, about their respective fields. They have no policy-making function." Thus, in Ludendorff's total war there is no place for the civilian statesman. The general rules supreme. And Ludendorff concludes: "All theories [*sic*] of Clausewitz have to be thrown overboard. War and politics serve the survival of the people, but war is the highest expression of the racial will to life."

Clausewitz had been of the opinion that the French Revolution had removed many of the limitations which in the *Ancien Régime* [former government], when cabinets rather than nations waged war, had prevented war from assuming its "abstract" or "absolute" character. Clausewitz had rejected the erroneous idea that war had "emancipated" itself from politics in consequence of the revolution. Instead, he insisted—in a passage which Ludendorff later quoted—that the political forces of the French Revolution had unleashed energies which subsequently changed the type of war. By thus attributing the change in the type of war to politics, Clausewitz defined the prevailing type of war in terms of the structure of the political community that wages it.

According to Ludendorff, on the other hand, total war is a product of demographic and technological developments. The increased size of populations and the improved efficiency of the means of destruction have inevitably created the totality of war. Total war, which has no political cause, absorbs politics.

There is not the slightest suggestion in Ludendorff's writings that he prefers total to limited war on moral or metaphysical grounds. Nor is there any explicit justification of total war in terms of an imperialistic doctrine, or of a value system in which pugnacity, heroism, and the love of sacrifice are so supreme as to demand war for their realization and glorification. Instead, Ludendorff goes so far as to contend that total war is essentially defensive. The people will not cooperate in waging it unless they know that war is waged to preserve their existence. To be sure, it would be expedient to make such contentions for the mere sake of appearance in a culture which, in E. M. Forster's words, "preaches idealism and practices brutality." Yet Ludendorff did not shrink from shocking the public by unorthodox opinions in the field of religion, and it would do injustice to his character to doubt that he meant what he said when he talked about the defensive character of total war. He insists that "the nature of total war requires that it be waged only if the whole people is really threatened in its existence, and determined to wage it." If this insistence upon the defensive nature of war were a mere attempt on the part of Ludendorff to conceal his true opinion as to its nature, he would have to be credited with a Machiavellian attitude toward the masses. There is no trace of such an attitude in his writings. In fact he rejects explicitly the opinion, characteristically to be found in the circles of National Socialist intellectuals, that the masses can and should be psychologically manipulated in the interest of the power holders. As has been pointed out, Ludendorff regarded attempts to manage the masses in this way as futile.

III

The National Socialists have not only organized German society for total war but have also written profusely about it. Their contributions to the development of the theory of total war are built upon Clausewitz' and Ludendorff's basic contention that in modern war all material and moral resources of the nation must be mobilized. The main difference between National Socialist literature and Ludendorff's writings on total war lies in the fact that the National Socialists have attempted to produce ideological justifications of modern war. Racial superiority and the law of nature, Darwinistically and geopolitically understood, are supposed to provide German war and the new militarism with a moral halo. Moreover, some National Socialist writers have pushed Ludendorff's theory to its logical end by denying the *existence* of peace altogether. They no longer regard war as a *phase* in the interrelations of states, preceded and followed by phases of peace, but as "the expression of a new political and social development in the life of peoples." Similarly, geopoliticians have written books about the forms which warfare assumes in times which according to common usage are designated as times of peace. Instead of speaking about peace between wars, they have found the formula of "the war between wars."

One of the most important changes of warfare, without which blitzkrieg methods and the coordination of different arms would have been impossible, was predicated upon a complete removal of resistance to technological change on the part of the new corps of officers. Karl Justrow, who criticized sharply the scarcity of engineers in the German armies of the first World War and contended that engineers had "not the slightest influence" on the conduct of the war, wrote shortly before the outbreak of the second World War, that "technology—once a stepchild in all organizations—is today treated with more and more understanding in the conduct of war."

This breakdown of resistance to technology has inevitably involved a greater equalization of society. The higher the demands for technological skill and physical fitness on the part of the expert operators of the means of destruction, the less important must be the respect paid to the status qualifications of the soldiers. Status consideration must be sacrificed in favor of high skill requirements, especially when there is a shortage of available personnel. Thus, the technology of total war favors the "egalitarian" militarism of Hitler's Germany. When Hitler reintroduced universal military service, he abolished the privilege of shorter service in the army which boys with a high school education had enjoyed under the kaiser. In this respect and also with respect to promotion from the ranks the military system of this modern despot is more egalitarian than was that of Imperial Germany. Hitler has proceeded in the spirit of what Oswald Spengler has called "Prussian Socialism," adapting this kind of socialism to the postdemocratic structure of his plebiscitarian dictatorship. With this resolution to liberate destructive techniques from humanitarian fetters and to sacrifice any tradition to military efficiency he has brought to a head the martial equalization of society that began in eighteenth century Prussia but required the rise of modern political mass movements to become truly effective.

When, in 1733, the so-called canton system of recruitment was introduced in Prussia, the enlargement of the social basis of the army was officially justified by the argument that the inequality among those enrolled should be abolished. Later the introduction of universal military service in Prussia was announced by a cabinet order which stated that "all privileges based on social status cease to exist with the army." This was in 1808, when the liberal Barthold Georg Niebuhr wrote that universal conscription, "this equality which disgusts the true friend of liberty," will lead to ". . . the demoralization and degeneration of the whole nation, universal brutality, the destruction of civilization and of the educated classes."

The two developments which have most incisively changed the social structure of German economy in this war were not discussed at great length before war broke out. The ruthless principle of turning the conquered territories into a reservoir of labor for the conqueror, from which, according to German claims, no less than twelve million foreign workers had been forced to migrate to Germany by 1943, was not fully anticipated in the *Wehrwirtschaft* [wartime economy] discussions before 1939. Nor did any German economist dare to reveal the possibility of a virtual destruction of the German middle classes in the war of the future.

The contribution of German intellectuals to the literature of "psychological warfare" has probably been grossly overrated. The contribution of German psychologists to the theories of political mass behavior is smaller than the many volumes written on that subject would have us believe. Nazi literature on political propaganda contains little that has not been known for centuries to less pedantic students of rhetoric and to modern specialists in advertising. The recent overestimation of the German contribution is to a large extent a consequence of the fact that talk about German "fifth columns" and propaganda gave intellectuals in the democratic countries a thrilling opportunity to offer an excuse for the military inferiority of the democracies at the beginning of this war. The prestige of propaganda waxes and wanes with military success and failure. The Nazis as leaders of a modern mass movement have undoubtedly realized more clearly than did the leaders of Imperial Germany in the last war the importance of propaganda. They have invested more money and talent in it and have organized it efficiently. They have not produced any new "theory."

As to their propaganda practice, it is often overlooked that in some respects the National Socialists are in a less favorable position than was Germany under the kaiser. For example, any attempt to create discord in the camp of the enemy coalition must necessarily appear as a move of the German propaganda machine, because the world knows that all German propaganda is centrally planned. The German anti-Bolshevist campaign can at once be recognized as Dr. Goebbels' campaign. It is interesting to compare this predicament with the greater freedom of operation which Ludendorff had in the first World War. In June 1918, Colonel Haeften, the representative of the supreme command at the foreign office, presented the plan of an anti-Bolshevist campaign to Ludendorff for approval. In order to strengthen Landsdowne's peace party in England, influential Germans, acting to all appearances in complete independence from the government, were to advocate in public speeches a united European front against Bolshevism. The less centralized setup of the German propaganda machine at that time permitted maneuvers in political warfare upon which National Socialist propaganda cannot embark without giving itself away.

Ludendorff's ideas on the supreme position of the general in total war, however, were buried with him. German generals are under the domination of the National Socialist Party led by Hitler, a charismatic corporal. So complete was that domination that on January 30, 1943 Goering could dare to refer in public to the weak German military leaders who "were whining" before Hitler when he "held" the Eastern front against the onslaught of the Russians.

The Great Depression in Europe
James Laux

The Great Depression threw many governments and societies into turmoil as millions of people became unemployed. The growing crisis forced leaders to develop full-scale relief policies. Some leaders recalled the mobilization efforts in World War I and advocated reviving them to deal with the human casualties of the depression. Once again the state started to intervene directly in the economy and society by creating public works projects to employ and pay able-bodied adults. In this reading (1974), James Laux, an economic historian, traces some changes in European economic thinking that were wrought by the Great Depression.

The Depression, perhaps, had the most serious impact in Europe on people's thinking about economic matters. Looking back on the experience, most Europeans agreed that the orthodoxy of laissez-faire no longer held. They would not again accept the view that a government must interfere as little as possible in the operation of the economic system. Governments must accept wider responsibilities than balancing their own budgets. The value of the currency in terms of gold must give way to economic expansion if the two appear to conflict. Laissez-faire already was wheezing and laboring in the 1920s; after the decade of the 1930s it was nearly prostrate. As so often happens, a philosophy came along to justify this changed attitude, a new approach to theoretical economics worked out by the Englishman John Maynard Keynes. The most influential economist of the twentieth century, Keynes published his classic work in 1936, *The General Theory of Employment, Interest and Money.* He argued that governments can and should manipulate capitalist economies, by running surpluses or deficits, by investing heavily in public works, by changing the size of the money and credit supply, and by altering rates of interest. In his analysis he emphasized the total economy, the relations among savings, investment, production, and consumption, what is called macroeconomics, rather than an investigation of a single firm

---

James Laux, *The Great Depression in Europe* (St. Louis: Forum Press, 1974), 13–14.

or sector. A critic of socialism, Keynes scorned the significance of government ownership of production facilities, but promoted government intervention in an economy to make capitalism work better.

Bolstering this view were the remarkable production achievements of many European industrial states during the two world wars. In these crises national economies expanded military production enormously under government direction. Many asked why such techniques could not be applied in peacetime also, but to make consumer products rather than tools of destruction.

The upshot was that by 1945 if not 1939 most Europeans abandoned the idea that they lived at the mercy of an impersonal economic system whose rules could not be changed and accepted the proposition that the economy could operate the way people wanted it to. From this it was a short step to the concept of planning the future development of the economy—both the whole and particular segments of it. Economic planning became an acceptable posture for capitalist societies and enjoyed a considerable reputation. Some of those who supported it perhaps underestimated the possible merits of free markets as guiding production decisions and did seem to assume that planners somehow possess more wisdom than ordinary human beings.

Economic nationalism was a more immediate result of the Depression—the policy that short-run national economic interests have highest priority and that international economic cooperation and trade must give way before narrowly conceived national interests. Economic nationalism showed its sharpest teeth in those European states where political nationalism reached a peak—Germany, Italy, and the Soviet Union. Its strength declined in western Europe after the Second World War as people saw once again that economic prosperity among one's neighbors could bring great benefits to oneself. In an expanding continental or world economy everyone can get richer. But one wonders if economic nationalism may not revive in western Europe, especially if it seems a popular policy in a crisis.

The Great Depression had important political repercussions too. In Germany, the Depression's tragic gloom made the dynamism of the Nazi movement seem more attractive. It is difficult to imagine the Nazis achieving power without the Depression and its pervasive unemployment in the background. In France, the Depression convinced many that the regime of the Third Republic had lost its elan and relevance to twentieth-century problems, but the lack of a widely popular alternative meant that the Republic could limp along until a disastrous military defeat brought it down. In Britain, the Depression was less serious and no fundamental challenge to the political regime developed. The Conservatives held power for most of the interwar period and their failure to work actively to absorb the large unemployment that continued there until late in the 1930s brought widespread rancor and bitterness against them. Doubts as to the Conservatives' ability to manage a peacetime economy led to the first majority Labour government in the 1945 election. More profoundly, the years of heavy unemployment bred a very strong anticapitalist sentiment in much of British labor, a sentiment that led them after the war to demand moves toward socialism, such as nationalization of major industries.

The Depression helped convince Europeans that their governments must try to manage their economies. Most agreed that full employment and expanding output should be the goals. They did not agree on the means to achieve these ends.

Origins of the New Deal
Clarence B. Carson

This selection from a 1986 U.S. history textbook shows the origins of the policies of developing a welfare state. General Hugh Johnson served in mobilization efforts in World War I and the depression. He used military terminology to characterize the crisis of the depression and its solution, urging women to enlist in the war against unemployment. Once again women were encouraged to work for victory.

Before proceeding with an account of New Deal legislation, some account of the sources may help to clarify what was going on. Roosevelt pushed much of the early legislation through on the grounds that America was confronted with an emergency of unprecedented dimensions and that the people wanted action. That is, he did not identify the ideological underpinnings of what he was proposing. On the contrary, he made it appear that he was moving swiftly on many fronts in response to the situation with which he was confronted. In the argot of those times, he was being "pragmatic," i.e., experimenting, trying first this and then that, ever seeking something that would work, or work better. Undoubtedly, there was, at least on the surface, much that was experimental about New Deal measures, but they had antecedents both in ideology and programs advanced in the past. In the broadest of terms, socialism was the origin of the New Deal, but it was socialism as it had been winnowed through the minds of American radicals and reformers and hammered out as programs.

There were at least four sources of the New Deal. Roosevelt, as it turned out, was an inflationist, and this bent traces back to Populism. Populist ideas had entered the Democratic Party in 1896 with William Jennings Bryan's candidacy, and some of the silverites were still very much in evidence in the New Deal. A broader current than that was

---

Clarence B. Carson, *The Welfare State* (Wadley, Ala.: American Textbook Committee, 1986), 36.

there, however, for the Populists had favored paper money as a device for inflation as well, and, as we shall see, that was used much more for inflation by the New Deal than silver.

A second stream came from Progressivism, particularly that of Theodore Roosevelt. The Progressives had, of course, been a faction within the Republican Party, still were as late as the early 1930s. But Franklin Roosevelt wooed them vigorously in his 1932 campaign and had the help of such men as George W. Norris in winning states in the trans-Mississippi West. Moreover, Roosevelt had been early influenced by his cousin Theodore. As one historian said, the much younger Franklin "looked up to Uncle Ted, and the relationship brought Franklin Roosevelt a continuous suggestion that politics was a permissible career for a patrician, that a patrician's politics should be reform, and that reform meant broad federal powers wielded by executive leadership in the pattern of the New Nationalism." Another historian has said that "There are many occasions in its history when the New Deal . . . seems to stand squarely in the tradition of the New Nationalism." Among his advisers, Rexford G. Tugwell was a vigorous advocate of government regulation of big businesses rather than breaking them up by applying antitrust laws. That had been very much the emphasis of Roosevelt's New Nationalism.

The term "progressive," however, was not used by New Dealers. Instead, they usually called themselves "liberals," thus borrowing a word from the 19th century and giving it a somewhat different meaning and thrust. "Liberalism" had come into widespread use in the 19th century to describe the position favoring individual liberty, free trade, national independence, expansion of the suffrage and the like. Nineteenth-century liberals were usually strongly opposed to government intervention in the economy. By contrast, 20th-century "liberals" have favored government regulation and control over the economy, been collectivists, tended to view government as a beneficial influence in all areas of life. They are distant cousins, at best, to those of the 19th century.

A third source of the New Deal was the mobilization experience during World War I. They were greatly impressed with what they conceived had been accomplished by the use of government power to control and direct economic activity. General Hugh Johnson, who headed the National Recovery Administration (NRA) in the early period of the New Deal, had been connected with the War Industries Board during World War I and was convinced that government could effectively direct the economy in peacetime as well. "If cooperation can do so much," he said, "maybe there is something wrong with the old competitive system." He was in favor, he declared, of "self-government in industry under government supervision." People with experience in wartime agencies were in great demand at the beginning of the New Deal. As one historian says, "Only the veterans of the war mobilization had much experience with the kind of massive undertaking Roosevelt had inaugurated." Such people flocked to Washington in large numbers, and, as one of those there said, "One cannot go into the Cosmos Club without meeting half a dozen persons whom he knew during the war."

Warlike terminology was widely used in the early days of the New Deal. Roosevelt had set the stage for this in his Inaugural Address by his references to Americans getting behind him like a disciplined army and making "a war against the emergency." None could outdo General Johnson, who even appealed to women to enlist in the cause, declaring that "this time, it is the women who must carry the whole fight of President Roosevelt's war against depression, perhaps the most dangerous war of all. It is women . . . who will . . . go over the top to as great a victory as the Argonne." Just exactly how one goes about making war against emergencies or depressions no one apparently paused to ponder. After all, except as a rather doubtful figure of speech, wars are made against flesh and blood people who are usually assembled in armies and identified as the enemy. How, we are entitled to wonder, is it possible to fire cannon or launch grenades against emergencies or depression? This militant language could, however, call up a collective effort, and that was undoubtedly its purpose.

Soviet Wartime Mobilization
John Barber and Mark Harrison

Historians John Barber and Mark Harrison teamed up to write an account (1991) of the Soviet mobilization in World War II. They concentrate on the home front, where millions of women and the young were enlisted in factory workforces. Much attention is devoted to prison labor and the extreme conditions under which the prisoners worked and often died. Barber and Harrison also single out the mobilization process itself, which was often inefficient but eventually helped defeat the invading Nazi forces.

Recruits to the work-force came from a variety of sources. Many came from the families of workers mobilised to fight: partly out of a desire to identify with the husbands, fathers or sons at the front, partly to provide much needed income for the remaining family, partly because of legal and moral pressures to work. There were continuous campaigns to attract housewives, pensioners and adolescents into the work-force. White-collar workers and people in service industry were drafted into production. The Commissariat of Defence sent conscripts unfit for mili-

John Barber and Mark Harrison, *The Soviet Home Front, 1941–1945* (New York: Longman Press, 1991), 96–99, 116–19, 147–52.

tary service to work in factories, on building sites, or on transport, and often reallocated wounded servicemen to production after recovery. In the last year and a half of the war, skilled workers and engineers were released from the armed forces to return to work, particularly in the newly liberated regions.

But as in the early 1930s the countryside increasingly became the main source of new workers during the war. While millions of its inhabitants were drafted into the armed forces, millions of others — kolkhoz and individual peasants, artisans, young people — became workers. Between 1942 and 1944, a wartime Committee for Registration and Allocation of Labour Power (hereafter Labour Committee) mobilised 3 million people for permanent work in industry, building and transport, of whom 49.6 per cent were from urban and 50.4 per cent from rural backgrounds. As time went on, the countryside became ever more important as the source of new workers, accounting in 1942 for 23 per cent of the total, in 1943 for 59 per cent, and in 1944 for 62 per cent. Much of this increase came from the population of the liberated regions.

The state of flux in the working class was not confined to the movement of millions of people in and out of the industrial workforce. Many others changed their position within it, either geographically or professionally or both. In the early stages of the war, hundreds of thousands of workers moved eastwards from the war zones to the rear. Whereas in 1940 the eastern areas of the country had accounted for 37 per cent of workers and employees, in 1942 this figure had risen to 70 per cent. Skilled workers in particular were evacuated with their factories to the Urals, Siberia or the Far East. Many more made their own way to the rear as refugees. Later there would be large-scale movement in the opposite direction, as workers were sent into the liberated territories to rebuild what had been destroyed and to get factories working again.

The most conspicuous features of Soviet workers in wartime were their youth, their inexperience and the great preponderance of women. In many factories the majority of workers were under 25; in the newly built or restored engineering factories by the end of the war, they comprised up to three-quarters. In Leningrad, according to one report, by June 1943, 80 per cent of all factory workers were 23 years or under. The proportion of juveniles under 18 in the work-force rose substantially, from 6 per cent of workers and employees in industry in 1940 to 15 per cent in 1942. Many workers were very young. Of 2,460,000 workers under 18 in 1944, 712,000 were only 14 or 15 years old. Official figures do not reveal the number who were younger still, but there were certainly many. At the age of 12 a child became a "dependant" and his or her food ration was reduced accordingly. Where food was scarce, sheer hunger, or the need to provide for other members of the family, thus forced children to seek work; and though it was illegal for an employer to hire anyone under the age of 14, children often found work.

The influx of new workers into the labour force produced a corresponding fall in its average *stazh* (length of employment). This was particularly true of the priority sectors, such as defence industry and
engineering, where expansion was greatest. In Leningrad, three-quarters
of the workers in defence industry at the end of 1942 had begun work
since the beginning of that year. By the beginning of 1943, 60–70 per
cent of all Leningrad workers had a *stazh* of between six months and
two years. By the end of the war, most had not more than three years,
and many had only one year. There was still a nucleus of older workers,
but it had shrunk enormously. At the Kirov works in Leningrad at the
beginning of 1943, 18 per cent of workers had a *stazh* of ten years or more.
In 1945 only 25 per cent of Kuzbass miners and 16 per cent of Karaganda
miners had been employed since before the war. Inevitably the reduced
length of work experience, combined with the much shorter amount of
time devoted to training, resulted in lower skill levels.

Women's participation in the work-force had been a conspicuous
feature of the industrialisation drive of the 1930s, as it had also been of
Russian industry during World War I. But in World War II it rose to new
heights. "Men to the front, women to the factories!" was a familiar slogan
in the early part of the war; the appeal to women to replace the con-
scripted male members of their families, together with the mobilisation
of women for work which allowed few exemptions, produced an influx
of women into the work-force. If they had comprised 41 per cent of
workers and employees in 1940, they were 52 per cent in 1942 and 53
per cent in 1943–4, declining slightly to 51 per cent in 1945. In many
factories women soon comprised the majority, and sometimes the overwhelming majority, of workers. In light industry, where they had always
predominated, 80–90 per cent of the work-force were generally women.
But their proportion in heavy industry rose very sharply. In 1942 over
half of all turbine operators in power stations were women, and over a
quarter of all workers in coal-mining. By the end of 1944, they comprised
41.5 per cent of workers in the restored Donbass mines.

Close to the front line, the female proportion of the work-force was
even greater. In Leningrad, merely between July and October 1941 in two
major engineering factories, it rose from approximately one-quarter to
three-quarters. At the giant Kirov works, two-thirds of workers by January
1943 were women. By the end of 1942, 80 per cent of all Leningrad industrial workers were women, and by February 1943, 84 per cent.

Like all Soviet citizens, workers saw their conditions deteriorate
sharply during the war. At work they faced a longer working day and compulsory overtime, the end of leave entitlement, continual pressure to
meet higher production targets, obligatory military training or civil defence duties, the virtual suspension of labour safety regulations, and a
lack of adequate heating, lighting and ventilation. At home, the scarcity

of food and other basic necessities was a continuous and often extreme feature of their lives. Worst off were workers in cities close to the front line (and above all Leningrad), to whose hardships was added the threat of death from enemy action, and evacuated workers, provision for whom tended to be minimal.

Yet workers were also to some extent cushioned against the worst effects of the war. Their rations were higher than non-manual employees, let alone adult dependants, while peasants on collective farms received no rations at all. Factory canteens, shops and allotments were also a vital source of food. The support available at the work-place, however, went well beyond this. Many workers and their families lived in factory barracks, or even in the factories themselves; cramped though conditions were, at least heating and lighting were more likely to be available there. Factories also provided clinics, nurseries, launderies, baths, libraries, reading rooms and other amenities. In Leningrad, brigades of young workers organised at factories by the Komsomol took responsibility for taking food and fuel to sick people, cleaning apartments, and even burying the dead. Working-class solidarity and mutual aid, empty phrases for many years, took on new meaning in wartime.

Prisoners

No account of Soviet society during the war would be complete without mention of those at the very bottom of the social pyramid—the population of the camps and prisons. Less is known about this group than any other. Until recently, it figured in no Soviet statistics or histories of war; even now evidence of its size, composition and conditions is fragmentary. What is clear, however, is that the number of prisoners was substantial and that their already wretched conditions worsened considerably with the outbreak of war.

Estimates of the total number of Soviet citizens engaged in forced labour during the war range from 5 million to over 20 million. This divergence reflects both the lack of firm data and the inclusion of different categories of people. Besides the inmates of prison and labour camps, the figures may, for example, include members of national minorities deported to remote areas as "special migrants" (*spetsposelentsy*); or people sentenced to compulsory work at their place of employment for breaches of labour discipline. All had their freedom seriously limited in one way or another.

But those sentenced to penal servitude were in a category of their own, and deserve discussing as such. Unlike the others, they had no control over where they lived, or what work they did, or how much. Their freedom was not only restricted; it was in all important respects extinguished. A small proportion served their sentences in prison; but the great majority were in labour camps or labour colonies run by the NKVD's Chief Administration of Camps (Gulags). Much is still unknown about their number and conditions, but statistics recently published in the USSR provide considerably more data than previously available. Although they may still be incomplete, they probably indicate the main trends.

Having risen in 1940 (largely because of arrests in the territories newly incorporated in the USSR), the number of Gulag prisoners declined steadily between 1941 and 1944. By the beginning of 1944, it was reportedly down to three-fifths of the level of three years earlier; although over the following year it appears to have risen sharply again. There appear to have been two main reasons for the decline. First, releases from the camps ran at a high level in 1941–3. At over 40 per cent of the average annual number of prisoners, this was nearly double the rate in the last year of peace. The first release of prisoners was decreed on 12 July 1941; it applied to those in areas near the war zone who had been convicted for relatively minor crimes. The scope of this decree was extended on 24 November, and as a result some 420,000 men were dispatched to the front. Altogether, 1 million ex-prisoners fought during the war, mainly in the "penal battalions." Used for the most dangerous operations (clearing minefields, storming well-fortified positions), their casualty rate was the highest in the Red Army. In many cases, perhaps most, release from the camps during the war meant a speedy release from the misery of this world. Even so, many prisoners volunteered for military service, preferring to die on the battlefield rather than in the camps, or clutching at the hope of distinguishing themselves and winning rehabilitation, as some did.

Second, the death-rate in the camps soared during the war. It rose seven-fold between 1940 and 1942. One in five of the camp population died in 1942 and 1943. The reasons are simple: "more work and less food and less heat and worse clothes and ferocious discipline and more severe punishment." In a situation of scarcity, prisoners were the lowest priority, and their rations were reduced accordingly. At the same time, like all civilians they were under great pressure to increase output. Despite their conditions, productivity in the camps increased by 80 per cent between 1941 and 1943. Cold and hunger, malnutrition and exhaustion took their inevitable toll. So bad were the conditions that the Soviet procuracy[1] is said to have made representations about them to Beriya.[2] Solzhenitsyn claims that in the wartime camps during winter "a death rate of one per cent per day was commonplace and common knowledge." In some camps at least this may not have been an exaggeration.

1. The procuracy was a bureaucratic watchdog agency. It investigated actions of various government bureaus.

2. Beriya (Lavrenti Beria) was head of the Soviet NKVD—the secret police and forerunner of the Soviet KGB.

One other factor may have contributed to the decline in the size of the camp population in 1941 and 1942, namely the loss of territory, and with it the loss of prisoners. At the outbreak of war, the NKVD decided to evacuate three-quarters of a million prisoners from the western part of the country eastwards. Lacking transport, many had to cover vast distances on foot. But the speed of the German advance prevented this in some areas, particularly in Belorussia, the Ukraine and the Baltic republics. Some prisoners may have escaped, others may have been captured by the Germans. What is certain is that prisoners were often executed by their NKVD guards. The "L'vov massacre" on 29–30 June 1941 was the first of many such cases.

Despite the fall in the number of prisoners, there was a constant stream of new arrivals. Although it was at its height in the first year of the war, the net inflow of prisoners was never less than a quarter of the average total, and it rose again as the end of the war approached, probably as a result of arrests in the newly liberated areas. This, plus a decline in the death-rate and, in 1944, in the number of prisoners released, produced an increase of nearly a quarter in the size of the Gulag work-force between 1 January 1944 and 1 January 1945.

On the other hand, the number of prisoners actually in the camps stayed relatively low; at the beginning of 1945 it was less than half what it had been four years earlier. The reason for this was the steady shift of prisoners from the camps to Gulag labour colonies attached to factories and construction sites. To cope with the worsening manpower shortage in industry, Gulag prisoners were increasingly used to supplement the free work-force. By 1945 there were more prisoners in the labour colonies than in the camps themselves. According to Victor Kravchenko, "few industrial enterprises were without slave contingents . . . in dozens of them coerced labor was the principal or sole reliance," and this may well have been the case. Prisoners could have constituted around one-tenth of the industrial work-force by the end of the war. They were employed in many areas of industry and construction. The NKVD provided labour amounting to a quarter of a million prisoners for 640 enterprises and building sites belonging to other commissariats. Other prisoners worked for the NKVD itself, in its mines, metalworks, farms, even fisheries.

Not all prisoners were victims of political repression. There were real criminals among them, guilty of treason, collaboration, personal violence, speculation, theft and the whole range of crimes known in every society. But there were also many who were punished on trumped-up charges of desertion from the Red Army, or for minor infractions of the draconian labour laws, or for spreading rumours, for making anti-Soviet statements or for the many other political offences which came under Article 58 of the RSFSR [the Russian Federation, or the Russian Soviet Federative Socialist Republic] Criminal Code. Guilty or innocent, whether working in factories, mines, forests, building sites, or fighting the enemy, they all contributed to Soviet victory. And they did so in conditions which were extreme even by the standards of the Gulag. As Solzhenitsyn writes, "whoever didn't serve time in wartime didn't know what camp was really like."

The Mobilisation Process

Where would the 13 million new soldiers and war workers come from? Initially reserves were mobilised from the urban population. Thus in the second half of 1941 half a million unemployed women volunteered for war work, together with 300,000 school children between the ages of 12 and 15, and thousands of students and veterans. In 1942 more than half a million more were found for war work from the same groups.

At the same time, the unemployed reserves of the urban economy were slight by comparison with the huge requirements of the war. The main source of additional war workers and soldiers was necessarily those already employed in the town and countryside.

As far as recruitment to war work was concerned, much of it did not require anyone to change their place of work or residence; it took place automatically, as a result of the conversion of civilian enterprises to war production. Steel-workers went on making steel, but their steel went to armour tanks rather than to plate road vehicles. Engineers continued to build machines, but the machines were for warlike not peaceful use. However, there was still a need to find many new workers for such enterprises because established workers joined the armed forces or were promoted to administrative grades. For this reason, and because of the need to expand converted defence factories and create new ones, there was also significant recruitment into war work out of light industry and services — 130,000 under the auspices of the wartime Labour Committee just in the second half of 1941. In subsequent years this channel would be greatly enlarged; in 1942–5 the Labour Committee directed nearly 12 million workers into war work or training, and half of them came from the urban economy.

The last major source of recruitment to the war was the rural population. Three-fifths of the Red Army's wartime strength (11.6 million at its peak) were of rural origin. Rural conscripts judged unfit for combat duty were directed by the defence commissariat into war work — 700,000 just in the second half of 1941. Of those mobilised in later years by the Labour Committee, a growing proportion was of rural origin; in 1943–4 three-fifths came from the countryside.

These recruits helped to fill the places of existing workers, mainly young men, taken into the armed forces. The result was major change in the composition of the Soviet work-force. The share of women in industrial employment, which stood at two-fifths in 1940, rose to over half during 1942 and nearly three-fifths in 1943. In beleaguered Leningrad, where virtually all male workers were enlisted in combat units, women's share in the factory work-force rose to 80 per cent or more. Age was affected as much as gender. In the public sector as a whole, the combined employment share of the very young (under 19 years) and the relatively mature (over 50) rose from one-sixth in 1939 to more than one-quarter in 1942. It is hardly an exaggeration to picture the typical Soviet workplace collective in wartime as schoolchildren, grandparents, mothers and aunts.

The impact on rural employment was also predictable. Young men vanished from the countryside. The total rural work-force on Soviet-controlled territory fell disastrously, and not just because of the loss of huge territories behind German lines. In the Soviet rear, in regions untouched by occupation, villages were stripped of working hands; there, the collective farm working population fell by more than one-third—in the Ural region and Siberia, by 45 per cent. Agriculture became the preserve of women, children, pensioners and evacuees. In the prewar village, women already formed a majority of the collective farm work-force (this is explained by the rapid prewar recruitment of young men from the village to new jobs in industry and construction during rapid industrialisation). The war sharply intensified the trend. By 1944 able-bodied women outnumbered men in the interior regions by almost four to one.

The destination of those mobilised was either military service or service as a war worker. On the whole, war work meant one of five different kinds of employment. There were millions of new jobs in *defence plants* making guns, shells, tanks and aircraft. War work could also mean employment in civilian *heavy industry*—in engineering factories, iron and steel works and chemicals plants, in coal-mines, oil-fields and power stations, producing the essential inputs for the manufacture and arming of weapons. Other branches of war work included *construction*—work on defensive fortifications, as well as building or rebuilding factories, power stations and railway lines. *Transport* itself became a branch of war work, with its immense significance for supply of the front, as well as of production. Lastly, there were times when even *agriculture* was given the status of war work because, without bread, meat and fats, soldiers could not fight and war workers could not go on working.

Few of these jobs were unskilled. At least half the unsatisfied labour requirements reported by the defence and heavy industry commissariats early in 1942 were for skilled workers, and in the aircraft and tank industries the proportion rose to two-thirds. At this early stage of the war, the skill deficit probably seemed much more alarming than the short supply of labour generally. To assemble modern aeroplanes and armoured vehicles demanded the steady hand and stamina of experienced craft workers in the prime of life, rather than housewives in middle age who had never seen the inside of a factory workshop, or raw youths from remote villages.

At the same time, the skills shortage was being aggravated by the uncoordinated mobilisation process which was stripping away the existing workforce from munitions factories, especially those in the front-line regions.

As long as more unskilled workers were available, however, the skill deficit could always be overcome. There were many traditional ways of adapting skilled occupations and the industrial environment to the needs of new unskilled war workers, for skilled labour had always been short in backward, agrarian Russia and this was no new problem. Ways of coping ranged from breaking down skilled processes or "deskilling" jobs to movements for "learning by doing" or training on the job.

At the same time, the principal reliance had to be placed on formal schemes for upgrading workers' skills, and the war saw a huge expansion of vocational training. In 1940 a total of 3.5 million manual workers in industry either underwent some kind of induction training on entering the work-force, or else trained for a higher level of skill qualification (this was out of a mid-year industrial work-force of 8.3 million). In 1942, when there were 2.8 million *fewer* industrial manual workers, the number undergoing training actually rose to 3.8 million. In addition, in 1942 some 600,000 school leavers entered full-time vocational training, compared to an insignificant number in 1940. In total, the number training for improved skills during the year was equivalent to fully four-fifths of the 1942 manual work-force in industry, compared to less than half of the work-force in 1940. Industrial training on this massive scale opened up new skilled trades to women. However, the new avenues for female advancement were restricted to the shop-floor; there does not seem to have been any wartime increase in women's share of managerial or administrative posts.

Taking the war years as a whole, therefore, the shortage of skilled labour was acute but could not be decisive. Ultimately, what constrained the Soviet productive effort was the shortage of working hands. Allocating the working population correctly between alternative employments, whether on the front line or in the rear, would help make the difference between defeat and victory.

There was already an absolute shortage of hands when war broke out. However, the civilian economy contained substantial reserves, both of "disguised" unemployment, and of workers in occupations which would be graded inessential in wartime. These reserves were quickly used up. The drain of workers out of civilian employment into the Soviet Army and defence production was so rapid that soon nothing was left that did not carry the status of war work—even in agriculture. Thus, in connection with the 1942 spring sowing campaign, the Soviet head of state M. I. Kalinin declared:

> If we evaluate the different kinds of work in our country at present, in the ninth month of the war, then we can rank spring sowing work as of first importance. With it can be compared only the production of ammunition and armament.

Nor was this rhetoric. A month later, a government decree ordered a reverse mobilisation of the non-employed back into farm work.

This was just one symptom of the general situation. The reserves of labour in inessential employment were running out; the remaining kinds of employment were all essential to the war effort, and all carried the highest priority. Construction work meant building war plant. Agricultural work meant growing food for soldiers and war workers. Work in transport meant carrying weapons, rations and machinery and fuel for war production around the country. Work in the clothing industry meant making uniforms for soldiers and work clothes for war workers. The relative priority of these jobs became more and more finely graded and, at times, even outranked the priority of military needs. Thus, in May 1942 the GKO [State Defense Committee] halted the conscription of railway workers and ordered the return to railway employment of Red Army personnel skilled in railway operations.

Thus, during 1942 the Soviet economy moved from full employment in the normal, peacetime sense to full wartime mobilisation. At the same time this was not a smooth, orderly transition. For a start, there was a great difference between the western regions and the interior. In the western regions where the threat of invasion and occupation was immediate, there was no question of a smooth, controlled mobilisation of the work-force for a prolonged war effort. Immediately, combat took priority over production.

In Leningrad, in Kiev and Odessa, in the Donbass, in Moscow and Tula, home defence militias were recruited from the factories. Their formation and training went on at work-places outside working hours. But with the enemy's approach, the workers left the factories to collect spades and rifles, to dig defensive fortifications and to fight the invader. This applied just as much to munitions workers as to teachers and pastry-cooks, and reflected the simple logic that there was no point carrying on war production if the factory could not be defended. (But none of it applied in the Baltic republics and the former territory of eastern Poland, where the mood of the population was anti-Soviet and the fighting was over in days rather than weeks.) The only activity which might be given still higher priority was to fulfill measures for the most desperate eventuality, that of giving up the town. In this case movable assets and civilians must be evacuated, fixed installations and road and rail links mined for destruction and papers burnt.

Thus in the western regions the immediate response was to pitch the work-force into a state of immediate combat mobilisation. This was a state of utter imbalance, a running crisis which could be sustained for more than a few days only by uninterrupted supply of food and munitions from the interior regions. When the enemy came the volunteer divisions, poorly led and virtually untrained, would suffer appalling losses. The casualties would include many skilled munitions, engineering and metal workers, who represented a severe loss to the war economy.

In the interior the situation was better, and the transition to wartime economic mobilisation was smoother, but only by comparison. Near the front line, the problem was that everyone was forced to become a soldier, leaving not enough workers to produce even the military goods, let alone to carry on civilian trades. In the interior, the problem was that, of those not taken by the army, nearly everyone became a war worker, leaving too few to carry on with producing food, fuel and basic materials. In the long run, this was just as threatening to continuity of the war effort. To correct it would take terrific restraint, and the task would occupy most of 1942.

Chinese Women in Revolution and War
Margery Wolf

In this selection (1985), Wolf and other scholars of modern Chinese history examine the fate of women in China during the communist period. They argue that while women were expected to become involved in revolutionary activities and labor movements, such as collectivization, they were also expected to sacrifice their interests and deny their problems for the greater goals of the Revolution. Some women began to believe that the Revolution had largely passed them by because women's issues were seldom considered, discussed, or acted on.

In February 1943, the [Chinese Communist] Party's decision to avoid discussions of women's social and political inequality was made explicit at the meeting of the Central Committee in a directive on women's work in the Anti-Japanese Base Areas. I quote again from [Kay Ann] Johnson's account:

> According to the directive, women were not to be called to mass political meetings. The village women's associations were to be de-emphasized and supplanted by small production groups as the basic unit for women's organization. Political, cultural and educational work was to be carried out among women only to the extent that it directly contributed to improving their production skills. There was no mention of the 1934 Marriage Law, no work to educate against child betrothal, no mention of oppressive traditional practices except those practices, such as foot-binding, which it said directly hindered production. Instead, women leaders were instructed to "lessen the unnecessary mobilization of rural women" so they could devote more energy to production.

> To justify this policy and defend its narrow focus against its feminist critics, the directive fully developed the notion that this singular em-

Margery Wolf, *Revolution Postponed* (Stanford, Calif.: Stanford University Press, 1985), 16–25.

phasis on production was not only necessary to the war and the peasants' livelihood, but was the best, indeed the only, way to further women's own liberation.

As Johnson goes on to point out, this directive became the standard for all subsequent policy decisions on the woman question. Where once the CCP had said that women's lot would be equalized through class struggle and revolution, it now seemed that the women must make their own way by proving that they could contribute to production equally with men; only by doing that could they change men's attitudes. At the same time, of course, as Ding Ling had pointed out, women were expected to bear the truly heavy burden of their traditional roles, economic and social, within the household. Throughout the Sino-Japanese War and the civil war that followed, the primary function of the women's organizations remained that of mobilizing women for production. Party leaders spoke from time to time of the need for village women to take part in political action, and they talked of the problems of mistreatment of women by husbands and mothers-in-law and the selling of women and children into (and out of) marriage. But any woman who seemed to be suggesting revolution rather than reform as a solution to the burdens of women was quickly accused of error, of neglecting the class struggle in favor of a narrow feminist one. This was an early manifestation of a pattern that would become all too familiar: the set of reform goals and social education projects that could and would most easily and most often be set aside until the current economic or social crises were solved were those pertaining to women.

Shortly after Liberation, however, such did not appear to be the case. One of the first major initiatives from the new government was the promulgation of the Marriage Law in May 1950. The features of the new law that received the greatest attention, both favorable and unfavorable, were the rights of women to demand divorces and the rights of young people to choose their own marriage partners without parental interference. Marriage by parental arrangement was forbidden, as were child betrothals and the selling of women or children into marriage. Initially, the right to divorce caused the greatest havoc as hundreds of thousands of unhappy women sought to assert their newly discovered rights. That this threatened many men and their mothers, also seeking to enjoy *their* newly discovered rights in the new society, goes without saying. And the local level cadre who might have wished to help women acquire a legal and morally justifiable divorce was caught in between. If the cadre (usually a man) carried out his duties under the Marriage Law, he might find himself faced with an angry village and a serious handicap in the "important" work to come. If he did not, he was returning women, illegally, to families who would undoubtedly make them feel their anger for the loss of face they had suffered. The cadre was in fact caught between two Maoist dicta: he (rarely she) must be sensitive to the will of the masses, and he must use the Maoist method of confrontation, struggle, and education, risking polarization to achieve eventual consensus.

For many cadres, the dilemma was resolved by the implementation of the Agrarian Reform Law, which was announced the following month. Why these two major campaigns were introduced in such quick succession remains a source of speculation among China scholars. As Kay Ann Johnson points out, one might think that they were intended to be mutually supporting: "Land reform redistributed property and power in the villages, marriage reform redistributed property and power in the family. The marriage reform law gave women and children equal property rights, the land reform law gave them real property." But this (as Johnson recognizes) seems not to be what they had in mind. Reform cadres were urged to bring women into the struggle against the landlords and to encourage them to speak out in public meetings on the land reform issues, but they were also warned explicitly not to let women's "special problems" interfere with the important land reform work. Land reform cadres were given special training and spent many hours of study before they went into the villages to mobilize the peasants for this very basic transformation of their society. Even local level cadre knew the law inside and out before they began to work with their fellow citizens. Their knowledge of the Marriage Law and its implications was quite another thing. Often as not they were ignorant of its basic content and, equally often, they were hostile to the ideas they understood it to be espousing. They had interpreted, probably correctly, the barrage of material on land reform coming to them as meaning that marriage reform was to be mentioned and forgotten while the land work proceeded.

Land reform apparently was to benefit women as much as men or more in that for the first time they too would receive a share of land equal to that of each man. The hidden benefit to women was the experience they would gain in speaking out as political beings in a public setting. For some this did occur, but I suspect most let their menfolk do the talking. Reports from some areas of China indicate that the women who did speak out were looked at askance or were reprimanded. Though land deeds were made out in women's names, they were handed over to the male heads of household just as women's wages were. The presumption that land ownership would increase women's power within the family is arguable under some circumstances, but since the land of all family members was soon turned into collective land, there was insufficient time for such changes to occur, let alone be documented. The failure of land ownership to automatically produce gender equalization is readily apparent in the debates that took place in the rural areas over who should be given the shares of land for unmarried women. This land became a new item in marriage negotiations.

If the kind of publicity and education given to the principles of land reform had been applied to the Marriage Law at the same time, the developing contradictions might eventually have been resolved. But at that point the government needed to convince the rural male community that the benefits associated with support for the CCP were immediate and personal. To give land was an enormous gift, but to take away male authority over the other half of society was a threat more basic than a new revolution could tolerate. So, the fact that women "owned" land was rendered impotent by the fact that women themselves remained the property of men who still could transfer them and their property with a fair amount of ease. Whatever women's legal rights, their actual control over the means of production or even over their own bodies did not change much as the result of land reform.

By 1953 reports of the failures in the implementation of the Marriage Law were made public, both as a nudge to factions within the government who preferred not to move at all on family reform issues and as the start of a campaign to spread knowledge about the law's intent. Statistics were published describing the tens of thousands of murders and suicides that had resulted from the lack of support for women who wished to annul betrothals or free themselves from unhappy marriages. The figures tell us little since we have no population baseline from which to judge them, but the fact that they were being collected and publicized indicates the determination of at least some section in the government to confront the issue. Even as cadres were being trained and pilot campaigns launched in rural areas, the Central Committee was still debating the wisdom of such a disruptive program and attempting to devise (or force through) moderating tactics.

The conservatives were successful. Mao's response in 1927 to criticism of "going too far" had been, "Proper limits have to be exceeded in order to right a wrong, or else the wrong cannot be righted"; here the marriage reform cadres were cautioned to tread carefully. Mass struggle meetings, which had been so successful in the land reform campaign, were not to be used. Individuals were not to be targeted for mass criticism unless they had caused a death or serious injury. Past failings were not to be investigated; instead, the good models were to be held up for emulation. And finally, to gain the cooperation of local cadres who were known to be a major stumbling block in the movement, cadres were to be investigated only by other cadres and not held up for public criticism and confession. The local cadres were also given broad discretionary powers to suspend or limit the campaign in case it produced major social conflicts, disrupted production, or the like. According to Elisabeth Croll, "The Women's Federation noted in a report on the state of affairs in southern China that to get a divorce, there were three obstacles to overcome: the obstacle of the husband, of the mother-in-law and of the cadres. Apparently it was the latter which was often the hardest to overcome." Once again, it seems, the continued cooperation of local cadres took precedence over marriage reform.

In other words, the goals of the much-touted campaign were long term and primarily "informational." If the provisions of the law were known widely but did not spread anxiety widely, the campaign would be considered a success. By those criteria, Johnson feels that it was:

> Even though the publicity month did not get off on schedule in many areas, more people learned about, studied and discussed the Marriage Law than at any time since the law was passed. . . . Not only does it seem that millions became more clearly aware of the major issues of marriage reform and women's rights, but people also became more aware of some degree of government determination in supporting such changes—something which, given the past behavior of local officials, may not have been clearly understood in many areas prior to the 1953 campaign."

It is worth noting, however, that when I asked a number of women in Jiangsu and Shaanxi to tell me about the marriage reform campaigns in their area, only one of them could remember such a campaign occurring and she was not at all sure of its content. "My children were small at that time, and I had no time to go to meetings," she said.

By 1956 the rhetoric and, one assumes, the emphasis on the new law had changed. Editorials supporting young people against the restrictions of the patriarchal family stopped appearing. Publications that dealt with the family spoke instead of the need to prevent sexual laxity and licentiousness and to guard against the bourgeois attitudes toward marriage that were creeping into the country. These latter included such failings as contracting marriages for monetary gain or security and the whimsical changing of marital partners. It seems rather unlikely that many such breaches of China's stern moral standards occurred during that early period, but the message being conveyed was unmistakable. The nation had important business ahead and was not to be distracted by the selfish individualistic needs of unhappy women. The first Five Year Program was under way, and while men were urged to push ahead, women were urged to "link up closely the household work with the work of constructing a socialist society" by way of the Five Goods Movement. Since the economy was not yet ready to provide full-time employment for women, they should (1) unite with the neighborhood families for mutual aid, (2) do housework well, (3) educate children well, (4) encourage family production, study, and work, and (5) study well themselves. Women's magazines concentrated on domestic topics, including fashion tips and self-beautification, leading presumably to a happier and more productive husband, not to bourgeois partner-switching.

In the countryside, collectivization was stepped up, and women were being liberated by labor—that is, if labor needs allowed. Where single-cropping created labor surpluses, women remained in reserve. And, as part of the developing Chinese pattern, efforts were made not to let women's issues interfere. As Judith Stacey describes it:

Where the demand for labor allowed the mobilization of women to proceed, the regime exercised concern to avoid undue threats to patriarchal sensibilities. Activists stressed the benefits to family prosperity peasants would derive if they allowed their women to work in the fields. Peasants with traditional beliefs about pollution — that menstruating women would harm the crops — were reassured by measures barring women from agricultural labor during their menses, this on the "scientific" ground of protection of health. Official investigation teams even published reports appreciative of local communities that excluded pregnant, lactating, and menstruating women from agricultural work. Likewise, peasant concern that women who labored in public were subject to immoral temptations was allayed when cadres organized separate female work teams for work conducted away from direct familial supervision. Even when the government conducted ideological campaigns to combat peasant resistance to female agricultural labor, it attempted to reassure the public that families had little to fear. . . . The collectivization of agriculture succeeded in expanding the contribution of female labor and in modifying the specific contents of the traditional sexual division of labor, but it leveled no fundamental challenge to the traditional view that female labor was naturally different from and subordinate to that of men.

The Great Leap was Mao's attempt to achieve dramatically higher levels of production within the limits of China's still backward technology. For the Great Leap to succeed, some 300 million women had to be mobilized, and that mobilization obviously required some new institutional arrangements. For the first time and only a few short years after the Five Goods had relegated women to the sidelines, the patriarchal citadels were to be challenged. This was apparent in the rural areas, less so in the cities. If women were to work long hours in the fields every day, they could not also take care of children and prepare and preserve food in the old time-consuming ways. The newly formed communes were instructed to set up child care facilities, communal kitchens, even service centers for mending. Since such needs were identified as women's needs, they did not receive the planning and funding associated with other aspects of production. The cafeterias were the cause of the most grumbling, producing poorly cooked food at the wrong times. More importantly for a staggering economy, they were wasteful not only of food but of fuel, since it was the firing of the stove for cooking that also provided necessary heat to the *kang* (sleeping platform) during the icy winter months. But many analysts suggest that in fact it was the pressure to change women's role and status that caused the most distress in the rural areas. Workpoints were not raised to the level of men's, but they were raised. Women were assigned tasks formerly done only by men; they were trained in male skills and performed them with ease. This did not make the Great Leap policies popular among rural males. As Phyllis Andors says, "Of all the policies adopted in the Great Leap the attempt to change the role and status of Chinese women probably resulted in the most widespread, consistent, and far-reaching opposition. It was both qualitatively and quantitatively different from other problems for it involved questioning basic traditional cultural values and institutions, and half the population was involved in its scope. Andors's conclusion fits the pattern that is the theme of this chapter. The policies underlying the Great Leap assumed that women's progress would come only as a result of their own labor: "But it is clear that at this stage the Chinese had decided that the advancement of women must not be at the expense of economic growth and technical change; i.e., the opportunity for female employment and participation must be within the context of increasing production and expansion of social services."

In the cities, the recruitment of women did not produce as much anxiety about patriarchal institutions as it did in the countryside. Partly this was because women were often brought in to take over simple basic tasks that would free men to do more technically advanced processes and were thus not a threat to the familiar sexual division of labor. And the neighborhood collectives wherein most women worked in the early days were by definition totally outside the male sector. Many of these small factories are still in operation today, and they are a tribute to the women who organized them and continue to keep them going. Some of them are a kind of collective jobber, doing piecework for a nearby factory. Others, such as one that binds sheets of paper into accounting books, produce a complete product. Still others have isolated and taken over a basic process through which raw materials must go before a factory can assimilate them.

The restrictions placed on these neighborhood organizations, which developed in response to the government's call for women to join the labor force, are indicative of how much sacrifice the policy makers were willing to make toward women's efforts. The women were told they could not ask the government for funds, raw materials, machines, premises, or workers from state-run factories. If with none of these things they could create a factory, they would be fulfilling their patriotic duty. But their achievements brought them no nearer to equality with male workers since the wages were very low, there were no benefits, and advancement was out of the question. If the entry of women into labor was the path to equality, it would appear that the government was unwilling to provide more than an ill-drawn map.

In the late 1950's a three-year drought combined with generally inadequate central planning turned the Great Leap Forward into an economic disaster from which the country was unable to recover for more than a decade. Retrenchment on all fronts again forced women out of the labor force. In the mid-1960's Mao launched the Great Proletarian Cultural Revolution in an attempt to regain among other things ideological control of his revolution and rid the nation of its crippling bureaucracy. Mao turned to the young people for support, but some effort was made to involve women. As Johnson puts it:

> Thus the Cultural Revolution, more than previous periods, placed emphasis on the need to mobilize women to participation in politics as well as production. Not only were barriers to women's rights of participation attacked, but intense normative pressure was also generated to impress upon women that they had an obligation to devote themselves more fully to social and political responsibilities outside the home. Red Guards and the mass media widely propagated norms of behavior which stressed that the individual's role and responsibilities to the collective should take precedence over more narrow and individualistic family roles and responsibilities.

PRIMARY SOURCES

VOICES OF WORKING WOMEN IN WORLD WAR I: SELECTIONS FROM ANGELA WOOLLACOTT'S *ON HER THEIR LIVES DEPEND*

In her 1994 book on British women munitions workers during World War I, *On Her Their Lives Depend,* historian Angela Woollacott collected some important writings by and about women, their work, and how it was perceived. The first selection reprinted here shows the growing self-esteem some women developed as a result of their new role as workers. Two accounts come from the diary of G. M. West, a member of the Women Police Service who visited several munitions factories, noting working conditions. One journalist's account suggests an evolving camaraderie, a kind of sisterhood. Other selections are songs or poems lamenting the plight of women in war. All provide vivid glimpses of a society forced to employ a broader segment of society to maintain the demands of an exhausting war.

An Assessment of the Impact of Working Women in World War I
Flora Annie Steel

Contemporary observers hailed the benefits of women's wartime opportunities. Flora Annie Steel's assessment of women's situation at the time of the Armistice was one of apocalyptic optimism:

> Verily and indeed, if we women have done something in this war, the war has done more for us women. It has taught us to recognise our-

Angela Woollacott, *On Her Their Lives Depend: Munitions Workers in the Great War* (Berkeley and Los Angeles: University of California Press, 1994), 5.

selves, to justify our existence. Ideas that for the most part were but the baseless fabric of a dreamer's vision have taken form and the world is fresh and new for womanhood. Why, our very carriage is different, as anyone with eyes can see! As Kipling puts it, we walk now as if we owned ourselves, and we stand closer to each other.

Working-class women benefited from the war in the gender-specific ways of increased employment opportunities, higher wages (up to three times their prewar rates of pay), and a chance to learn new skills. Not all women experienced greater gender consciousness during the war, but the evidence suggests that, at least for some women, wartime work created gender-related growth in self-esteem and assertiveness. The gender consciousness that existed among women munitions workers was not, however, an identity that cut across class lines. Rather, their sense of themselves as women was constructed around options available to them as members of the working class.

Working Conditions in World War I Factories
G. M. West

Miss G. M. West joined the Women Police Service during the war and was sent to police four different munitions factories employing women, each of which she described in her diary. At the government factory at Queen's Ferry outside Chester, which made sulphuric acid, nitric acid, guncotton, TNT, and oleum, her strongest reaction was to the middle section where sulphuric acid was turned into nitric acid and nitric acid into oleum (a corrosive, oily solution):

> The particles of acid land on your face & make you nearly mad, like pins & needles only much more so; & they land on your clothes & make brown specks all over them, & they rot your handkerchiefs & get up your nose & down your throat, & into your eyes, so that you are blind & speechless by the time your hour is up & you make your escape. . . .

Her next assignment was to a factory at Pembrey, a little coal-mining village in South Wales, where TNT, guncotton, cordite, and ballistite were being manufactured:

> The ether in the cordite affects the girls. It gives some headaches, hysteria, & sometimes fits. If a worker has the least tendency to epilepsy, even if she has never shown it before, the ether will bring it out. . . . [I]f they stay on in the cordite sheds, they become confirmed epileptics & have the fits even when not exposed to the fumes. Some of the girls have 12 fits or more one after the other.

Angela Woollacott, *On Her Their Lives Depend: Munitions Workers in the Great War* (Berkeley and Los Angeles: University of California Press, 1994), 35.

Working Women at Leisure
Anonymous

According to a Weybridge printer, who was appealing before a conscription tribunal to allow him to keep his "last man" in July 1918, it was impossible for him to obtain female labor because "girls will not work anywhere except in munitions, where they can sing, dance and play." Apparently, he failed to consider that wage levels in munitions had anything to do with the predilections of women workers. Journalists were responsible, in good part, for this public image of women munitions workers, proffering descriptions of munitions factories such as the following one of the scene during a dinner hour:

> Away in one corner of the yard are two lines of merry dancers, their arms linked, dancing their favourite "Knees up, Mother Brown," while sturdy women, obviously picked for their strength and size for heavy machines, stand by with folded arms and nod to each other with a smiling "It-does-your-heart-good-to-see-them" look.

> Some there are who "keep themselves to themselves," and sit apart with a chosen friend and crochet antimacassars. Others have precious letters to be read again and again, even perhaps read out. . . .

> On the staircase is a moving stream of gay-coloured overalls, for the munition girl loves brightness, as the old deaf flower seller who sits outside the works has discovered, and in many breasts are bunches of fresh primroses.

> The procession pauses while its leaders gaze over the rail and throw a laughing word at a self-conscious group who are being photographed — very trying this, for the interruption has sent Elsie off into hysterical giggles again. But no matter, for Mrs. Bunce, who has worked her heavy lathe for "three years come May" and who means to send this group, with herself as the central figure, to a certain stalwart sergeant, father to seven small Bunces, has soon silenced her with a peremptory "Don't act so silly!" and the required fixed look has returned to all faces.

Dangerous Working Conditions
G. M. West

While legislation such as the 1901 Consolidation Act, which laid down standards for ventilation and sanitary accommodation, continued to improve the work environment in factories, working conditions at the

---

Angela Woollacott, *On Her Their Lives Depend: Munitions Workers in the Great War* (Berkeley and Los Angeles: University of California Press, 1994), 44–45.

Angela Woollacott, *On Her Their Lives Depend: Munitions Workers in the Great War* (Berkeley and Los Angeles: University of California Press, 1994), 69.

start of the war were often very poor. Long hours, a stuffy and over-crowded atmosphere, and a lack of canteen, toilet, washing, and first aid facilities obtained in the majority of factories, especially smaller ones. As the *Woman's Dreadnought* frequently pointed out, many women workers continued to work under conditions of "sweating." Isolated or remote factories were sufficiently invisible that they could evade regulation: even in April 1917 Miss West recorded the horrific conditions in the explosive factory at Pembrey, South Wales, a place she dubbed "the back of beyond":

> This factory is very badly equipped as regards the welfare of the girls. The change rooms are fearfully crowded, long troughs are provided instead of wash basins, & there is always a scarcity of soap & towels. The girls [*sic*] danger clothes are often horribly dirty & in rags, many of the outdoor workers, who should have top boots, oilskins & s.westers [*sic*], haven't them. Although the fumes often mean 16 or 18 "casualties" a night, there are only 4 beds in the surgery for men & women & they are all in the same room. . . . There are no drains owing to the ground being below sea level. . . . The result is horrible & smelly swamps. There were until recently no lights in the lavatories, & as these same lavatories are generally full of rats & often very dirty the girls are afraid to go in.

In contrast to this revolting state of affairs, some of the national factories built during the war were exemplary about providing lavatory, washing, changing, first aid, canteen, and other facilities.

A Musical Parody
Madeline Ida Bedford

In 1917 Madeline Ida Bedford parodied a munitions worker's high living, purportedly in the worker's voice:

Munition Wages

Earning high wages? Yus,
    Five quid a week.
A woman, too, mind you,
    I calls it dim sweet.

Ye'are asking some questions—
    But bless yer, here goes:
I spends the whole racket
    On good times and clothes.

* * *

Angela Woollacott, *On Her Their Lives Depend: Munitions Workers in the Great War* (Berkeley and Los Angeles: University of California Press, 1994), 125.

We're all here today, mate,
    Tomorrow—perhaps dead,
If Fate tumbles on us
    And blows up our shed.

Afraid! Are yer kidding?
    With money to spend!
Years back I wore tatters,
    Now—silk stockings, mi friend!

I've bracelets and jewellery,
    Rings envied by friends;
A sergeant to swank with,
    And something to lend.

I drive out in taxis,
    Do theatres in style.
And this is mi verdict—
    It is jolly worth while.

Worth while, for tomorrow
    If I'm blown to the sky,
I'll have repaid mi wages
    In death—and pass by.

A Factory Song
Anonymous

To cheer themselves during the long monotony of their shifts, especially on night shift, women munitions workers sang the songs of wartime popular culture. Some of the songs they repetitively sang were the same as those sung by soldiers while marching. In addition, women munitions workers took well-known tunes and made up new lyrics that featured themselves as heroines. Part of the purpose of these was to commemorate their own work group or unit, to distinguish themselves from the women workers in the next shed, factory, or process. In the lyrics they invented, however, they often portrayed themselves as performing a direct, heroic role in the business of the war, in the bloodshed and the vanquishing of the enemy. The songs indicate a vivid awareness of the nature of munitions work and of the war at the front, as well as a desire to valorize their own role in it. A song from an explosives factory at Faversham in Kent went as follows:

Angela Woollacott, *On Her Their Lives Depend: Munitions Workers in the Great War* (Berkeley and Los Angeles: University of California Press, 1994), 192–93.

The Girls with Yellow Hands

The guns out there are roaring fast, the bullets fly like rain;
The aeroplanes are curvetting, they go and come again;
The bombs talk loud; the mines crash out; no trench their might
    withstands.
Who helped them all to do their job? The girls with yellow hands.

The boys out there have hands of red; it's German blood, and warm.
The Germans know what's coming when the English swarm—
Canadians and British, and the men from Southern lands.
Who helped them all to do their job? The girls with yellow hands.

The boys are smiling though they rush against a barb'ed trench;
The girls are smiling though destruction hovers o'er their bench;
And when the soldiers sweep along through lines of shattered strands,
Who helped them all to do their job? The girls with yellow hands.

Lyrics to such songs often referred specifically to working with TNT and its emblematic yellowing, presumably to arrogate whatever glamor was possible to a discoloration that must have been a social embarrassment as well as an indication of poisoning. The song below is from the south of Scotland:

Give honour to the Gretna girls,
Give honour where honour is due,
Don't forget the Gretna girls
Who are doing their duty for you.

And when they are in the factory
Midst the cordite and the smell,
We'll give three cheers for the Gretna girls
And the others can come as well.

Come boys and do your little bit,
We'll meet you by-and-by

THE SOVIET UNION AND CHINA IN REVOLUTION AND WAR

The leaders of the Soviet Union and Communist China committed ever greater numbers of their people to building socialism and fighting counterrevolutionaries. Josef Stalin collectivized peasants, forcing them to work in huge agricultural complexes controlled by the state. Practically every Soviet citizen was enlisted in the fight against the Nazis during World War II, and the government relied heavily on forced labor. Similar pressures in China forced the government to encourage women to enter the workforce. Chairman Mao Zedong spoke about "the other half of the sky" to suggest that women should make up a greater part of a labor force devoted to building socialism and communism.

Soviet Peasants and Women in 1929
Joseph Stalin

Written with his approval, a biography about Stalin published in 1949
discusses the Soviet leader's view about effectively employing peasants
and women in the national workforce. In 1929, he argued that the middle
peasants supported the collectivization movement, thereby isolating the
rich peasants (kulaks), *who, from the state's perspective, were the enemy.*
Stalin also paid tribute to women, saying that they had played important
roles in past struggles. He urged the party to form armies of laboring
women to usher in the new historical stage of socialism. During the collec-
tivization program, millions were mobilized and millions more, peasants,
including many women, perished in their struggle against the Soviet state
or languished in the gulags.

Stalin rallied the whole party for the fight against the Rights and led it in
the assault against the last stronghold of capitalist exploitation in the
country. Stalin's genius, his inflexible will, and brilliant perspicacity advanced the revolution to a new and higher stage. In "A Year of Great
Change," the article he wrote in 1929 on the occasion of the twelfth anniversary of the October Revolution, he said:

"The past year witnessed a great change on all fronts of socialist construction. The change expressed itself, and is still expressing itself, in a
determined *offensive* of socialism against the capitalist elements in town
and country. The characteristic feature of this offensive is that it has already brought us a number of decisive *successes* in the principal spheres
of the socialist reconstruction of our national economy."

The party secured a radical improvement in the productivity of labor.
In the main, it solved one of the most difficult problems of socialist industrialization — the problem of accumulating financial resources for
the development of heavy industry. It succeeded in bringing about a
radical improvement in the development of Soviet agriculture and of
the Soviet peasantry. The collective farm movement began to advance by
leaps and bounds, even surpassing large-scale industry in rate of development. It was becoming a mass movement.

"The new and decisive feature of the present collective farm movement," Stalin wrote, "is that the peasants are joining the collective farms
not in separate groups, as was formerly the case, but in whole villages,
whole volosts [subdistricts], whole districts, and even whole areas. And
what does that mean? It means that *the middle peasant has joined the
collective farm movement.* And that is the basis of that radical change in

Marx-Engels-Lenin Institute, *Joseph Stalin: A Political Biography* (New York: International
Publishers, 1949), 64–67.

the development of agriculture which represents the most important achievement of the Soviet government. . . ."

Thus, under Stalin's guidance, the way was paved for the historic transition from the policy of restricting and squeezing out the kulak elements to the policy of eliminating the kulaks as a class, on the basis of solid collectivization.

This was a period when industrialization and collectivization were only gathering momentum, and when it was necessary to muster the productive forces of the people to the utmost for the accomplishment of tasks of the greatest magnitude. And it is characteristic of Stalin's wisdom that he chose this moment to bring prominently to the fore the question of the status of woman, of her position in society and her contribution to the labor effort as a worker or peasant, and to stress the important role she had to play in public and social life. Having given the problem of women the salience it deserved, Stalin indicated the only correct lines to solve it.

There has not been a single great movement of the oppressed in history in which working women have not played a part. Working women, who are the most oppressed of all the oppressed, have never stood aloof, and could not stand aloof, from the great march of emancipation. We know that the movement for the emancipation of the slaves had its hundreds and thousands of women martyrs and heroines. Tens of thousands of working women took their place in the ranks of the fighters for the emancipation of the serfs. And it is not surprising that the revolutionary movement of the working class, the most powerful of all the emancipatory movements of the oppressed masses, has attracted millions of working women to its standard.

"The working women," Stalin further said, "the female industrial workers and peasants, constitute one of the biggest reserves of the working class, a reserve that represents a good half of the population. Whether this female reserve goes with the working class or against it will determine the fate of the proletarian movement, the victory or defeat of the proletarian revolution, the victory or defeat of the proletarian government. The first task of the proletariat and of its vanguard, the Communist Party, therefore is to wage a resolute struggle to wrest women, the women workers and peasants, from the influence of the bourgeoisie, politically to educate and to organize the women workers and peasants under the banner of the proletariat.

"But working women," Stalin went on to say, "are something more than a reserve. They may become and should become—if the working class pursues a correct policy—a regular army of the working class operating against the bourgeoisie. To mold the woman labor reserve into an army of women workers and peasants fighting shoulder to shoulder with the great army of the proletariat—that is the second and all-important task of the working class."

As for the role and significance of women in the collective farms, Stalin expressed his views on this subject at the first congress of collective-farm shock workers. He said:

"The woman question in the collective farms is a big question, comrades. I know that many of you underrate the women and even laugh at them. That is a mistake, comrades, a serious mistake. The point is not only that women comprise half the population. Primarily, the point is that the collective farm movement has advanced a number of remarkable and capable women to leading positions. Look at this congress, at the delegates, and you will realize that women have long since advanced from the ranks of the backward to the ranks of the forward. The women in the collective farms are a great force. To keep this force down would be criminal. It is our duty to bring the women in the collective farms forward and to make use of this great force.

"As for the women collective farmers themselves," Stalin went on, "they must remember the power and significance of the collective farms for women; they must remember that only in the collective farm do they have the opportunity of becoming equal with men. Without collective farms—inequality; in the collective farms—equal rights. Let our comrades, the women collective farmers, remember this and let them cherish the collective farm system as the apple of their eye."

The enlistment of the broad masses of the country, including the working people of the formerly oppressed and backward nations in the work of building socialism, was a signal triumph for the Soviet ideology, which regards the masses as the real makers of history, over the bourgeois ideology, which insistently inculcates the absurd idea that the masses are incapable of independent constructive endeavor in any sphere of life. Stalin exposed the reactionary essence of the "theory" that the exploited cannot get along without the exploiters. "One of the most important results of the October Revolution is that it dealt this false 'theory' a mortal blow," Stalin said.

Stalin likewise exposed the reactionary legend that nations are divided into superior and inferior races.

"It was formerly the 'accepted idea' that the world has been divided from time immemorial into inferior and superior races, into blacks and whites, of whom the former are unfit for civilization and are doomed to be objects of exploitation, while the latter are the only vehicles of civilization, whose mission it is to exploit the former. This legend must now be regarded as shattered and discarded. One of the most important results of the October Revolution is that it dealt this legend a mortal blow, having demonstrated in practice that liberated non-European nations, drawn into the channel of Soviet development, are not a bit less capable of promoting a *really* progressive culture and a *really* progressive civilization than are the European nations."

Life in a Soviet Labor Camp
Alexander Solzhenitsyn

Solzhenitsyn wrote a series of novels and works based on his life experiences and research about the Soviet gulags. One of his most powerful works is One Day in the Life of Ivan Denisovich *(1963). The selection from this novel depicts part of a working day when Ivan and his coworkers built part of a wall in a factory. The scene captures the cold working conditions and the workers' humanity in the face of their captors' attempts to dehumanize them.*

Trust old moonface. If he'd been working for himself, he'd have been on his feet even sooner. (And another reason Shukhov was in a hurry—he wanted to grab the plumb line before Kilgas. They'd only gotten one from the tool shop.)

"Will there be three laying the bricks?" Pavlo asked the boss. "Should we put another man on? Or won't there be enough mortar?"

The boss frowned and thought a while. "I'll be the fourth man myself, Pavlo. And what's that about the mortar? The mixer's so big you could put six men on the job. You take the stuff out at one end while it's being mixed at the other. You just see we're not held up a single minute!"

Pavlo jumped up. He was a young fellow and he had a good color. He still hadn't been too hard hit by life in the camps. And his cheeks were still round from eating those Ukrainian dumplings back home. "If you lay bricks," he said, "I'll make the mortar. And we'll see who works the fastest! Where's the biggest shovel around here?"

That's what these gangs did to a man. There was Pavlo who used to carry a gun in the forests and make raids on villages. Why the hell should he kill himself with work in this place? But there's nothing you wouldn't do for your boss.

Shukhov went up with Kilgas. They could hear Senka coming up the ladder after them. He'd gotten the idea, deaf as he was.

The walls for the second story had only just been started. Three rows of bricks all around and a little higher in places. This was the quickest part of the job—from knee level up to your chest and no need to stand on scaffolds.

The scaffolds had all been carted off by the other prisoners—either taken away to other buildings or burned—just so nobody else could have them. Now, to do a decent job, they'd have to make new ones the next day. If not they'd be stymied.

Alexander Solzhenitsyn, *One Day in the Life of Ivan Denisovich*, trans. Max Hayward and Ronald Hingley (New York: Bantam Books, 1963), 104–11.

You could see a lot from the top of the plant—the whole compound covered with snow and not a soul in sight (the prisoners were all under cover, trying to get warm before the whistle blew), the black watchtowers, and the pointed poles with barbed wire. You couldn't see the wire if you looked into the sun, only if you looked away from it. It was shining bright and your eyes couldn't stand the light.

And close by, you could see the steam engine that made the power. It was smoking like hell and making the sky black. Then it started breathing hard. It always wheezed like a sick man before it sounded the whistle. There it came now. They hadn't put in that much overtime after all.

"Hey, Stakhanovite! Hurry up with that plumb line!" Kilgas tried to hustle him.

"Look at all that ice on your part of the wall!" Shukhov jeered back at him. "Do you think you can clear it off by the evening? That trowel won't be much good to you if you don't!"

They were going to lay the walls they'd settled on in the morning, but then the boss shouted up at them:

"Hey there! We'll work two to a wall so the mortar doesn't freeze in the hods. You take Senka on your wall, Shukhov, and I'll work with Kilgas. Meanwhile Pavlo'll clean off Kilgas' wall for me."

Shukhov and Kilgas looked at each other. He was right. It would be easier like that. They grabbed their picks.

Shukhov no longer saw the view with the glare of sun on the snow. And he didn't see the prisoners leaving their shelters either and fanning out over the compound, some to finish digging holes started in the morning and others to put up the rafters on the roofs of the workshops. All he saw now was the wall in front of him—from the left-hand corner where it was waist-high to the right-hand corner where it joined up with Kilgas'. He showed Senka where to hack off the ice and he hacked away at it himself for all he was worth with the head and blade of his pick, so that chips of ice were flying all around and in his face too. He was doing a good job and he was fast, but his mind wasn't on it. In his mind, he could see the wall under the ice, the outside wall of the power plant that was two bricks thick. He didn't know the man who'd worked on it in his place before. But that guy sure didn't know his job. He'd messed it up. Shukhov was now getting used to the wall like it was his own. One brick was too far in, and he'd have to lay three rows all over again to make it flush and also lay the mortar on thicker. Then in another spot the wall was bulging out a little, and he'd have to make that flush too. He figured how he'd split up the wall. The part he'd lay himself from the beginning, on the left, and what Senka'd lay as far as Kilgas, to the right. There on the corner, he guessed, Kilgas wouldn't be able to hold back and he'd do some of Senka's job for him so it would be a little easier on Senka. And while they were busy at the corner, he'd put up more than half the wall here so they wouldn't get behind. And he figured out how many bricks he'd lay where. The minute they started bringing bricks up, he grabbed hold of Alyoshka: "Bring 'em over to me! Put 'em right over here!"

Senka was hacking off the last of the ice, and Shukhov picked up a wire brush and started scrubbing the wall with it all over. He cleaned the top layer of bricks till they were a light gray color like dirty snow and got the ice out of the grooves. While he was still busy with his brush Tyurin came up and set his yardstick up at the corner. Shukhov and Kilgas had put theirs up a long time ago.

"Hey!" Pavlo shouted from down below. "Anybody still alive up there? Here we come with the mortar!"

Shukhov got in a sweat. He hadn't put up his leveling string yet. He figured he'd put it high enough for three rows at once, and some to spare. And to make things easier for Senka, he took part of the outside row and left him a little of the inside. While he was putting up the string, he told Senka with words and signs where to start laying. He got it, deaf as he was. He bit his lips and squinted over at the boss's wall as if to say, "We'll show 'em. We'll keep up with 'em." And he laughed.

Now they were bringing the mortar up the ladder. There'd be eight men on the job, working in twos. The boss told them not to put troughs with mortar near the bricklayers—the mortar'd only freeze before they got to use it—but to have the stuff brought up to them in the hods so they could take it out right away, two at a time, and slap it on the wall. And so the guys who brought up the hods wouldn't stand around freezing up here on top, they'd carry bricks over to the layers. And when their hods were empty, the next two came up from down below without wasting any time, and the first two went down again. Then they thawed out their hod by the stove to get the frozen mortar off it and try to get as warm as they could themselves.

Two hods came up together, one for Kilgas' wall and the other for Shukhov's. The mortar was steaming in the freezing cold, though there wasn't much warmth in it. When you slapped it on the wall with your trowel you had to work quick so it wouldn't freeze. If it did, you couldn't get it off again, either with your trowel or the back of your gavel, and if you laid a brick a little out of place it froze to the spot and stuck there. Then the only thing to do was pry it off with the back of the pick and hack the mortar away again.

But Shukhov never made a mistake. His bricks were always right in line. If one of them was broken or had a fault, Shukhov spotted it right off the bat and found the place on the wall where it would fit.

He'd scoop up some steaming mortar with his trowel, throw it on, and remember how the groove of the brick ran so he'd get the next one on dead center. He always put on just enough mortar for each brick. Then he'd pick up a brick out of the pile, but with great care so he wouldn't get a hole in his mitten—they were pretty rough, these bricks. Then he'd level off the mortar with a trowel and drop the brick on top. He had to even it out fast and tap it in place with his trowel if it wasn't right, so the outside wall would be straight as a die and the bricks level both cross-ways and lengthways, and then they froze in place. If any mortar was squeezed out from under a brick, you had to scrape it off with the edge of your trowel fast as you could and throw it away (in summer you could use it for the next brick, but not in this weather). This could happen when you had a brick with a piece broken off the end, so you had to lay on a lot more mortar to fill in. You couldn't just lay a brick like that, but you had to slide it up to the next one, and that's when you'd get this extra mortar running out.

He was hard at work now. Once he ironed out the snags left by the guy who'd worked here before and laid a couple of rows of his own, it'd be easy going. But right now he had to watch things like a hawk.

He was working like crazy on the outside row to meet Senka halfway. Now Senka was getting closer to Shukhov. He'd started together with the boss at the corner, but the boss was now going the other way. Shukhov signaled the fellows carrying the hods to bring the stuff up to him on the double. He was so busy he didn't have time to wipe his nose.

When he and Senka came together, they started taking mortar out of the same hod. There wasn't enough to go around.

"Mortar!" Shukhov yelled over the wall.

"Here she comes!" Pavlo shouted back.

Another hod came along, and they used up what was still soft. But a lot of it was frozen to the sides and they told the fellows to scrape it off themselves. There was no sense in them carrying all the frozen stuff down again.

"Okay, that's it. Next one."

Shukhov and the other bricklayers didn't feel the cold any more. They were now going all out and they were hot—the way you are at the start of a job like this when you get soaking wet under your coat and jacket and both shirts. But they didn't stop for a second and went on working like crazy. After an hour, they got so hot the sweat dried on them. The main thing was they didn't get the cold in their feet. Nothing else mattered. The slight cutting wind didn't take their minds off the work. Only Klevshin kept banging one foot against the other. He wore size nine, but each boot was a different size and both were tight.

Tyurin kept shouting for more mortar and so did Shukhov. Any fellow who really worked hard always became a sort of gang boss for a time. The main thing for Shukhov was not to lag behind, and for this he'd have chased his own brother up and down that ladder with a hod.

At first it was the Captain and Fetyukov who carried the stuff up to-gether. The ladder was steep and slippery, and for a time the Captain went pretty slow. Shukhov tried to push him a little: "Come on there, Captain. We need more bricks, Captain."

A Rural Base for the Chinese Revolution
Mao Zedong

In this 1939 essay, Mao discusses the need to develop a rural base for the Chinese revolution. Since the Chinese nationalists controlled the cities of China, the revolutionaries had little choice but to work with the peasants. Mao and his collaborators formed a mostly peasant revolutionary force which he led to victory in 1949. China's was the first Marxist revolution in which peasants played a prominent role.

In the War of Resistance a section of the big landlord class and big bourgeoisie, represented by Wang Ching-wei [Wang Qingwei], has turned traitor and deserted to the enemy. Consequently, the anti-Japanese people cannot but regard these big bourgeois elements who have betrayed our national interests as one of the targets of the revolution.

It is evident, then, that the enemies of the Chinese revolution are very powerful. They include not only powerful imperialists and powerful feudal forces, but also, at times, the bourgeois reactionaries who collaborate with the imperialist and feudal forces to oppose the people. Therefore, it is wrong to underestimate the strength of the enemies of the revolutionary Chinese people.

In the face of such enemies, the Chinese revolution cannot be other than protracted and ruthless. With such powerful enemies, the revolutionary forces cannot be built up and tempered into a power capable of crushing them except over a long period of time. With enemies who so ruthlessly suppress the Chinese revolution, the revolutionary forces cannot hold their own positions, let alone capture those of the enemy, unless they steel themselves and display their tenacity to the full. It is therefore wrong to think that the forces of the Chinese revolution can be built up in the twinkling of an eye, or that China's revolutionary struggle can triumph overnight.

In the face of such enemies, the principal means or form of the Chinese revolution must be armed struggle, not peaceful struggle. For our enemies have made peaceful activity impossible for the Chinese people and have deprived them of all political freedom and democratic rights. Stalin says, "In China the armed revolution is fighting the armed counter-revolution. That is one of the specific features and one of the advantages of the Chinese revolution." This formulation is perfectly correct. Therefore, it is wrong to belittle armed struggle, revolutionary war, guerrilla war and army work.

In the face of such enemies, there arises the question of revolutionary base areas. Since China's key cities have long been occupied by the

Mao Zedong, *The Chinese Revolution: 1900–1950* (Boston: Houghton Mifflin, 1974), 132–34.

powerful imperialists and their reactionary Chinese allies, it is imperative for the revolutionary ranks to turn the backward villages into advanced, consolidated base areas, into great military, political, economic
and cultural bastions of the revolution from which to fight their vicious
enemies who are using the cities for attacks on the rural districts, and in
this way gradually to achieve the complete victory of the revolution
through protracted fighting; it is imperative for them to do so if they do
not wish to compromise with imperialism and its lackeys but are determined to fight on, and if they intend to build up and temper their forces,
and avoid decisive battles with a powerful enemy while their own
strength is inadequate. Such being the case, victory in the Chinese
revolution can be won first in the rural areas, and this is possible because China's economic development is uneven (her economy not being a unified capitalist economy), because her territory is extensive
(which gives the revolutionary forces room to manoeuvre), because the
counter-revolutionary camp is disunited and full of contradictions, and
because the struggle of the peasants who are the main force in the revolution is led by the Communist Party, the party of the proletariat; but on
the other hand, these very circumstances make the revolution uneven and
render the task of winning complete victory protracted and arduous.
Clearly then the protracted revolutionary struggle in the revolutionary
base areas consists mainly in peasant guerrilla warfare led by the Chinese Communist Party. Therefore, it is wrong to ignore the necessity of
using rural districts as revolutionary base areas, to neglect painstaking
work among the peasants, and to neglect guerrilla warfare.

However, stressing armed struggle does not mean abandoning other
forms of struggle; on the contrary, armed struggle cannot succeed unless co-ordinated with other forms of struggle. And stressing the work in
the rural base areas does not mean abandoning our work in the cities
and in the other vast rural areas which are still under the enemy's rule;
on the contrary, without the work in the cities and in these other rural
areas, our own rural base areas would be isolated and the revolution
would suffer defeat. Moreover, the final objective of the revolution is the
capture of the cities, the enemy's main bases, and this objective cannot
be achieved without adequate work in the cities.

PRISONER OF WAR LABOR

Prisoners of war were extensively used as labor during World War II.
Some worked in concentration camps, others in the jungles of Southeast Asia, and millions more labored in Germany and Japan. Although
the intent of the Germans and Japanese was to extract work from the
prisoners to accomplish various tasks, prisoners were frequently not fed
enough to sustain energy levels needed for work. The death rates of prisoner of war laborers were often appalling.

A Japanese Officer Speaks to Prisoners of War
Y. Nagatomo

This selection is a speech by a Japanese officer given in late 1942 to prisoners working on the Burmese-Thai Railroad. The officer explains that World War II was caused by centuries of American and British aggression in Asia. The tone is civil, but the message is clear: Work or starve. Do not expect favors. The prisoners are "pitiful victims," many of whom died laboring for their captors.

Speech delivered by Lt. Col. Y. Nagatomo to Allied Prisoners of War at Thanbyuzayat, Burma on October 28th 1942.

It is a great pleasure to me to see you at this place as I am appointed Chief of the war prisoners camp obedient to the Imperial Command issued by His Majesty the Emperor. The great East Asiatic war has broken out due to the rising of the East Asiatic Nations whose hearts were burnt with the desire to live and preserve their nations on account of the intrusion of the British and Americans for the past many years.

There is therefore no other reason for Japan to drive out the Anti-Asiatic powers of the arrogant and insolent British and Americans from East Asia in cooperation with our neighbors of China and other East Asiatic Nations and establish the Great East Asia Co-Prosperity Sphere for the benefit of all human beings and establish lasting great peace in the world. During the past few centuries, Nippon has made great sacrifices and extreme endeavors to become the leader of the East Asiatic Nations, who were mercilessly and pitifully treated by the outside forces of the British and Americans, and the Nippon Army [Imperial Japanese Army], without disgracing anybody, has been doing her best until now for fostering Nippon's real power.

You are only a few remaining skeletons after the invasion of East Asia for the past few centuries, and are pitiful victims. It is not your fault, but until your governments do not wake up from their dreams and discontinue their resistance, all of you will not be released. However, I shall not treat you badly for the sake of humanity as you have no fighting power left at all.

His Majesty the Emperor has been deeply anxious about all prisoners of war, and has ordered us to enable the opening of War Prisoner camps at almost all the places in the SW countries.

The Imperial Thoughts are unestimable and the Imperial Favors are infinite, and as such, you should weep with gratitude at the greatness of

---

The Burma-Thailand Railway, ed. Gavan McCormack and Hank Nelson (St. Leonards, Australia: Allen and Unwin, 1993), 195–97.

them. I shall correct or mend the misleading and improper Anti-Japanese ideas. I shall meet with you hereafter and at the beginning I shall require of you the four following points:

1. I heard that you complain about the insufficiency of various items. Although there may be lack of materials it is difficult to meet your requirements. Just turn your eyes to the present conditions of the world. It is entirely different from the pre war times. In all lands and countries materials are considerably short and it is not easy to obtain even a small piece of cigarette and the present position is such that it is not possible even for needy women and children to get sufficient food. Needless to say, therefore at such inconvenient places even our respectable Imperial Army is also not able to get mosquito nets, foodstuffs, medicines and cigarettes. As conditions are such, how can you expect me to treat you better than the Imperial Army? I do not prosecute according to my own wishes and it is not due to the expense but due to the shortage of materials at such difficult places. In spite of our wishes to meet their requirements, I cannot do so with money. I shall supply you, however, if I can do so with my best efforts and I hope you will rely upon me and render your wishes before me. We will build the railroad if we have to build it over the white man's body. It gives me great pleasure to have a fast moving defeated nation in my power. You are merely rabble but I will not feel bad because it is your rulers. If you want anything you will have to come through me for same and there will be many of you who will not see your homes again. Work cheerfully at my command.

2. I shall strictly manage all of your going out, coming back, meeting with friends, communications. Possessions of money shall be limited, living manners, deportment, salutation, and attitude shall be strictly according to the rules of the Nippon Army, because it is only possible to manage you all, who are merely rabble, by the order of military regulations. By this time I shall issue separate pamphlets of house rules of War prisoners and you are required to act strictly in accordance with these rules and you shall not infringe on them by any means.

3. My biggest requirement from you is escape. The rules of escape shall naturally be severe. This rule may be quite useless and only binding to some of the war prisoners, but it is most important for all of you in the management of the camp. You should therefore be contented accordingly. If there is a man here who has at least 1% of a chance of escape, we shall make him face the extreme penalty. If there is one foolish man who is trying to escape, he shall see big jungles toward the East which are impossible for communication. Towards the West he shall see boundless ocean and above all, in the main points of

the North, South, our Nippon Armies are guarding. You will easily understand the difficulty of complete escape. A few such cases of ill-omened matters which happened in Singapore (execution of over a thousand Chinese civilians) shall prove the above and you should not repeat such foolish things although it is a lost chance after great embarrassment.

4. Hereafter, I shall require all of you to work as nobody is permitted to do nothing and eat the present. In addition, the Imperial Japanese have great work to promote at the places newly occupied by them, and this is an essential and important matter. At the time of such shortness of materials your lives are preserved by the military, and all of you must award them with your labor. By the hand of the Nippon Army Railway Construction Corps to connect Thailand and Burma, the work has started to the great interest of the world. There are deep jungles where no man ever came to clear them by cutting the trees. There are also countless difficulties and suffering, but you shall have the honor to join in this great work which was never done before, and you shall also do your best effort. I shall investigate and check carefully about your coming back, attendance so that all of you except those who are unable to work shall be taken out for labor. At the same time I shall expect all of you to work earnestly and confidently henceforth you shall be guided by this motto.

Y. Nagatomo
Lieutenant Colonel, Nippon
Exp. Force

Chief No. 3 Branch
Thailand POW Administration

A Nazi Official Speaks to SS Officers
Heinrich Himmler

Heinrich Himmler was head of the SS (Schutzstaffel, or "protection echelon"), one of the most powerful police agencies of the German state. The SS were the elite of the militia raised by the Nazi Party for its own purposes of intimidation, coercion, and security; as such their loyalty was first to Adolf Hitler as head of the party and only secondly to Germany. In this 1943 speech, Himmler outlines the course of the war and the role of the SS. Himmler presents a code of behavior for the SS man. At the same time, he makes it clear that he cares not a whit for the lives of non-German peoples. His code of conduct applies only to actions taken in support of other Germans. Racism permeates this discourse wherein non-Germans

A Holocaust Reader, ed. Lucy Dawidowicz (New York: Berman House, 1976), 130–35.

*are considered to be animals or beasts, and Germans justified in being
indifferent to their fate. He also coldly discusses the extermination of the
Jews and the confiscation of their property. Racist metaphors are employed likening Jews to germs, both needing eradication before they infect
others.*

. . . In 1941 the Führer attacked Russia. That was, as we probably can assert now, shortly—perhaps three to six months—before Stalin was
winding up for his great push into Central and Western Europe. I can sketch
this first year in a very few lines. The attack cut through. The Russian
army was herded together in great pockets, ground down, captured. At
that time we did not value this human mass the way we value it today,
as raw material, as labor. In the long run, viewed in terms of generations, it is no loss, but today, because of the loss of manpower, it is re-
grettable that the prisoners died by the tens and hundreds of thousands
of exhaustion, of hunger. . . .

Good Nature in the Wrong Place

It is a basic mistake for us to infuse our inoffensive soul and feeling, our
good nature, our idealism, into alien peoples. This has been true since
the time of Herder, who must have written *Stimmen der Völker* in a boozy
hour,[1] and who thereby brought such immeasurable sorrow and misery
on us later generations. This has been true since the case of the Czechs
and Slovenes, to whom, after all, we gave their sense of nationality. They
themselves were not capable of achieving it; we invented it for them.

One basic principle must be absolute for the SS man: we must be
honest, decent, loyal, and comradely to members of our own blood and to
nobody else. What happens to the Russians, what happens to the Czechs,
is a matter of total indifference to me. What there is among the nations in
the way of good blood of our kind, we will take for ourselves—if necessary, by kidnapping their children and raising them among us. Whether
the other nations live in prosperity or croak from hunger interests me
only insofar as we need them as slaves for our culture; otherwise, it does
not interest me. Whether 10,000 Russian females drop from exhaustion
while building an anti-tank ditch interests me only insofar as the anti-
tank ditch gets finished for Germany's sake. We shall never be brutal and
heartless where it is not necessary—obviously not. We Germans, the
only people in the world who have a decent attitude toward animals,
will also take a decent attitude toward these human animals. But it is a
crime against our own blood to worry about them and to give them
ideals that will make it still harder for our sons and grandsons to cope

1. Johann Gottfried von Herder (1744–1803), German philosopher and poet, has been
called the father of German nationalism. As a champion of the idea of nationalism, he
published an anthology of folk songs of various peoples called *Stimmen der Völker* (Voices
of the Peoples).

with them. If someone were to come to me and say, "I cannot build the anti-tank ditch with women or children; it is inhuman, they will die in the process," then I would have to say, "You are a murderer of your own blood, for if the anti-tank ditch is not built, German soldiers will die, and they are sons of German mothers. They are our own blood." This is what I want to instill into the SS and what I believe I have instilled into them as one of the most sacred laws of the future: Our concern, our duty is to our people and our blood; it is for them that we have to provide and to plan, to work and to fight, and for nothing else. Toward anything else we can be indifferent. I wish the SS to take this attitude in confronting the problem of all alien, non-Germanic peoples, especially the Russians. All else is just soap bubbles, is a fraud against our own nation and an obstacle to the earlier winning of the war. . . .

Foreigners in the Reich

We must also realize that we have between six and seven million foreigners in Germany, perhaps even eight million by now. We have prisoners in Germany. They are none of them dangerous so long as we hit them hard at the smallest trifle. Shooting ten Poles today is a mere nothing when compared with the fact that we might later have to shoot tens of thousands in their place, and that the shooting of these tens of thousands would also cost German blood. Every little fire will immediately be stamped out and quenched and extinguished; otherwise — as with a real conflagration — a political and psychological fire may break out among the people.

The Communists in the Reich

I do not believe the Communists could risk any action, for their leading elements, like most criminals, are in our concentration camps. Here something needs saying: After the war it will be possible to see what a blessing it was for Germany that, regardless of all humanitarian sentimentality, we imprisoned this whole criminal substratum of the German people in the concentration camps; and for this I claim the credit. If these people were going about free, we would be having a harder time of it. For then the subhumans would have their NCO's and commanding officers, they would have their workers' and soldiers' councils. As it is, they are locked up, and are making shells or projectile cases or other important things, and are very useful members of human society. . . .

The Evacuation of the Jews

I also want to make reference before you here, in complete frankness, to a really grave matter. Among ourselves, this once, it shall be uttered quite frankly; but in public we will never speak of it. Just as we did not hesitate on June 30, 1934, to do our duty as ordered, to stand up against the wall comrades who had transgressed, and shoot them,[2] so we have never talked about this and never will. It was the tact which I am glad to say is a matter of course to us that made us never discuss it among ourselves, never talk about it. Each of us shuddered, and yet each one knew that he would do it again if it were ordered and if it were necessary.

I am referring to the evacuation of the Jews, the annihilation of the Jewish people. This is one of those things that are easily said. "The Jewish people is going to be annihilated," says every party member. "Sure, it's in our program, elimination of the Jews, annihilation—we'll take care of it." And then they all come trudging, 80 million worthy Germans, and each one has his one decent Jew. Sure, the others are swine, but this one is an A-1 Jew. Of all those who talk this way, not one has seen it happen, not one has been through it. Most of you must know what it means to see a hundred corpses lie side by side, or five hundred, or a thousand. To have stuck this out and—excepting cases of human weakness—to have kept our integrity, that is what has made us hard. In our history, this is an unwritten and never-to-be-written page of glory, for we know how difficult we would have made it for ourselves if today—amid the bombing raids, the hardships and the deprivations of war—we still had the Jews in every city as secret saboteurs, agitators, and demagogues. If the Jews were still ensconced in the body of the German nation, we probably would have reached the 1916–17 stage by now.[3]

The wealth they had we have taken from them. I have issued a strict order, carried out by SS-Obergruppenführer Pohl, that this wealth in its entirety is to be turned over to the Reich as a matter of course. We have taken none of it for ourselves. Individuals who transgress will be punished in accordance with an order I issued at the beginning, threatening that whoever takes so much as a mark of it for himself is a dead man. A number of SS men—not very many—have transgressed, and they will die, without mercy. We had the moral right, we had the duty toward our people, to kill this people which wanted to kill us. But we do not have the right to enrich ourselves with so much as a fur, a watch, a mark, or a cigarette or anything else. Having exterminated a germ, we do not want, in the end, to be infected by the germ, and die of it. I will not stand by and let even a small rotten spot develop or take hold. Wherever it may form, we together will cauterize it. All in all, however, we can say that we have carried out this heaviest of our tasks in a spirit of love for our people. And our inward being, our soul, our character has not suffered injury from it.

2. A reference to the purge of the SA [*Sturmabteilung,* "storm troopers," the Nazi Party militia] and the murder of its top leaders by SS officers and men.

3. The reference is to the time when the tide of World War I began to turn against Germany. German nationalists and rightists then attributed Germany's losses and ultimate defeat to the *Dolchstoss,* the "stab in the back" by the Jews.

QUESTIONS TO CONSIDER

1. What were the connections between the warfare state created in World War I and the welfare state created during the Great Depression around the world?

2. Women became increasingly important to twentieth-century workforces. How were they viewed and treated, especially in totalitarian states such as China and the Soviet Union?

3. Discuss the growing role of peasants in the workforce. How were they regarded by their rulers?

4. Discuss the use of forced labor, especially in wartime. What were working conditions like in the various camps?

5. What kinds of injustices were imposed by totalitarian states on some of their subject peoples?

ACCELERATING CHANGE

INTRODUCTION

The post – World War II era was characterized by rapid and pervasive change in many arenas of life. Were these changes any greater in magnitude than those of the eighteenth century or nineteenth century, or does every contemporary period seem to be more dynamic and volatile than the past?

This question is impossible to answer fully, but many scholars argue that the current era is qualitatively different from all (or virtually all) periods that have preceded it. Their opinion is based largely on a comparison of the pace of change in earlier times with the pace today. To explain this difference, scholars look to a number of continuing historical trends that started some time ago that have profoundly affected our era.

The rate of population growth, for example, has been increasing more or less steadily since the development of agriculture several thousand years ago. The increases in population during the past fifty years, however, have far outstripped those of the preceding centuries, partly because population growth is cumulative and the base population from which increase comes is so much larger than before. Equally important, however, are the medical and green revolutions, which have produced means of improving health and food supplies. These improvements have affected every place on earth, but Third World countries — former colonies — have seen the most dramatic improvements and resulting population increases.

Similarly, resentment indigenous peoples hold toward colonial-imperialist seizure and exploitation of their lands has existed since the beginning of the early modern colonial system in the sixteenth century. By the early twentieth century, resentments had increased in many places, leading to the birth of independence movements. By the latter half of the twentieth century, many of these movements had become serious threats to colonial rule, and overseas colonies demanded and received political independence.

There can be no doubt that the pace of technological change in the late twentieth century is incredibly fast, and most historians believe that this pace has been increasing ever since the Industrial Revolution. The electronic computer is only one example of a technology that was unknown fifty years ago, a novelty twenty-five years ago, and a necessity for many businesses and individuals today. Communications satellites, electric automobiles, solar-powered equipment, and other recently developed devices have either fundamentally changed the way significant numbers of people live their lives or have the potential to do so. Will the increasing pace of technological development continue, or have we experienced a relatively brief spurt of development that will be followed by a slower rate of change? Will technological change demand radical social or economic change? Will we be able to control our destinies, or will we be driven forward by exigencies created by technology? Future historians may be able to attempt to answer these questions, but we who are experiencing this episode of history can only speculate.

A final example of the rapid change of twentieth-century life is the growth of the middle class. From time to time in various parts of the world an intermediate class that was neither rich nor poor has developed. However, after a few centuries of existence, as political and economic conditions changed, the middle class often dwindled or disappeared. In medieval Europe, in contrast, the development of a middle class was followed by a sustained growth of its size and power that has continued to the present and has spread to many other parts of the world. According to some scholars, these and many other trends have culminated in the era following World War II and have made this era unlike any other in terms of the pace and depth of worldwide change.

These ongoing processes have combined with a series of unique events to make the post–1945 era a volatile historical period. In this environment there developed a phenomenon that dominated most of the latter half of the twentieth century, affecting nearly every aspect of life: the Cold War. The Cold War was a rivalry between capitalist and communist countries that characterized the period between 1945 — when World War II and the alliance of these countries against the Axis powers ended — and 1989 — when the Soviet Union dissolved itself and largely abandoned communism. While the Cold War rarely erupted into violent confrontation, as in the Korean and Vietnam Wars, it manifested itself in adversarial foreign relations, massive military budgets built up in anticipation of a possible "hot" war, and insidious propaganda campaigns against the opponent's core ideology. The Cold War spawned such diverse spin-offs as:

- major improvements in technology, often resulting from military technology development.
- the provision of funds of various sorts to independence movements within colonies and to newly independent countries. These funds were largely intended to curry favor and induce the newly independent countries to join one's own political bloc.

- purges to find and remove those who might sympathize with the rival camp. These campaigns often destroyed the lives of innocent people who had no such sympathies.
- an undercurrent of fear and alienation, based on the knowledge that a war with nuclear weapons would be far more devastating than any war in history.
- various movements, which may have been founded in reaction to alienation, that rejected traditional values.

All of these phenomena occurred in both the communist and the capitalist blocs, although in different forms.

Part Nine of the reader considers a few of the changes that have characterized the period from 1945 to the present. To reduce the wealth of possible readings from this era to a manageable, focused collection, only a few arenas will be considered: the Cold War, independence movements, and the role of technology in broader change. The political rivalry of the Cold War looms over this entire era, its repercussions rippling through social life, technology, and the arts around the world. In the Third World, movements to gain political independence also dominated the era. Everywhere, technology was developing apace, reaching far into many spheres of life.

SCHOLARLY WORKS

Technology as Cause or Effect?
Carlo M. Cipolla

Carlo Cipolla is a historian of technology who has directed most of his efforts to the period before the Industrial Revolution. Many of his works have explored whether technological progress has brought about changes in society, culture, and economics or whether it has been the reverse. In this brief essay, he notes that this basic question underlies the way we frame our considerations of the history of technology.

Many anthropologists place the beginning of the human adventure at the moment when some primitive creature began to produce and use tools. If so, the earliest flaked flints, the most ancient polished stones mark the beginning of our history. All that followed can hardly be understood without reference to a growing number of increasingly complex tools. As Thomas Carlyle described him, "Man stands on a basis, at most of the flattest soled, of some half square foot insecurely enough.

Carlo M. Cipolla and Derek Birdsall, *The Technology of Man: A Visual History* (New York: Holt, Rinehart and Winston, 1979), 17–19.

Three quintals are a crushing load for him; the steer of the field tosses him aloft like a wasterag. Nevertheless he can use tools. Without tools he is nothing. With tools he is all." The role of tools and technology in shaping our destiny is so dramatically obvious, though, that it may distort our sense of the relative importance of the factors at play. In the presence of so many technical miracles, we may be blinded to the fact that it is not technology which is truly miraculous, but the mind behind it.

Technology is not the parent of human activity: it is its stepchild. Both technology and invention arise from historical circumstances of an altogether peculiar character and are part of the total human experience. When we try to explain why a given technological development occurred at a certain place and a certain time it is very easy to fall prey to facile determinism: with hindsight many a development may look simply like the natural, almost inevitable product of some need. But necessity is itself often man-made: and even where an unarguable, objective necessity has been an important ingredient, it has represented a challenge, but hardly the full explanation. We are frequently told this or that society developed labor-saving machinery *because* it faced shortages of labor; or that the mechanical clock was invented *because* the sun did not always shine on sundials, and in winter the water in water clocks turned into ice. In fact, when faced by a shortage of labor, one society may fatalistically accept the consequences; another may launch raids to capture slaves; another may develop labor-saving machinery. The response depends largely on the prevailing culture. Clouds and cold weather have existed always and nearly everywhere; the reason why the clock was invented in medieval Europe can be explained only in human terms.

In fact when we speak of the challenges of a given environment or the needs of a given society, we must beware of thinking in terms of purely objective, exogenous factors. The challenge counts insofar as it is perceived by man, and what matters is how it is perceived.

Actually, the characteristics of a culture not only condition the appearance of tools but also their use, destination, and spread. The microscope was invented in the 17th century: but it was another two centuries before microbiology was born. Until the development of a new philosophy and new methods of systematic empirical inquiry, the doctors who looked through microscopes at microbes could not make sense of what they saw. In the 17th and 18th centuries, when Europeans took clocks and scientific instruments to China to impress the Imperial Court and the Mandarinate, the Chinese were eager to acquire such pieces, but mostly as toys.

To say the development and spread of technology can only be explained in human terms does not, however, imply that technology is a neutral stepchild of human activity. Technology deeply affects the material culture of a society, the size and composition of its population, the composition of the labor force and its work patterns, and the physical environment. Most important of all, it affects human minds. A boy playing with a mechanical toy and a scientist using a computer will both be deeply affected in the workings of their minds, their inclinations and their curiosities by the gadgetry they are using. The technologies nurtured by a culture may easily have a cumulative effect on it.

The Third Wave
Alvin Toffler

Alvin Toffler is a "futurist," a writer who examines trends to predict what the future will bring. He has written several popular books that explore the impact of technology in the recent past and the influence he expects it to have on society in the future. This selection, excerpted from The Third Wave *(1980), expresses his confidence that technology will force massive reorganizations of society.*

A new civilization is emerging in our lives, and blind men everywhere are trying to suppress it. This new civilization brings with it new family styles; changed ways of working, loving, and living; a new economy; new political conflicts; and beyond all this an altered consciousness as well. Pieces of this new civilization exist today. Millions are already attuning their lives to the rhythms of tomorrow. Others, terrified of the future, are engaged in a desperate, futile flight into the past and are trying to restore the dying world that gave them birth.

The dawn of this new civilization is the single most explosive fact of our lifetimes.

It is the central event—the key to understanding the years immediately ahead. It is an event as profound as that First Wave of change unleashed ten thousand years ago by the invention of agriculture, or the earthshaking Second Wave of change touched off by the industrial revolution. We are the children of the next transformation, the Third Wave.

We grope for words to describe the full power and reach of this extraordinary change. Some speak of a looming Space Age, Information Age, Electronic Era, or Global Village. Zbigniew Brzezinski has told us we face a "technetronic age." Sociologist Daniel Bell describes the coming of a "post-industrial society." Soviet futurists speak of the S.T.R.—the "scientific-technological revolution." I myself have written extensively about the arrival of a "super-industrial society." Yet none of these terms, including my own, is adequate.

Some of these phrases, by focusing on a single factor, narrow rather than expand our understanding. Others are static, implying that a new

Alvin Toffler, *The Third Wave* (New York: William Morrow, 1980), 25–30.

society can come into our lives smoothly, without conflict or stress. None of these terms even begins to convey the full force, scope, and dynamism of the changes rushing toward us or of the pressures and conflicts they trigger.

Humanity faces a quantum leap forward. It faces the deepest social upheaval and creative restructuring of all time. Without clearly recognizing it, we are engaged in building a remarkable new civilization from the ground up. This is the meaning of the Third Wave.

Until now the human race has undergone two great waves of change, each one largely obliterating earlier cultures or civilizations and replacing them with ways of life inconceivable to those who came before. The First Wave of change—the agricultural revolution—took thousands of years to play itself out. The Second Wave—the rise of industrial civilization—took a mere three hundred years. Today history is even more accelerative, and it is likely that the Third Wave will sweep across history and complete itself in a few decades. We, who happen to share the planet at this explosive moment, will therefore feel the full impact of the Third Wave in our own lifetimes.

Tearing our families apart, rocking our economy, paralyzing our political systems, shattering our values, the Third Wave affects everyone. It challenges all the old power relationships, the privileges and prerogatives of the endangered elites of today, and provides the backdrop against which the key power struggles of tomorrow will be fought.

Much in this emerging civilization contradicts the old traditional industrial civilization. It is, at one and the same time, highly technological and anti-industrial.

The Third Wave brings with it a genuinely new way of life based on diversified, renewable energy sources; on methods of production that make most factory assembly lines obsolete; on new, non-nuclear families; on a novel institution that might be called the "electronic cottage"; and on radically changed schools and corporations of the future. The emergent civilization writes a new code of behavior for us and carries us beyond standardization, synchronization, and centralization, beyond the concentration of energy, money, and power.

This new civilization, as it challenges the old, will topple bureaucracies, reduce the role of the nation-state, and give rise to semiautonomous economies in a postimperialist world. It requires governments that are simpler, more effective, yet more democratic than any we know today. It is a civilization with its own distinctive world outlook, its own ways of dealing with time, space, logic, and causality.

Above all, as we shall see, Third Wave civilization begins to heal the historic breach between producer and consumer, giving rise to the "prosumer" economics of tomorrow. For this reason, among many, it could—with some intelligent help from us—turn out to be the first truly humane civilization in recorded history.

The Revolutionary Premise

Two apparently contrasting images of the future grip the popular imagination today. Most people — to the extent that they bother to think about the future at all — assume the world they know will last indefinitely. They find it difficult to imagine a truly different way of life for themselves, let alone a totally new civilization. Of course they recognize that things are changing. But they assume today's changes will somehow pass them by and that nothing will shake the familiar economic framework and political structure. They confidently expect the future to continue the present.

This straight-line thinking comes in various packages. At one level it appears as an unexamined assumption lying behind the decisions of businessmen, teachers, parents, and politicians. At a more sophisticated level it comes dressed up in statistics, computerized data, and forecasters' jargon. Either way it adds up to a vision of a future world that is essentially "more of the same" — Second Wave industrialism writ even larger and spread over more of this planet.

Recent events have severely shaken this confident image of the future. As crisis after crisis has crackled across the headlines, as Iran erupted, as Mao was de-deified, as oil prices skyrocketed and inflation ran wild, as terrorism spread and governments seemed helpless to stop it, a bleaker vision has become increasingly popular. Thus, large numbers of people — fed on a steady diet of bad news, disaster movies, apocalyptic Bible stories, and nightmare scenarios issued by prestigious think tanks — have apparently concluded that today's society cannot be projected into the future because there is no future. For them, Armageddon is only minutes away. The earth is racing toward its final cataclysmic shudder.

On the surface these two visions of the future seem very different. Yet both produce similar psychological and political effects. For both lead to the paralysis of imagination and will.

If tomorrow's society is simply an enlarged, Cinerama version of the present, there is little we *need* do to prepare for it. If, on the other hand, society is inevitably destined to self-destruct within our lifetime, there is nothing we *can* do about it. In short, both these ways of looking at the future generate privatism and passivity. Both freeze us into inaction.

Yet, in trying to understand what is happening to us, we are not limited to this simpleminded choice between Armageddon and More-of-the-Same. There are many more clarifying and constructive ways to think about tomorrow — ways that prepare us for the future and, more important, help us to change the present.

This book is based on what I call the "revolutionary premise." It assumes that, even though the decades immediately ahead are likely to be filled with upheavals, turbulence, perhaps even widespread violence, we will not totally destroy ourselves. It assumes that the jolting changes we are now experiencing are not chaotic or random but that, in fact, they form a sharp, clearly discernible pattern. It assumes, moreover, that these changes are cumulative—that they add up to a giant transformation in the way we live, work, play, and think, and that a sane and desirable future is possible. In short, what follows begins with the premise that what is happening now is nothing less than a global revolution, a quantum jump in history.

Put differently, this book flows from the assumption that we are the final generation of an old civilization and the first generation of a new one, and that much of our personal confusion, anguish, and disorientation can be traced directly to the conflict within us, and within our political institutions, between the dying Second Wave civilization and the emergent Third Wave civilization that is thundering in to take its place.

When we finally understand this, many seemingly senseless events become suddenly comprehensible. The broad patterns of change begin to emerge clearly. Action for survival becomes possible and plausible again. In short, the revolutionary premise liberates our intellect and our will.

The Leading Edge

To say the changes we face will be revolutionary, however, is not enough. Before we can control or channel them we need a fresh way to identify and analyze them. Without this we are hopelessly lost.

One powerful new approach might be called social "wave-front" analysis. It looks at history as a succession of rolling waves of change and asks where the leading edge of each wave is carrying us. It focuses our attention not so much on the continuities of history (important as they are) as on the discontinuities—the innovations and breakpoints. It identifies key change patterns as they emerge, so that we can influence them.

Beginning with the very simple idea that the rise of agriculture was the first turning point in human social development, and that the industrial revolution was the second great breakthrough, it views each of these not as a discrete, one-time event but as a wave of change moving at a certain velocity.

Before the First Wave of change, most humans lived in small, often migratory groups and fed themselves by foraging, fishing, hunting, or herding. At some point, roughly ten millennia ago, the agricultural revolution began, and it crept slowly across the planet spreading villages, settlements, cultivated land, and a new way of life.

This First Wave of change had not yet exhausted itself by the end of the seventeenth century, when the industrial revolution broke over Europe and unleashed the second great wave of planetary change. This new process—industrialization—began moving much more rapidly across nations and continents. Thus two separate and distinct change processes were rolling across the earth simultaneously, at different speeds.

Today the First Wave has virtually subsided. Only a few tiny tribal populations, in South America or Papua New Guinea, for example, remain to be reached by agriculture. But the force of this great First Wave has basically been spent.

Meanwhile, the Second Wave, having revolutionized life in Europe, North America, and some other parts of the globe in a few short centuries, continues to spread, as many countries, until now basically agricultural, scramble to build steel mills, auto plants, textile factories, railroads, and food processing plants. The momentum of industrialization is still felt. The Second Wave has not entirely spent its force.

But even as this process continues, another, even more important, has begun. For as the tide of industrialism peaked in the decades after World War II, a little-understood Third Wave began to surge across the earth, transforming everything it touched.

Many countries, therefore, are feeling the simultaneous impact of two, even three, quite different waves of change, all moving at different rates of speed and with different degrees of force behind them.

For the purposes of this book we shall consider the First Wave era to have begun sometime around 8000 B.C. and to have dominated the earth unchallenged until sometime around A.D. 1650–1750. From this moment on, the First Wave lost momentum as the Second Wave picked up steam. Industrial civilization, the product of this Second Wave, then dominated the planet in its turn until it, too, crested. This latest historical turning point arrived in the United States during the decade beginning about 1955—the decade that saw white-collar and service workers outnumber blue-collar workers for the first time. This was the same decade that saw the widespread introduction of the computer, commercial jet travel, the birth control pill, and many other high-impact innovations. It was precisely during this decade that the Third Wave began to gather its force in the United States. Since then it has arrived—at slightly different dates—in most of the other industrial nations, including Britain, France, Sweden, Germany, the Soviet Union, and Japan. Today all the high-technology nations are reeling from the collision between the Third Wave and the obsolete, encrusted economies and institutions of the Second.

Understanding this is the secret to making sense of much of the political and social conflict we see around us.

Technology as Progress, Technology as Threat
Edward Wenk Jr.

Edward Wenk is a critic of Alvin Toffler and others who express confidence that technology will create progress and improve the human condition. He agrees that the pace of technological change has been staggering in the last decades of the twentieth century, but he is less sure that this

---

Wenk, Edward Jr., *Tradeoffs: Imperatives of Choice in a High-tech World* (Baltimore: Johns Hopkins University Press, 1986), 6–13.

*change will necessarily continue or that it is to our advantage to have it
do so. While Toffler sees humanity as being swept forward by a wave of
technological development, Wenk argues that we actively steer a course
rather than be passively propelled by technological change. This excerpt
(1979) is taken from a book addressed to national leaders, urging them to
take an active role in directing the ways technology shapes society.*

Change is one of the most compelling truths of living. Some changes reflect the inescapable and irrevocable stages of natural law. Biological
aging is inevitable. Continental drift is uncontrollable. But some elements of change derive from calculated human endeavor. Fundamental
and dramatic shifts in individual and social behavior have occurred with
charismatic leadership, some of it religious, some ideological, some
purely exploitive of the human condition.

In contemporary society, the most powerful engines of change are
human invention, innovation, and applications of scientific knowledge.
Collectively, we call these functions "technology."

Technology has always been a source of cultural transformation.
The artifacts left by our predecessors have become treasures of insight
as to how people coped with their strenuous, hostile, and capricious
natural environment. Indeed, we define these cultures by their tools and
their material achievements. Technology was the springboard for change,
from hunting and gathering to agriculture, from use of fire and the arrow
to the intercontinental, nuclear-tipped missile. Once, the wheel was high-
tech. Interactions between culture and technology are so powerful that
we are spontaneously but wrongly inclined to equate technology with
civilization.

In the modern world, we continue to employ these instruments of
human processing to gain control over our environment—to such a degree that we not only live *with* technology; we *live* technology. Indeed,
technology has demonstrated a fabulous capacity to generate new
wealth even faster than capital alone, with a conspicuous virtue of en-
hancing material standards of living. By both developed and developing
nations, it is regarded as a crucible for economic growth. Partly, this
arises because technology has proven to be a key to abundance. Partly,
too, this admiration is accentuated because economic growth is itself
heralded as desirable. The products of a technological society entice exuberant consumerism, further pumped by technological leverage in advertising. And when changes occur in our economic situation, changes
also occur in the way we look at technology.

Technology has also functioned as a source of treasured freedoms:
freedom from the back-breaking labor of chopping wood, pumping water, and carting ice, and from slavery in the mines; freedom from disease and disability; freedom from geographical and cultural isolation
and social immobility; freedom to spend more adult years on educa-

tion; freedom to plan families. Technology has given more people than ever before the freedom to choose; and it has provided more choices: how and where we live; what we work at; what we eat; how we vacation. In short, technology has vastly enhanced the quality of life.

That propinquity of technology and culture has led to our taking technology almost for granted. Consider a typical working day. We awake to a radio alarm clock; switch off the electric blanket; dress in clothes of synthetic fiber; defrost orange juice and microwave our breakfast with electricity generated by nuclear power; commute to the office in a high-powered car listening to a forty-watt hi-fi stereo; travel up by elevator in time to receive a telephone call relayed by satellite from ten time zones away. These are machines for living. Their impacts do not stop at the end of the day. At night, it's the contraceptive and sleeping pills. Weekends, it's the high-tech sandbox: television; Atari games; helicopter ski lifts; power tools and power boats.

At a different scale, consider technology's impact on culture in reducing agricultural employment from 30 percent of the work force to 3; in facilitating both the congested, high-rise central business district and the traffic-strewn flight to the suburbs; in equipping a civilian population with more TV sets than toilets.

We began to glorify technology over a century ago, with its cascade of inventions: the steam engine, electric lights, farm machinery, the sewing machine, even running water. Then came the automobile, the telephone, radio, television, jet aircraft, modern medicine, and nuclear energy. Along with these inventions came a manufacturing and marketing infrastructure, soft technology to foster penetration into all of society.

In World War II, technology became the great equalizer, helping purchase victory with a minimum loss of life[1] by superiority in industrial production and sophisticated weapons. That heyday of science as an endless frontier was further excited by the 1957 Soviet space surprise. We entered the competition with gusto. We adopted technology as our chosen vehicle to global superiority in the race for people's minds, as well as to domestic social progress.

Today we are hooked on technology. It underpins every aspect of life: national security; the energy supply; industrial productivity; food production; health care delivery; urban habitation and infrastructure; education, entertainment, and telecommunications. We refer to ourselves as the information society, a condition made feasible only by new advances in computer virtuosity.

Yet, we are not comfortable with all the changes wrought by technology. Every technology introduced for its intended benefits carries inadvertent side effects, direct and indirect. The direct by-products may

---

1. Few scholars join Wenk in considering the 60 million or more deaths in World War II as "minimal," though presumably technology might have prevented still greater losses.

be benign, or they may be harmful; or they may be both, but to different people. They are all the more bewildering because they are usually hidden, and may hibernate only to burst on the scene unexpectedly, endangering life, health, property, or the environment. Pesticides to improve agricultural productivity are poisonous; nuclear plants generate both power and dangerous waste; swift jet aircraft create objectionable airport noise; computers invade privacy. The list of direct side effects is endless, literally endless, because *every* technology plays Jekyll and Hyde. To these chronic disabilities must be added the risk of catastrophic accident involving hazardous materials in routine transit, chemical plant leakage, or nuclear plant meltdown.

The indirect side effects may be more subtle but, in the long run, even more potent. Technology has profoundly altered human institutions, life-styles, and basic values; witness the impact of the automobile and the pill on sexual mores. Because the pace of technology evolves more swiftly than social institutions that husband it, it has sparked disharmony in purpose and economic and social instability. Look at what has happened to the family farmer, selling out to the agrobusinesses. Indeed, technology has promoted the growth and power of industrial enterprises. Then, it has forced growth in government to regulate private initiatives so as to mitigate hazardous impacts. It has tended to nurture social as well as technical complexity so as to hinder public understanding, then to engender deep feelings of anxiety. In trying to cope, some people have turned to spiritual inspiration in a quest for a more comprehensible world, some to cults for the comfort of simplistic explanations.

Like any love affair, ours with technology has been carried on with euphoric highs, periodically tempered by cycles of reality testing. While achievements of ingenuity constitute an expression of our most treasured creative instincts, they also pose challenges in the management of technological change so as to extract its blessings without sacrificing our cultural ideals.

Given our complex and confusing society, we need to have someone demystify technology. I don't mean trying to explain how complex machines work. We can leave understanding the insides of TV and the laser, the nuclear reactor and the CAT scanner, to scientists and engineers. What we need to know more transparently is how these discoveries influence our lives and the lives of our children. In other words, we need to be able to test the optimistic claims of technology's advocates that novelty and change always nurture progress, to understand whether the promised benefits are imperceptively accompanied by new or higher risks.

Healthy skepticism doesn't mean rejecting technology. New scientific discoveries are exciting. The human psyche seems tickled by unmasking nature's secrets. It's like solving a puzzle or deciphering a code. Applying that new knowledge to everyday dilemmas stirs the blood. We tend to love innovation, sometimes for its own sake. And furthermore, we get addicted because human experience has confirmed that technology contributes substantially to the American dream.

A search is then necessary to match the satisfaction of our needs and wants with the most appropriate technological means. Technology should be an instrument to achieve social ends, and not an end in itself. So we must inquire as to how we prioritize goals, set criteria for choosing means, and illuminate tradeoffs, say between solar and nuclear energy, between energy extraction and conservation, or between a new weapon system in space and arms control.

As I have said, *all* technologies can breed trouble. They carry a hidden load of unintended surprises. These side effects may be social, economic, cultural, or environmental. Some may turn out to be benign, a form of serendipity; yet others may be inimical to human life and the human spirit. To add to the few examples previously cited, the automobile, intended to provide swift and economical personal transport, entails a huge bill for premature death, disability, and urban air pollution, and an appetite for unlimited supplies of petroleum. Medical apparatus to increase the power of diagnosis and treatment is so expensive that bills for the nation's health care now exceed 10 percent of our GNP and lower-income citizens are excluded from a quality system.

In the 1960s, partly because of Rachel Carson's shocker, *Silent Spring*, about how pesticides were wiping out birds, we discovered that technologically induced risks to the natural environment had been quietly increasing. Here was the first cycle of reality testing in this technological century. To be sure, there had been a nagging anxiety about machines replacing jobs, and indeed, about the bomb opening a lethal Pandora's box. But because the political behavior of a society reflects the prevailing cultural focus, these concerns had to await the arrival in the 1960s of the countercultural revolution.

Some called technology a new social disease, so potent in its adverse effects that there were impetuous cries to turn it off. But technology was too tightly interwoven with our culture, indeed with almost every function in our society. We were not about to cut off our noses to spite our faces and abandon technological pursuits. Society thus had to deal with the adverse side effects by *social* innovation. In a primitive and innocent way, we instituted a doctrine of anticipation. By law, we required environmental impact analysis of all new projects *before* they were put in place. Later, we demanded total impact analysis. We used the legislative process to help us look before we leap, to seek answers to the simple question, "What might happen, if?"

In a remarkably short time, that love affair with the machine that had been going on for a hundred years in adolescent attitudes of unquestioning esteem suddenly matured to a more balanced perception: with the potential of technology to enrich people's lives come uncertainties and dangers. Society discovered that we had to do more than cope by the skin of our teeth; we had to exercise critical judgment.

For decades, we had been asking only, "Can we do it?" In the 1960s, we began asking, "Ought we to do it?" That deeper perception, however, is still accompanied neither by credible methodology nor by a durable commitment to harmony between, say, economy and ecology.

Consequently, in the 1980s, we wrestle with a different challenge concerning technology: "Can we manage it?" What we mean is the social management of technology. Since that phrase may be unfamiliar, we must draw on the analogy with "industrial management." That interdisciplinary body of knowledge is concerned with decision making, largely within the industrial firm, regarding how to achieve intended production of goods and services with optimum economy and efficiency. The social management of technology is also concerned with decision making and with the outcomes of technological initiatives. But unlike industrial management, it focuses on the broader consequences of technology and on the broader participation of society as a whole in the acts of management.

We thus develop an argument for the sharpening of civic competence to manage technology more adroitly. Otherwise, we may breed serious inequities as to benefits and beneficiaries, or inadvertently squander our natural legacy. Even worse, in being deaf to signals about the future, we may unwittingly disregard emerging threats to human society.

People have two fundamental misconceptions about technology. In the first place, many think that technology is hardware—ubiquitous automobiles, 747s, telephones, Polaroid cameras, VCRs, and home refrigerators. These are devices we can see, touch, hear, and experience. We forget that technology is also software, or perhaps squishyware; people and their institutions must furnish instructions as to its use. So, at its root, technology is more than technique. This concept is consistent with Webster's definition as "the totality of specialized knowledge and means to provide goods and services necessary for human sustenance and comfort." Technology is thus a process, a social process of generating and utilizing knowledge so deeply engraved in our culture that everyone is now profoundly affected.

The second misconception arises because we forget that everyone is also directly involved in technology. That's obvious for the mechanic, the industrial manager, the scientist, or the engineer. All have a hands-on affiliation. But we neglect the bankers who decide on investment capital for plant expansion, or policy officials who make choices and allocate resources for weapon systems and for urban mass transit, or who set standards for water quality. And we disregard just plain citizens. They are involved in four different ways: as consumers of technological products, as voters on referenda for nuclear power, as investors in fledgling high-tech enterprises, and as unknowing victims of unfavorable impacts. Technology is not a spectator sport.

Almost all contemporary organizations, both public and corporate, are engaged in technology. GM produces cars; Exxon sells gasoline; RCA makes radios and television sets; AT&T and many other firms market communication services. Most government agencies also deal with technology: with armaments, nuclear power development, medical research, food production, water supply, toxic waste disposal, transportation safety, purity of food, effectiveness of pharmaceuticals, census information, and production incentives. Virtually all agencies created since World War II are rooted in some aspect of technology.

In advancing beyond notions of hardware, we discover technology's full significance in human affairs. Technology has altered risks to individuals and to society as a whole. For example, it has reduced infant mortality and infectious disease. Indeed, immunization and sanitary engineering to purify water and dispose of human waste have reduced premature deaths worldwide more than have any other medical achievements. But because of side effects, technology also has generated a new portfolio of risks such as those outlined previously.

There are other overarching repercussions. First, with swift transportation and instant communication, nations are now locked together as one world, technologically, if not politically. Events anywhere have effects everywhere. Second, technology increasingly intermingles people and nature, exposing the natural environment to human insults, accelerating uncritical consumption of nonrenewable resources and increasing the risk of a change in climate.

Next, through technology, cultures that were previously isolated by geography have been brought into contact and into conflict; remember the enigma of Americans held hostage in Iran. Within cultures, generations are being split by the pulse of change because some thrive on it and others are inordinately stressed. Severe collisions erupt between humanists and those enchanted by technologically pulsed materialism and indifferent to technology's social impacts. Tensions may be further aggravated by scientific contributions to longevity that increase the proportion of elderly.

In addition, at the institutional scale, technology acts as a mobilizing agent to concentrate wealth and power. It then plays a political role in every society, developed and developing, capitalist and socialist. It starkly accentuates distinctions between who wins and who loses, and how much. Indeed, technology tends to discriminate against the unrepresented and the disadvantaged, and to support the elitist establishment. Technology, at least in its impacts, is not neutral. Then, because of the choices involved regarding beneficiaries, technology has become more political. Conversely, through TV campaigning and computerized voter lists, politics have become more technological.

Next, we find that the grand decisions on technology are no longer made in the marketplace. They are made by public policy. Choosing those goals to which a technology is directed, creating an atmosphere for industrial innovation, setting priorities for research, making trade-offs between employment and environmental protection, committing funds for massive civil projects or expensive weapon systems — these are today's salient choices. And the major actors in this process are not scientists and engineers. They are politicians, the people you and I elect.

These characteristic linkages with society are generic, applicable to almost every technology, whether television or nuclear weapons. The existence of such encompassing patterns may seem remarkable, but exceptions are rare.

Tomorrow, we should expect more technology, not less. To shape that future we need to acquire this sharper image of technology as more than technique or products. It entails a tangled skein of familiar social processes, communication networks, and institutions, along with natural processes and technical facilities, a blend of science and human values.

To visualize its social, economic, and cultural impacts, consider technology as an amplifier. With lever and wheel and bomb, technology amplifies human muscle. With the computer, it amplifies the human mind and human memory. Indeed, in various ways technology amplifies human senses, enabling us to see invisible objects close by or enormous ones at great distances; to hear the inaudible; to measure infinitesimal moments of time. Almost all of the hardware that we deploy today amplifies something tangible.

Less apparent is the role of technology as *social amplifier*. It has spawned the population explosion, but it also magnifies the less tangible. Technology may either elevate or imperil the human spirit, facilitate or threaten freedom and self-esteem; it exalts the economic machine and expands material appetites and inequalities in their satisfaction; it stretches the boundaries of interpersonal transactions, the span, volume, and complexity of communication networks. It intensifies the potential for conflict. As technology increases demands on our social institutions, it exposes their weaknesses. Technology expands the number of options that confront our decision makers, increases risks to them, and heightens the cost from error. Not too surprisingly, technology amplifies the power of organizations and individuals who control it.

Inadvertently, technology increases the role of government. Indeed, technology and government have grown together and, given heavy government funding of research, somewhat because of each other. So technology amplifies brawn, brain, and bureaucracy.

The only feature of human experience not amplified by technology is time. With human affairs speeded up by technology, including change itself, and with our culture unwittingly applauding that achievement, we find a paradox. Technology furnishes more choices but less time to choose. With that situation comes stress, stress from the tyranny of the clock, stress from anxiety over the unexplored consequences of a hasty decision, and stress from fears that technology is out of control.

To avoid the penalties of impetuous decisions, we are obliged to ask how to steer technology to extract the most socially satisfactory outcomes. In building on the concept of collision avoidance, driving defensively means continuous anticipation. That is the basis of another fundamental connection of technology—beyond society and politics to its linkage with the future.

PRIMARY SOURCES AND SCHOLARLY WORKS

THE COLD WAR AND THE PARTITION OF TRIESTE

While the Cold War was fueled by competing ideologies of global significance, it was often manifested in regional and even local disputes and rivalries. Any one of these can serve as a window into the Cold War, and the following readings deal with the partition of Trieste.

Trieste is a city and region at the north end of the Adriatic Sea, the traditional frontier between the Italian and Balkan states. Previously independent, Trieste became a part of Italy in 1920. Following World War II, both Italy and Yugoslavia claimed Trieste, and the Allies deferred settling this dispute by establishing temporary Anglo-American military rule.

In 1953, Great Britain and the United States decided that it was time to end their rule, and the dispute resurfaced. Despite ethnic, historical, and ideological antagonisms, Italy and Yugoslavia were able to reach a mutually acceptable agreement on October 5, 1954, and it was ratified by both countries shortly thereafter. This agreement, brokered by Great Britain and the United States, provided for the partition of Trieste and the absorption of its parts into Italy and Yugoslavia, which took place without serious incident in the months following the agreement. Yugoslavia was a communist country, though it had broken with the Soviet Union. Nonetheless, many government policy makers grouped all communists together and considered the partition of Trieste an example of Cold War diplomacy.

Statement by the Yugoslav Ambassador to Washington, 11 March 1954
Vladimir Popovic

Yugoslav ambassador to the United States, Vladimir Popovic, was an important spokesperson for the Yugoslavian position on Trieste. In the months between the announcement that Anglo-American administration

Documents on International Affairs, 1954, ed. Denise Folliot (London: Oxford University Press, 1957), 213–14.

would end and the conclusion of an agreement, he released many concilia-
tory statements like the one presented here. Such statements from Popovic
and his Italian counterparts encouraged the traditional historical inter-
pretation that the Trieste Agreement arose primarily out of a bipartisan
desire to achieve consensus.

I continue to hope that a friendly solution of the Trieste question may
be possible. Yugoslavia is making further efforts and is ready to make
sacrifices in order to bring about good relations with Italy, thus strengthening friendly co-operation in this part of the world. It has been seen
that a solution cannot be found on the basis of the decision of 8 October
[a preliminary proposal for settlement] and that other ways and means
must be sought to satisfy and respect Yugoslav interests. Only thus will
the negative impression made in Yugoslavia by the October announcement on Yugoslavia's relations with the western allies gradually disappear. All that Yugoslavia demands in Zone A is the return of a certain
number of Slovene villages which are of no significance to Italy from political or economic point of view and which belong ethnically and his-
torically to Yugoslavia. This means that with a little more understanding
the Trieste problem might be easily and quickly solved. This solution
depends solely on the Italian Government's wish to reach an agreement.
The Italian Government's wish to obtain similar concessions refers to
important towns in Zone B and it is impossible to discuss this.

   Yugoslavia continues to wish for a conference to find a solution to
the Trieste question, but it is also ready to solve the problem through
diplomatic channels. The content is more important than the form, and
Yugoslavia is prepared to seek this content through any kind of form. At
the moment negotiations are more or less at a standstill, but contact is
maintained, and the best thing would be for direct Italo-Yugoslav negotiations to take place if the Italian Government showed a sincere wish
for them. However there has been no reaction on the part of the Italian
Government to show that our true desire is meeting with an echo from
the other side.

Trieste: Ethnicity and the Cold War, 1945–1954
Glenda Sluga

In this scholarly article published in 1994, Glenda Sluga suggests that earlier
historians oversimplified their interpretation of the Trieste partition, fo-
cusing too narrowly on an interest in fostering cooperation between Cold
War antagonists. She argues that ethnicity was a crucial factor in Trieste
and played a significant role in the achievement of an agreement over its
partition.

Journal of Contemporary History 29 (1994): 285–303.

In many histories of Trieste the city is located in the south-eastern corner of a geopolitical area comprising northern Italy, Austria and northern Yugoslavia, at the head of the Adriatic Sea, and at the heart of a region known variously as Venezia Giulia, Julijska Krajina, or the Julian March. A Habsburg port in the nineteenth century, Trieste was brought within Italian borders in 1920. Following the second world war, the liberated city's status was contested by supporters of an independent territory of Trieste, by pro-Italian nationalists and by pro-Yugoslav communists. Some historians have hailed the political settlement reached in 1954 as a model case of conflict resolution and border delineation. Their histories have reduced the complexity of Trieste's post-war political and cultural disarray to the East-West, 'Slav'-Italian, and communist-democratic oppositions that dominated political and historical assumptions during the Cold War. Moreover, they have propounded the view that "ethnic identity" should ideally coincide with, and *ipso facto* legitimate, "national identity," and that "self-determination" is best achieved when the boundaries of ethnically-defined territories coincide with those of homonymous nations.

When the British-U.S. Allies decided to co-operate with Tito's [Josip Tito, president of Yugoslavia] partisans in the final years of the war to expel nazi forces from areas bordering Yugoslavia and Italy, patriotic Italians were already wary of Tito's communist motives and objectives. As Slovene partisans wrested control of the occupied areas in the region of Trieste, the Slovene Osvobodilna Fronta (OF), or Liberation Front, set up local administrations called Liberation Committees on behalf of Tito's government. Although the Committees enjoyed considerable support in Trieste and surrounding villages, their allegiance with Yugoslavia made them unacceptable to the Allies. The Committees were also opposed by a section of the Italian-speaking middle class who feared not only communism, but *Slavs*. Pro-Italian intellectuals reserved the term "Slav" for Trieste's Slovene-speaking population, but by it they also wished to connote a broader "Eastern" threat to the city's cultural *italianità* [italian character]. The British-U.S. representatives who took over the administration of Trieste in June 1945 accepted and reinforced the identification of partisans and "Slavs." To them Slavs were a political communist threat from the East. The two connotations of the term overlapped politically and emotionally, enabling a rapport to be formed between the Allies and pro-Italian Triestines.

In 1945, Tito-led partisans included Italians, Slovenes, Croats and even Greeks—men and women. In ethnic, gender, as well as political terms their make-up was mixed. Being the first and most influential resistance organization within Venezia Giulia, the partisans attracted a large number of anti-fascists, including many without specifically communist sentiments. After assuming control of Trieste on 1 May 1945 (the day before the arrival of the British 8th Army), the partisan administration turned its attention to relations between Italians and Slovenes in the region. In the wake of twenty-three years of Italian fascist rule, the partisans' concern with "ethnic" relations was inevitable. In Mussolini's Italy "Slavs" were openly portrayed as the nemesis of Italian *civiltà* [civilization] and *patria* [homeland]. Fascist assimilationist policies incorporating theories of Italian historical and cultural superiority aimed at the annihilation of "Slavic" culture.

The anti-slavic ideology of the fascist period swayed even anti-fascist Triestines, in particular the members of the Venezia Giulia branch of the resistance organization Comitato di Liberazione Nazionale (CLN). For the pro-Italian CLN, Tito's Osvobodilna Fronta was the embodiment of Slavic imperialism, threatening the identity of Trieste as western, democratic, civilized and Italian. Though anti-fascist, the purpose of the CLN was to offer an "Italian" alternative to the undesirable diversity of ethnicities represented by the pro-Yugoslav OF. Dominated by members of the Italian Republican Party, the Giulian CLN sought to secure the *italianità* of Trieste within the Italian nation state, although it also emphasized European federation and the autonomy of Venezia Giulia within an Italian federation.

In 1943, the CLN appointed the Triestine historian Carlo Schiffrer to assess the likelihood of collaboration between "Slavs" and Italians. Reporting later on his attempts to liaise between the CLN and the Osvobodilna Fronta, Schiffrer noted that already in 1944 there was a feeling among the CLN that an anti-Italian nationalist Slav front was well established:

> The eventuality of an occupation of the city on the part of . . . a ferocious Balkan militia, animated by sentiments of hatred against Italians, was not to be taken lightly. Certainly looking back, we could say that no such thing happened, but this does not make the CLN's preoccupations any less real in their contribution to the disturbance of the local political ambience.

For Schiffrer himself, the possibility of a union of Italian culture in Trieste with communist Yugoslavia was *"un orribile imbastardimento di forma"* [a horrible bastardization of form]. Referring to an encounter with an Italian-speaking member of the pro-Yugoslav OF called Pino, Schiffrer remarked that "even he must be a Slovene who is attempting to pass himself off as an Italian on the occasion." CLN sympathizers could not conceive of the possibility of an authentically Italian pro-Yugoslav.

In 1946, against the background of peace conferences, Schiffrer took an academic approach to issues of essential *italianità*, language, and culture, in his *Historic Glance at the Relations Between Italians and Slavs in Venezia Giulia*. The pamphlet traces the continuity of the Roman population of Venezia Giulia and sets up an antagonistic relationship between "Slavs" and "Italians" of the region. Modes of identification of these two groups, and their territorial ambitions, are set in stark contrast. "The two nations who are disputing the region could not be more different," Schiffrer wrote, "because one is an *urban* nation and the other a *rustic* one." The ethnography of Slavs—an "amorphous multitude"—was said to be the antithesis of "vital" Italian culture. Schiffrer interrelates history, geography, and economics in a narrative of "national" oppositions:

> For the Italian, sentiments, traditions, education lead to extend the "holy soil of the fatherland" as far as the mountain-range of the Alps or, to be more precise, even as far as the principal watershed of the Alps. . . . And if within these limits there are rustic populations of another tongue, the psychology of the Italian, derived from a thousand years old traditions [sic], finds it quite natural that the country must follow the lot of the towns and not the other way about. The more so, as a similar solution seems to him more than justified by history, by his own undisputed past predominance, by his own culture which is more antique and richer than that most recent one of the Slave [sic] populations.

With the nazis expelled from Trieste, the CLN became the Osvobodilna Fronta's main opposition. On 1 May 1945, the day on which the partisans declared Venezia Giulia liberated, pro-Yugoslav posters written in Italian stressed the theme of Italo-Slovene fraternity. They also identified fascism, and the CLN, as the enemy. They suggested that Trieste's future lay within the Yugoslav federation, and that the Allies were to be consulted on this matter. Such proclamations elicited an enthusiastic response from those who regarded the partisan troops as liberators. Yet festivities were taking place amid social disorder. The first weeks of "liberation" were marred by daily skirmishes and violent, often fatal, confrontations.

After two weeks of military rule by the Osvobodilna Fronta, a partisan civilian "Liberation Council" was appointed. The new administration's ideology aspired to a citizenship that would obliterate the political significance of class and ethnic difference. Trieste was to be given a new identity "as a city of mixed inhabitants, each with respected rights regardless of their nationality." This new identity, it was claimed, would not only be characteristic of the non-fascist order, it would be a safeguard against fascism and racism. While the army would retain some powers, the stated aim was an autonomous democratic Trieste (city and region), to be the seventh republic of federal Yugoslavia.

Despite overt communist ambitions, the new administration sought to bring its main opponents, the Italian-speaking middle class, into its fold, in order to gain international credibility at the peace talks. Middle-class support was never won. The Liberation Council was instead associated by its opponents with mass disappearances of Italians who, it was claimed, had been thrown into *foibe*—large holes of indeterminate depth dotting the local limestone landscape. Such disappearances and chilling stories of random summary justice fed fears of Slav barbarism. Leading Triestine intellectuals charged that the partisan government was "the most shameful, most humiliating, saddest scar and insult that the *italianità* of the city has ever suffered in the long millenia of its existence."

The Giulian Comitato di Liberazione Nazionale vacillated between declarations of Trieste's autonomy and nostalgic reaffirmations of its prosperity under Italian rule. There was concern about the number of Italians joining Tito's partisans (the "new nationalists," as they were called). On 3 May 1945, the CLN made public its position on the "Yugoslav occupation": the sole legitimate local representative of Italian democratic government was the CLN; the Osvobodilna Fronta was a Trojan horse of Yugoslav nationalism. "Italian" citizens of Trieste were invited to exercise their *alta civiltà* [high culture] to distance themselves from the barbarism of the Yugoslavs, and to remain *"padrone del proprio Destino"* [master of one's destiny]. The work of the CLN in this period popularized certain accounts of the Resistance. These included printed accounts of Trieste's actual liberation in editions that could be circulated among the British-U.S. Allies, the Peace Commission and other relevant interest groups. Authentic citizenship was seen to depend on Roman ancestry, and the partisans' role in the liberation of Trieste was contested.

Assumptions of a natural cultural antagonism between Italians and Slavs are abundant in British-U.S. documentation of the partisan forces and their administration in Trieste. Such assumptions are especially well illustrated in a memoir from the period, Geoffrey Cox's *The Road to Trieste*. Cox was an Intelligence Officer with the New Zealand 2nd Division of the British 8th Army. Late in April 1945 his division was advancing eastward across northern Italy, with orders to take Trieste for the Allies. Cox's account of the war, as it appears in *The Road to Trieste*, has been received generally as an authoritative account of events, of cultural relations in Venezia Giulia, and of the Allied troops' perceptions of local populations. In the course of his eastward advance, Cox conjured up a boundary between the Italy through which he travelled and what he designated the "Balkans." In attempting to orientate the cultural and political terrain of Venezia Giulia, Cox relied on a distinction between Western Europe, to which Italy belonged, and eastern Balkan Europe, which was "Slav." His impression of the partisans in Trieste, who had arrived one day before the Allies, was of occupying alien Slav forces:

> You only had to drive through the [western approaches to Trieste] to see tension at every turn. At the crossroads, on every bridge, the local partisans and the Tito troops stood in irritated silence alongside the [advance parties of] British and American sentries. On the great cornice road which is cut into the rock above the sea between Monfalcone and Trieste, our supply trucks wound in and out of columns of marching Tito troops, some of them Mohammedans with faces as dark as Moors.

Elsewhere in Cox's account, partisans strike up friendships with "dark" soldiers among Cox's own division, fellow New Zealanders, the Maori battalion. Cox maintained that such friendships were inexplicable and contrary to general feelings. The relationship between Allied soldiers and "Yugoslav" partisans was said to be normally hostile and politically and culturally antagonistic:

> It may have been only that here and there a girl to whom [the New Zealand soldiers] waved would turn aside instead of waving back, it may have been that the men shook their heads at our dog-Italian, but it was unmistakeable. We felt like strangers in a strange land, as if at the Isonzo [river] we had passed some unmarked but distinct frontier. As indeed we had. We had driven from Italy into what was to become a No Man's Land between Eastern and Western Europe, and like any No Man's Land it was extremely unpleasant.

Although the dominant theme in *The Road to Trieste* is the high probability of a border that would eventually and naturally separate Italy from Yugoslavia, West from East and democracy from communism in Venezia Giulia, it is clear that Cox's conception of an inevitable and proper border was often shaken by the observed political and cultural complexity of the region, seen at such times by him as a No Man's Land, an area that could not be claimed or named absolutely.

Sylvia Sprigge, the *Manchester Guardian*'s war correspondent who entered Trieste with Cox's division, reported comparable conceptions for a contemporary issue of *The World Today*. Like Cox, Sprigge has had an influence on the ways in which the history of Trieste continues to be written. The structure of her "Diary" (divided into two parts: "From the West" and "From the East") was the framework within which Trieste's past, present and future had to be understood. For Sprigge, the problem of Trieste was the problem of communism inspired by "Slavs":

> The communists would make a tabula rasa of our civilisation and start "fresh," as though "freshness" were a privilege belonging only to the dockyard workers, tramwaymen, and shipbuilding hands of Trieste and Monfalcone. . . . To the Slovenes . . . tradition means very little, since it has been for centuries associated in their minds with oppression. So they were ready to scrap everything, just as Soviet Russia nearly thirty years ago was prepared to do without a penal or civil code, a stock exchange, landlords, and factory owners and managers, in order to create a new order.

However, Sprigge also noted that

> the workers of Trieste and the peasants in the region for the first time in many years felt they were the most important people in the city, whose hopes and ideals would at last be realised and how in the [Osvobodilna Fronta] and under Yugoslav occupation, fraternisation between Italians and Yugoslavs really existed.

Sprigge included this observation but did not explore its implications in her report, explaining that she could not be expected to deal with all aspects of the problem. The observation that a certain section of the population supported a new egalitarian relationship between Italians and Slovenes had to give way to a consistent East-West model.

After forty-two days of partisan rule, the British-U.S. forces assumed power in Trieste, following an agreement between Field Marshal Alexander and Tito. Trieste's pro-Yugoslav civilian government, the Liberation Council, was not invited to participate in the negotiations. In June 1945 the Yugoslav army withdrew and an "Allied Military Government" was established in the newly created "Zone A" of Venezia Giulia. "Zone B," the area surrounding Trieste and outlying villages and towns, including the Istrian coastline (with the exception of Pula), was placed under Yugoslav trusteeship. Despite Tito's condition that existing administrations be maintained where they were functioning, Allied directives slowly forced Trieste's Liberation Council to disband.

Although the Allies were of the impression that the Allied Military Government (AMG) had replaced an unpopular administration, a week after the departure of the Yugoslav army an Allied intelligence officer reported that in "Slav" areas of Zone A the "Yugoslavs" were in fact popular, without recourse to "political intimidation." As late as September 1945, 19 out of the 37 communes comprising Zone A, including four communes with a population of over 90 per cent Italian-speakers, were refusing Allied government-appointed administrations. The Senior Civil Affairs Officer for Zone A alleged that, "in each case the people of these Communes are either extremely Communistic or completely over-awed by the Communist elements."

The AMG policies intended to weaken pro-communist forces endangered the government's proclaimed neutrality, as well as its claims to represent a more pluralist, democratic political order—the so-called British and American political way of life. The AMG's brief for Zone A was to replace communist-inspired innovations with a legal and administrative framework inherited from the Italian state as it existed on 8 September 1943. The reinstatement of fascist laws (purged of anti-semitic clauses) together with the rejection of the policies of the May administration, negated Italo-Slovene fraternity encouraged by the communists. Reaching an equitable political solution for Trieste was rendered more difficult by the Allied government's reduction of political affiliation to ethnicity. While pro-Yugoslav groups saw ethnic hostility in Trieste to be the result of a capitalist conspiracy to disunite the working classes by encouraging nationalism, the Allied government concluded that anti-nationalism, or the policy of Italian and Slovene fraternity, was an ideological ploy, a manoeuvre to convince workers that their interests lay with communism. Hence AMG officials concluded that sloganeering speeches asserting the themes of co-operation among ethnic groups were eccentric and devious.

At a meeting in September 1945 with France Bevk, president of the pro-Yugoslav administration responsible for Zone B, Colonel Robertson, the Zone A Deputy Civil Affairs Officer, concluded that he and Bevk would never agree on how to define "the people" of Trieste and Venezia Giulia. As far as Robertson was concerned, the partisans, by appealing to the working classes and peasants and calling for Slav-Italian unity, were hiding behind sham claims to political representation. Bevk, on the other hand, regarded as insidious Robertson's assertion that the partisans were all "Slavs" and only represented Yugoslav interests:

> B: You keep asserting that we only represent Slovenes, this is not precise, since we also represent Italians.
>
> R: But you get your instructions for your point of view from Belgrade.
>
> B: We work alone and independently and we do not acknowledge any instructions from there.
>
> R: We cannot have two governments here. So one has to go.

AMG intelligence was, of course, quite capable of putting together complex and politically sensitive accounts of post-partisan Trieste, of a kind indicating that differences among Triestines depended as much on their political views as on ethnic identity. In September 1945 Colonel Cripps, the Director of the Local Government Subcommission, and his deputy, Major Temple, conducted a survey of Zone A in an attempt to determine just who the people of that area were and what they stood for. Cripps and Temple concluded that Zone A was composed of Italian towns surrounded by Slovene hinterlands. On the grounds of a 1921 Italian census they supposed that in the city of Trieste the ratio of Italians to Slovenes was roughly six to one. Political affiliations of Italians that they identified were said to be "still in the process of changing and dependent on economic factors to a large extent and on nationalistic factors to a smaller extent." The authors of the survey sensed that "high pressure" and "propaganda" had distorted local politics: "Even the attitude of the populace might not reflect their true feelings. Daily there has been a fluctuation of opinion, tempered by world as well as local events." Contrary to the Trieste of Sprigge and Cox, Cripps and Temple stressed that "ideological and nationalist aspirations" were very much intertwined, while "ethnic differences" were being overemphasized when economic or political differences were just as, if not more, significant. They considered that membership of communist organizations was usually taken up for social rather than national reasons.

The following year, in May 1946, Graham Bower of the Foreign Office Research Department reported that no more than 10 per cent of Trieste's industrial workers were of "Slavic" origin, on the grounds that few spoke "Slav" or thought of themselves as Slav. At the same time, the majority of industrial workers were self-declared communists, and so pro-Tito and pro-Yugoslavia, and sent their children to the "Slav schools" originally set up by the partisans. For them Italy meant fascism. Bower's association of the Italian working class with communism should have cast doubt

on Allied assumptions about the near-coincidence of ethnicity and political identity. It should have suggested that "Italians" were sending their
children to "Slovene" schools because they agreed with the political education offered there, and that there existed Slovenes who considered
themselves Italian workers and bilingual Triestines.

However, the Allied government saw it in its interest to disregard local
attempts at negotiation across boundaries of ethnic definition. Its own
presence was partially explained by the supposed need for an arbitrator
between the two ethnic groups of Zone A. Discordant voices could be
checked by calling into question the possibility of Italian support for
pro-Yugoslav communism. After reading an AMG "ethnological survey"
released in October 1945, a member of the Foreign Office staff noted
that popular support for the partisans was being manipulated by the
communists, "persuading the working class of Trieste and Monfalcone
that Yugoslavia will assure the workers' paradise." Another un-Italian
activity, according to Allied Information Service reports, was the local
communist party's effort to "submerge" the national issue, a course of
action regarded as quite reprehensible. Public demonstrations in support of Trieste's incorporation into Yugoslavia were undermined by the
identification of the demonstrators as Slovenes, peasants (for it was assumed that these were Slovenes) or women (who could not be acting
spontaneously). The Senior Civil Affairs Officer, Colonel Bowman, high-
lights this stratagem in his memoirs:

> In the case of the pro-Yugoslav demonstrations, it simply was too much
> to expect us to swallow that hundreds or even thousands of people from
> the hinterland, who in the normal course of their lives had not been in
> the city half-a-dozen times, should just happen to be there, moved by
> similar emotions, after a gruelling, all-night march on foot from outlying
> communities where they lived and worked.

When, on 16 June 1945, women and children were reported to have
participated in communist demonstrations, Col. Bowman claimed that
they were probably demonstrating in exchange for food. In a revised
1977 version of *The Road to Trieste* (renamed *The Race for Trieste*), Cox
similarly dismisses a demonstration in support of a partisan administration for Monfalcone as inauthentic, on the grounds that it was formally organized, rather than a "spontaneous uprush of feeling as in the
Italian towns and villages": "There was a sense of individualism being
directed, if not crushed, of wariness if not fear mixed with the rejoicing."

AMG officials in Trieste purposefully controlled symbolic means of
expression and identification. When, in 1945, enquiries were made by
Allied personnel as to the administration's policy on "national flags"
(outlawed as manifestations of nationalism by the pro-Yugoslav Liberation
Council), the AMG answered that only officially recognized national flags
were acceptable: an Italian flag with a red star in the middle (viz., the

flag that represented Italian communism and which had appeared in liberation celebrations throughout Italy) was definitely not a national flag and could not be raised.

In 1947 the Union of Anti-fascist Italians and Slovenes (UAIS), descendants of the old pro-Yugoslav Liberation Council, complained that their May Day plans had been sabotaged by the Allied government's decision not to allow their celebrations to take place at the Piazza Unità. It was widely accepted that the Piazza Unità, the city's main square, added to the impact of demonstrations occurring in it. Fronting the Adriatic, with Trieste and its hinterland ranged about it, that particular square was the grandest of all symbolic spaces in Trieste. The AMG had decided to divide up the city for the 1947 May Day celebrations, allocating the main square to pro-Italian groups. The anti-fascist UAIS was allocated what was defined as working-class, communist and "Slav" spaces of the city, which included, ironically, the Piazza Garibaldi. Such a division absolutely defined the Piazza Unità, the heart of the city, as Italian.

The Allied government changed its policy regarding flags for the occasion. It instructed the UAIS to use the red flag, and none other, in their festivities, a tactic that the UAIS believed was meant to undermine their credibility as a mainstream political organization. For the May Day festival provided the UAIS with an occasion to make a political statement about their general representativeness. By demanding that they use the red flag and no national flags, and by confining UAIS activities to parts of the city identified as "Slavic," Trieste's Allied government hoped to lessen the number of people finding the symbolic substance of UAIS activities acceptable, and thereby divide the left-leaning anti-fascist community. The banner of communism was to be seen to represent Slavs wholly and exclusively. National identities were to be reinforced through the continued depiction of communism as a political-cultural phenomenon, culturally "Slavic" and politically "Yugoslav"—despite, or indeed because of, the strength of communist organizations in Italy proper.

The assumption that ethnicity (or "race") determined political affiliations was generally held in conjunction with the assumption that ethnic relations in Trieste were fundamentally hostile. So long as the question of Trieste remained unresolved, and its importance in the unfolding Cold War increased, the assertion of the inevitability of hatred between Italians and Slavs was usefully employed by the military, politicians and historians to underpin arguments relating to the area's political future or, more precisely, to the protection of Slovenes from Italian prejudice, or of Italians from Slovene ruthlessness. The Allied government's reluctance to hold democratic elections, promised since June 1945, was justified by representing the relationship between Slav and Italian as so "racially" antagonistic that such concessions would lead to widespread violence (especially if the pro-Italian constitution of local government was upset).

Thus, in 1949, General Airey (AMG Senior Commanding Administrative Officer), having told his political advisers that "the Slovene problem was of course the primary reason for our presence in Trieste," added:

> My policy has been and still is, directed towards complete equality for the Slovene population and to encourage the dangerous inflammation caused by the Slav-Communist influx of 1945 to heal up . . . I am determined that nothing shall be done to retard the healing process or to open old wounds by reviving lost causes and stimulating excessive Slovene nationalism.

The peace talks envisaged three possibilities for Trieste's political future: its return to Italian rule, in spite of Italy's role in the war until 1943; its return to partisan rule, leading to its federation with the newly constituted communist Yugoslavia; or its independence as the Free Territory of Trieste. The first two options faced widespread resistance. Opponents of Trieste's return to Italy argued that not only would the Italian solution reward Italy for its aggressive fascism, it would be unacceptable to those who held the *Italian state* (not just Mussolini) responsible for the atrocities and oppression of the past decades. On the other hand, the option of granting Trieste to Yugoslavia was opposed by those who saw it as a precedent recognizing the claims of Soviet-influenced communism.

In light of the failure in 1946 of the internationally appointed Boundary Commission to draw a line separating the two major ethnic communities with minimum displacement, the solution of a Free Territory of Trieste was adopted in the same year at the peace talks to resolve the issues of political and ethnic representation. The solution was shortlived. It foundered on British-U.S. fears that the Free Territory might ultimately enjoy too much freedom. Sterndale Bennett, the British delegate to the peace talks, argued that Italians would be outnumbered by Slavs, thereby leading to a domination of the Territory's government by communist sympathizers.

The Free Territory's constitution, drawn up in 1947, provided for a governor with near-absolute power, appointed by the UN Security Council. In practice the governor was to act in accordance with British-U.S. interests. However, British-U.S. resistance to the idea meant that by the end of 1947 a governor had yet to be appointed. In December 1947, Geoffrey Wallinger, head of the Southern Department of the British Foreign Office, remarked that: "Even an impartial governor might represent a danger to the Italianate majority in the Anglo-American zone . . . the Americans rather hoped that the direct Italian-Yugoslav consultations would produce no agreed candidate.

As early as 1946 William Sullivan, the Allied government's British Political Adviser, had warned the Foreign Office about the preponderance of racial, national and ideological "fanaticism" in Trieste, and that support for the Free Territory was being utilized as a means of expanding the pro-Yugoslav organizations' popular base and planting a pro-Yugoslav bias in the future governor. The real fear, however, was not of a racial war between Italians and Slavs but of *co-operation* across ethnic boundaries —particularly under the impulse of communism. An intelligence report for October 1946 emphasized the possibility that the Free Territory might inspire a "Democratic Front," "uniting all left-wing and progressive elements . . . under communist auspices." The Foreign Office encouraged the belief that Yugoslavs were in "the classic slav manner" creating an efficient and widespread network of agents trained to usurp political control, and that it was only the presence of the Allied government which ensured that civil war would not break out. When the plan for a Free Territory of Trieste was finally dispensed with in March 1948, the AMG's official comment blamed a Yugoslav-Russian conspiracy to disable a truly international Trieste.

In July 1947, the U.S. State Department asked Trieste's Allied government to increase its support for pro-Italian groups, including the Lega Nazionale (which AMG reports had described as neo-fascist), so as to control the spread of communist Yugoslav influence. The University of Trieste (founded in 1938) was to be treated as an enclave for developing closer relations between the AMG and pro-Italian groups. An AMG "Study on morale and confidence" for October 1947 recommended the programming of "constant and effective anti-communistic propaganda by radio," and (despite the stipulations of the February 1947 Peace Treaty which made Italian, Slovene and even Croatian if necessary, official languages in Trieste) the discouragement of bilingualism, which would have made the use of Slovene official, "as this immediately brings in the national aspect."

Not everyone interpreted the relationship between Italians and Slovenes in Cold War terms. In 1949, the U.S. Political Adviser, Charles Baldwin, suggested that antagonism between "the Slovene and Italian elements of the population" was "deeply rooted" in the "accumulated resentments of centuries." But he also recommended that one way of reducing ill-feeling was to recognize Slovene minority rights, in the courts and in Allied government policy, thus combining "considerations of practical political importance with established American principles of justice and fair treatment." Although Baldwin's statement of principle was accepted on behalf of the U.S. Secretary of State, his recommendations were dismissed on the grounds that they would ultimately threaten freedom for Slovenes by arousing Italian hostility.

Similarly, in a Foreign Office Research Department review of "Italy's treatment of her Yugoslav minority in the period between 1918 to 1949," Margaret Carlyle suggested that minority rights in Trieste would have to be safeguarded before any handover to Italy could take place. An official recommendation required a second version of her paper to omit suggestions that Italian retaliatory measures against minorities would have to

be actively prevented. The issue of minority rights had no place in the consolidation of the anti-communist Allied government's order in Trieste.

The conception of Trieste as an Italian space with a troublesome nationalist Slovene population thwarted the Allied government's efforts to
allocate a building for a Slovene cultural centre in 1954, the final year of
AMG rule. A new cultural centre was to replace the original venue which
had been burnt down by Italian extremists in 1920. It was to be offered
as a form of compensation for Yugoslavia's losing Trieste in the final settlement decided between Britain, the U.S. and France. While the perceived
need to compensate the Slovene community for incorporation with Italy
could be seen to suggest that Slovenes were, after all, rightful citizens of
Trieste, it also reaffirmed the ordering of Triestine political space along
ethnic lines: Slovenes needed a separate cultural space because Trieste's
incorporation with Italy meant the disproportional satisfaction of Italian
needs.

When Allied government personnel had located a property at Trieste's
seaside suburb of Barcola, on the road leading west to Monfalcone,
Colonel Broad defended the executive's rejection of the proposed site
on the grounds that Trieste was composed of separate and distinct Italian and Slovene areas, and Italians would not tolerate a Slovene incursion. Thus a Slovene building (presumably along with its inhabitants)
could not be introduced into an Italian space:

> [The site] cannot now be accurately described as being in a predomi-
> nantly Slovene area. This has in fact become largely an Italian residen-
> tial district. Furthermore, the building is located on the main road from
> Italy into Trieste which would make it unsuitably conspicuous for use
> as a Slovene centre.

It is hardly necessary to state that there were AMG personnel who saw
Slovenes as cultural and political underdogs and sympathized with their
condition, or that ethnic relations in Trieste might have deteriorated
anyway had the communist Osvobodilna Fronta survived its few weeks
in government. What is noteworthy is that simple equations of "nationality" with a particular political outlook were ultimately undermined by
the political ends of anti-communism itself, even though both anti-
communism and the equations were aspects of the same Cold War
rhetoric. Anti-communist policies almost invariably amounted to support of the pro-Italian cause and, therefore, failure to act on complaints
of discrimination against Slovenes, or on requests to support Slovene cultural projects. But those policies also relied heavily on support from anti-
communist "Slavs," not to mention the marginalization of communist
"Italians."

Even if the Cold War in Trieste did not preoccupy all Allied government officials to the same extent, it directed AMG policies and the terms
in which the problems of political and geographical identity were under-

stood. As the Cold War began to affect the language of international diplomacy, fitting Europe into a schema of cultural and political oppositions gravitating around the assignations of East and West, Trieste provided a space to elaborate that language. The Iron Curtain reinforced discursive boundaries between Latins and Slavs, West and East, between civilized and barbarian, enlightened liberal democratic and totalitarian worlds, and as a result stifled alternative cultural and political negotiations between Italians and Slovenes in post-war Trieste. The anti-pluralist consequences of this way of thinking continue to be evident in the intellectual and popular prejudices of Triestine culture and of the region as a whole.

Special Statute from the Trieste Agreement
Manlio Brosio and Dr. Vladimir Velebit

The Trieste Agreement, signed in London on October 5, 1954, was written largely along formulaic lines. The first article presented a discussion of why the treaty had become necessary, the second article established responsibilities of the parties involved, the third article drew boundaries, and so forth. Appended to these articles, however, was the following "Special Statute" dealing with the issue of ethnicity (sometimes termed "race" in the document). This statute demonstrates the growing postwar concern of the world community for human rights and underscores Sluga's focus on ethnicity in her reinterpretation of the Trieste Agreement.

Whereas it is the common intention of the Italian and Yugoslav Governments to ensure human rights and fundamental freedoms without discrimination of race, sex, language and religion in the areas coming under their administration under the terms of the present Memorandum of Understanding [that is, the Trieste Agreement], it is agreed: —

1. In the administration of their respective areas the Italian and Yugoslav authorities shall act in accordance with the principles of the Universal Declaration of Human Rights adopted by the General Assembly of the United Nations on the 10th of December, 1948, so that all inhabitants of the two areas without discrimination may fully enjoy the fundamental rights and freedoms laid down in the aforesaid Declaration.
2. The members of the Yugoslav ethnic group in the area administered by Italy and members of the Italian ethnic group in the area administered by Yugoslavia shall enjoy equality of rights and treatment with the other inhabitants of the two areas.

Documents on International Affairs, 1954, ed. Denise Folliot (London: Oxford University Press, 1957), 216–19.

This equality implies that they shall enjoy: —

a. equality with other citizens regarding political and civil rights as well as other human rights and fundamental freedoms guaranteed by Article 1 [Article 1 of the Declaration of Human Rights];

b. equal rights in acquiring or performing any public services, functions, professions and honours;

c. equality of access to public and administrative office; in this regard the Italian and Yugoslav administrations will be guided by the principle of facilitating for the Yugoslav ethnic group and for the Italian ethnic group, respectively, under their administration a fair representation in administrative positions, and especially in those fields, such as the inspectorate of schools, where the interests of such inhabitants are particularly involved;

d. equality of treatment in following their trade or profession in agriculture, commerce, industry or any other field, and in organising and operating economic associations and organisations for this purpose. Such equality of treatment shall concern also taxation. In this regard persons now engaged in a trade or profession who do not possess the requisite diploma or certificate for carrying on such activities, shall have four years from the date of initialling of the present Memorandum of Understanding within which to acquire the necessary diploma or certificate. They will not be prevented from exercising their trade or profession because of failure to have the requisite documents unless they have failed to acquire them within the aforementioned four-year period;

e. equality of treatment in the use of languages as defined in Article 5 below;

f. equality with other citizens in the general field of social assistance and pensions (sickness benefits, old age and disability pensions, including disabilities resulting from war, and pensions to the dependants of those killed in war).

3. Incitement to national and racial hatred in the two areas is forbidden and any such act shall be punished.

4. The ethnic character and the unhampered cultural development of the Yugoslav ethnic group in the Italian-administered area and of the Italian ethnic group in the Yugoslav-administered area shall be safeguarded.

a. They shall enjoy the right to their own press in their mother tongue;

b. the educational, cultural, social and sports organisations of both groups shall be free to function in accordance with the existing laws. Such organisations shall be granted the same treatment as those accorded to other corresponding organisations in their respective areas, especially as regards the use of public buildings and radio and assistance from public financial means; and the

Italian and Yugoslav authorities will endeavour to ensure to such organisations the continued use of the facilities they now enjoy, or of comparable facilities;

c. kindergarten, primary, secondary and professional school teaching in the mother tongue shall be accorded to both groups. Such schools shall be maintained in all localities in the Italian-administered area where there are children members of the Yugoslav ethnic group, and in all localities in the Yugoslav-administered area where there are children members of the Italian ethnic group. The Italian and Yugoslav Governments agree to maintain the existing schools as set out in the list attached hereto for the ethnic groups in the area under their administration and will consult in the Mixed Committee provided for in the final Article of this Statute before closing any of these schools.

Such schools shall enjoy equality of treatment with other schools of the same type in the area administered, respectively, by Italy and Yugoslavia as regards provision of textbooks, buildings and other material means, the number and position of teachers and the recognition of diplomas. The Italian and Yugoslav authorities shall endeavour to ensure that the teaching in such schools will be performed by teachers of the same mother-tongue as the pupils.

The Italian and Yugoslav authorities will promptly introduce whatever legal prescriptions may be necessary so that the permanent organisation of such schools will be regulated in accordance with the foregoing provisions. Italian-speaking teachers, who on the date of the initialling of the present Memorandum of Understanding are employed as teachers in the educational system of the Yugoslav administered area and Slovene-speaking teachers who on the said date are employed as teachers in the educational system of the Italian administered area shall not be dismissed from their positions for the reason that they do not possess the requisite teaching diploma. This extraordinary provision shall not be used as a precedent or be claimed to apply to any cases other than the categories specified above. Within the framework of their existing laws the Yugoslav and Italian authorities will take all reasonable measures to give the aforementioned teachers an opportunity, as provided in Article 2 (d) above, to qualify for the same status as regular members of the teaching staff.

The educational programmes of such schools must not be directed at interfering with the national character of the pupils.

5. Members of the Yugoslav ethnic group in the area administered by Italy and members of the Italian ethnic group in the area administered by Yugoslavia shall be free to use their language in their personal and official relations with the administrative and judicial authorities of the

two areas. They shall have the right to receive from the authorities a reply in the same language; in verbal replies, either directly or through an interpreter; in correspondence, a translation of the replies at least is to be provided by the authorities.

Public documents concerning members of these ethnic groups, including court sentences, shall be accompanied by a translation in the appropriate language. The same shall apply to official announcements, public proclamations and publications.

In the area under Italian administration inscriptions on public institutions and the names of localities and streets shall be in the language of the Yugoslav ethnic group as well as in the language of the administering authority in those electoral districts of the Commune of Trieste and in those other communes where the members of that ethnic group constitute a significant element (at least one-quarter) of the population; in those communes in the area under Yugoslav administration where the members of the Italian ethnic group are a significant element (at least one-quarter) of the population such inscriptions and names shall be in Italian as well as in the language of the administering authority.

6. The economic development of the Yugoslav ethnic population in the Italian administered area and of the Italian ethnic population in the Yugoslav administered area shall be secured without discrimination and with a fair distribution of the available financial means.

7. No change should be made in the boundaries of the basic administrative units in the areas which come under the civilian administration of Italy or Yugoslavia with a view to prejudicing the ethnic composition of the units concerned.

8. A special Mixed Yugoslav-Italian Committee shall be established for the purpose of assistance and consultation concerning problems relating to the protection of the Yugoslav ethnic group in the area under Italian administration and of the Italian ethnic group in the area under Yugoslav administration. The Committee shall also examine complaints and questions raised by individuals belonging to the respective ethnic groups concerning the implementation of this Statute.

The Yugoslav and Italian Governments shall facilitate visits by the Committee to the area under their administration and grant it every facility for carrying out its responsibilities.

Both Governments undertake to negotiate forthwith detailed regulations governing the functioning of the Committee.

London, the 5th of October, 1954.

THE KIKUYU UPRISING AND MAU MAU

With the end of World War II, the forces that led to the breakup of European colonial holdings and the downfall of the imperialist system grew in strength. Indigenous peoples around the world were anxious to achieve independence and to partake of the opportunities of the post-war era, including aid from either side in the Cold War to help fund independence movements.

Kenya was one of the places where strong independence sentiments developed early. The British in Africa considered Kenya to be blessed with the richest resources, the most healthful climate, and the most breathtaking scenery in East Africa. As a result, it became a haven for British settlers, who formed a much larger population in Kenya (around 60,000 persons) than anywhere else in East Africa. The task of gaining independence became that much more difficult because of the fears and opposing interests of this large body of Euro-Africans. The growth of the indigenous Kenyan population, however, put mounting pressure on the colonial government, which had reserved certain lands for Africans. The conflict over land is what sparked the Kenyan independence movement.

The Kenya Central Association (KCA) came into being in 1922, dedicated to the recovery of lands that had been lost to the Kikuyu people, the most numerous and prominent tribal group in Kenya. Other associations with similar goals followed, most notably the Kenya African Union (KAU), which ultimately engineered the successful independence movement. In the early 1950s, a parallel organization developed: Mau Mau. Opponents of the KAU claimed that Mau Mau was simply the KAU's militant branch, and friends of the KAU declared Mau Mau a renegade faction. As usually used by scholars today, "Mau Mau" refers to the military-terrorist movement in Kenya, while "Kikuyu Uprising" usually refers to the range of military, terrorist, diplomatic, and other movements that worked for Kenyan independence.

Mau Mau built its numbers by having initiates take oaths of secrecy and loyalty, which were viewed as unbreakable ties in Kikuyu society. Because of successful recruiting, the movement swelled into a serious military force that conducted guerrilla warfare and executed terrorist acts. The Mau Maus then melted back into the Kenyan forests when British troops responded. Mau Mau forces called themselves the "Land and Freedom Army" in recognition of their twofold goals of securing the return of land seized by the British and gaining independence.

Numerous atrocities were attributed to Mau Mau, including massacres and torture estimated to have resulted in 1,700 deaths. In response, the British authorities declared "the Mau Mau Emergency" in 1952. By declaring this state of emergency, the government gave itself the right to use military forces for policing and restoring order and to suspend the legal rights of the accused. The colonial authorities increasingly used military force and detention without legal charges as they perceived the situation to be growing more desperate. As a result, about 10,000 Africans were killed by the military and another 90,000 were sent to prison ("detention camps") for as long as eleven years; the state of emergency meant that charges and trials were dispensed with. After a decade of conflict, bloodshed, diplomatic negotiations, and drain on the British budget, Kenya gained its independence in 1963.

Much as the Haiti Revolution had shown slave owners in the early-nineteenth-century Americas that slaves were a force to be reckoned with, the Mau Mau movement showed European colonials throughout Africa that indigenous Africans had the power and will to regain their independence. This was the first large-scale armed uprising by Africans against a European colonial power, and its tenacity and ferocity traumatized many residents of European descent. To make sense of this new phenomenon, they often invoked racist or psychopathological explanations; a political and economic confrontation was interpreted as an irrational rampage of violence for its own sake.

The following readings focus on differing views of Mau Mau held by persons in different circumstances. Some express the views of Kenyans of different descent and political inclinations, and others are scholars' analyses of how the myth of Mau Mau developed. Historians have to analyze their primary sources for bias, self-interest, and other factors that could color an account.

What, Then, Was the Mau Mau?
Michael Twaddle, in collaboration with Lucile Rabearimanana and Isaria N. Kimambo

Michael Twaddle and his colleagues provide a general interpretation of Mau Mau and its place within the larger struggle for Kenyan independence. Written for the UNESCO General History of Africa *and published in 1993, this article attempts to present a consensus view that takes advantage of recent scholarship. No historian can produce a completely dispassionate interpretation of any event or process, of course, but this article was intended to avoid partisan advocacy.*

What, then, was the Mau Mau? On present evidence it seems to have been a number of separate things, sometimes overlapping, at other times going off in different directions: a squatters' revolt; resistance against enforced agricultural improvement policies; a cultural revival; an internal war; and an anti-colonial movement that echoed earlier primary resistance against the imposition of British colonial rule half a century earlier.

To begin with, the Mau Mau was a squatters' revolt. When white settlers first established farms in the White Highlands of Kenya in the early twentieth century they were frequently assisted by Africans who exchanged their labour services for herding and cultivation rights, but with the eco-

---

General History of Africa, vol. 8, *Africa since 1935*, ed. Ali A. Mazrui (Paris: UNESCO; Oxford: Heinemann; Berkeley and Los Angeles: University of California Press, 1993), 237–41.

nomic boom that began at the end of the 1930s many white farmers became increasingly specialized and mechanized and as a result threw many squatters off their farms. Some ex-squatters were settled by the colonial administration at Olenguruone in the Rift Valley, but at the end of the 1940s many of these were expelled for disobeying agricultural instructions. And it was at Olenguruone that secret oathing was widely employed as a form of popular solidarity and resistance.

Oathing also erupted in the Kikuyu Reserve, where land consolidation was also proceeding apace as a result of population growth as well as the continuing boom in commodity prices; the Kikuyu Reserve being unusual in white-settled Africa in being comparatively central as regards roads and railways for an African reserve, and in having good soils. "It was this double peculiarity of the Kikuyu," comments John Lonsdale, "land consolidation at home and a farm tenantry outside, which determined that they, and they only, would be the seat of a violent agrarian revolt which not only set Africans against whites, but Kikuyu against Kikuyu too."

In Nairobi, by 1952 a city of nearly 100,000 people, and in other urban areas of upland Kenya such as Nakuru were other Africans, frequently called "spivs" in British documents of the time, who provided passive support and supplies for the forest fighters until Operation Anvil [a military operation conducted by the British forces] in 1954 completely cleared them out of Nairobi. It has been suggested that this alliance of workers and peasants against imperialism provides evidence of a growing proletarian consciousness in colonial Kenya, but such evidence as there is from contemporary Mau Mau hymns and subsequent memoirs suggests more a protest by recently displaced peasants against proletarianization than proletarian consciousness itself.

On yet another level, the Mau Mau must be seen as cultural assertion. But here we must be careful. The British colonial government saw oathing and opposition to terracing as back-looking conservatism, when it did not consider these things to have been deliberately provoked by "agitators" such Jomo Kenyatta. Oathing was obviously loaded with "culture." To be sure, some of the most bizarre evidence about the cultural aspects of the Mau Mau comes from Europeans of the time concerned sometimes to project their own fantasies onto Africans themselves. Nonetheless, through all the Mau Mau oathing ran certain irreducible cultural elements which appear to have acted as effectively as deterrents to recruitment of activists amongst non-Kikuyu as they assisted it amongst Kikuyu. In Mau Mau hymns too there were cultural elements which have led Professor Ogot to argue that "because of their exclusiveness they cannot be regarded as the national freedom songs which every Kenyan youth can sing with pride and conviction."

Finally, the Mau Mau must be seen as an anti-colonial movement, albeit a regionally paradoxical one. The areas of Kikuyuland most affected by colonial penetration and "stolen lands," namely Kiambu and its environs, were ones displaying the least overt support for the insurgents, while other areas away from Nairobi like Nyeri and Fort Hall proved much more militant though much less disrupted by either British colonialism or white settlers. But Robert Buijtenhuijs points out that Fort Hall and Nyeri were also areas of Kikuyuland where the British colonial entry at the start of this century was very brutal. Kiambu by comparison was pacified much more gently. If this is so, Ali Mazrui may well also be right to call the Mau Mau "the first major resurrection of the warrior tradition in recent East African history."

Nevertheless, resurrection or regression, what most concerned British politicians in the 1950s was the difficulty of keeping such a tumultuous area under colonial control. The British probably overestimated the actual military threat posed by the Mau Mau rebels, as well as underestimating the extent to which the British reaction itself would lead to mayhem and murder in which "private property was left to the care of thieves and Providence." But violence was violence, and the sheer expense of continuing to support white settlers could not be continued indefinitely within the British political tradition. And so it was that, after the Conservative Party won its third election in a row in Britain in 1959, Iain Macleod was appointed colonial secretary and the Mau Mau emergency was ended and a constitutional conference arranged.

This conference led to a 65-member legislative assembly in Kenya, 33 of them elected from open seats. The KAU was resurrected as KANU (the Kenya African National Union) and won 67 per cent of the votes in the ensuing election with a still-detained Jomo Kenyatta as the national president, Odinga as vice-president, and Mboya as general secretary. KANU was opposed by KADU (the Kenya African Democratic Union), formed by an alliance of coastal politicians and up-country notables from the smaller ethnic groups. However, it was not until after his release from detention (August 1961), a second Lancaster House conference, and a landslide victory for KANU in the May 1963 general election, that Kenyatta became prime minister and, six months later, leader of a fully independent country.

The Growth of Mau Mau

L. S. B. Leakey

Louis Leakey is best known for his research into early hominids in East Africa, but his earliest African research was a study of the customs and culture of the modern Kikuyu. A lifelong resident of Kenya, Leakey felt threatened by Mau Mau, as did most other residents of European extraction. Leakey, however, was fundamentally sympathetic to the Kikuyu and

L. S. B. Leakey, *Mau Mau and the Kikuyu* (London: Methuen, 1952), 95–100.

their situation. Leakey's account of Mau Mau, presented here, reflects his ambivalence about the movement. Other Euro-African writers typically were much more extreme in attributing Mau Mau atrocities to the savagery of the Kikuyu people or to some sort of group hysteria.

It is not absolutely certain exactly when the Mau Mau movement started, nor yet how it came to get this name. I have not been able to find any meaning, or any reasonable explanation of the name, while most of the Kikuyu that I have asked say it is just a "name without meaning."

There is a certain amount of reason to believe that it was in the latter part of 1948 or early in 1949 that Mau Mau really got under way, and that this was linked with the news that the Duke of Gloucester was coming out to Kenya, as His Majesty's representative, to confer city status upon Nairobi.

It is certain that as soon as the news of this decision to grant city status to Nairobi was released, a number of Kikuyu agitators, most of them former members of the banned Kenya Central Association, started spreading the fantastic story that the raising of Nairobi to city status was to be accompanied by further "thefts of land" from the Kikuyu by the British authorities. Since "save the land" is the battle-cry that can stir a Kikuyu more than anything else, it was not surprising that a number of people, more particularly those who already felt a strong grievance about land matters, rallied to the call. Many meetings were held and people were called upon to boycott the city celebrations and everything to do with them.

It seems most unlikely that the leaders of this movement to boycott the city celebrations seriously believed that there was to be any further alienation of native land for European settlement, for they must have been fully aware that under the Natives' Land Trust Ordinance the lands that had formally been called "Native Reserves" and which had once ranked as "Crown Lands" were now fully safeguarded.

However, the leaders of this movement were for some reason anxious to stir up further anti-British feeling, and they were fully aware that by saying that the land was in danger they were sure to get a following.

Certainly, at about that time and shortly before the Duke of Gloucester actually arrived, a big ceremony was performed in the Kiambu district at a place called Kiambaa, at which, according to many reasonably reliable accounts, a number of prominent Kikuyu took part in a solemn oath-taking ceremony, which included many, but probably not all, of the clauses of the oath ceremony that has more recently been shown to be associated with the Mau Mau.

That the persons who were organizing this movement would not stop short of violence, if they thought that their orders were being flouted, was shown by the fact that a Kikuyu member of the City Council, who not merely attended, but took a prominent part in the city celebrations, was shot at, though fortunately his assailants failed to kill him.

The vast majority of the Kikuyu regard the Mau Mau Association as nothing more than the old Kikuyu Central Association under another name. That this interpretation is correct seems to be supported by the fact that there is a remarkable similarity between the wording of the oath that was formerly taken by the K.C.A. (and which was one of the reasons that led to the banning of the Association) and the new Mau Mau oath. Moreover, the leaders of the old Kikuyu Central Association, who had been released from internment at the end of the war, tried in 1946 to revive the banned movement under the old name at the time when Jomo Kenyatta, the former General Secretary of the movement, came back to Kenya from England after a very long absence. This attempt failed and Government made it quite clear that the K.C.A., as such, would not be allowed to come back into existence. After this, for a time, the K.C.A. was never mentioned by Kikuyus either in speeches, or in the vernacular newspapers, but, under very thin disguise, the movement went on and was referred to as the "Association of three initials" or, as the Kikuyu had it, the *Kiama Kia Ndemwa Ithatu*. If the authorities tried to suggest that the meetings of the "Association of three initials" were illegal, on the grounds that it was, really, the banned organization, it was always possible for those taking part to reply that they were, in fact, referring to the three initials of some other political organization such as the Kenya African Union (K.A.U.) or the Kikuyu General Union (K.G.U.) which were bodies recognized by Government. They could thus avoid trouble, since it was almost impossible to prove that the "Association of three initials" was the old K.C.A. and not one of the others.

If we accept the view that is widely held by loyal Kikuyu that Mau Mau is only another name for the old K.C.A. and for the later "Association of three initials," we must not consider that all the former members of the K.C.A. became, automatically, members of Mau Mau. There were certainly some former K.C.A. members who had come to realize that the organization had done more harm than good to their cause, in its desire to get their land grievances settled, and who no longer gave their support to such movements.

At first, the Mau Mau movement was little heard of, and it probably only worked, in the early days, among people who were likely to approve of what was being planned. Obviously, it would have been most dangerous to approach really loyal Kikuyu and ask them to take the Mau Mau oath, for they would have refused and at once reported the movement to the authorities. Since, for the various reasons which we have examined, there were a great number of discontented Kikuyu among the squatters on European farms, the Mau Mau movement, from its probable start among a few leaders at Kiambu, was spread, first of all, in the farming areas. But, even among the squatters, there were many who were loyal to the British and who were not willing to take the Mau Mau oath, and so, very soon, it became necessary to do a number of things that were contrary to native custom, if the movement were not to be discovered and stopped by the authorities before it became too strong.

It became necessary, in the first place, to force people to take the oath once they had been approached about it and had signified their unwillingness to participate on a voluntary basis. Unless such people were coerced into taking this oath, they would be a menace to the movement, but, if they could be frightened and forced into taking it, then the movement was safe.

This may sound very illogical to the English mind, for if one of us were forced to do such a thing, either by physical force or by threatening all sorts of reprisals to our family if we did not submit, or by actual acts of violence and torture, our first reaction, afterwards, would be to go and report the matter to the nearest police station. The leaders of the movement, however, knew the psychology of their fellow tribesmen so well that they felt reasonably safe in taking such action. We have already seen that a Kikuyu who takes a solemn oath is punished by supernatural powers if he breaks that oath, or if he has perjured himself. One of the phrases used in the Mau Mau oath ceremony is to the effect that "if I do anything to give away this organization to the enemy, may I be killed by the oath." Having once made such an oath, even under pressure, no ordinary Kikuyu would dare to go and make a report to the police or to his employer, because, were he to do so, he would be breaking the oath and thus calling down upon himself, or upon members of his family, supernatural penalties. But—the reader will argue—if a man had taken a Mau Mau oath against his will, why could he not then arrange for an immediate "cleansing ceremony" and, having been cleansed and absolved from the effects of his oath, go and make a report to the authorities?

The answer to this question is really quite a simple one. While it is true that a person could be cleansed from the effects of a Mau Mau oath, participation in such a ceremony could not be kept quiet for long, since, to be effective, it must be carried out in public and before many witnesses. The Mau Mau people made it very clear to their victims that if they tried to get out of their obligations under the oath by such means, they would be victimized and even, if necessary, murdered.

From the Mau Mau point of view, therefore, the step that was taken of forcing people to take the oath against their will was a safe one, even though, by so doing, they were acting in a manner that was utterly and completely contrary to native law and custom, which has always laid down that an oath must be taken voluntarily and with the consent of members of the family of the person concerned.

It next became necessary to hold the oath-taking ceremonies at night, inside huts. This move was necessitated by the fact that, at this time, the movement was mainly being organized among squatters on European farms and there was always the likelihood that if an oath-taking ceremony was organized by day, the owner of the farm might come along and want to know what was being done. Moreover, if force were used at such a ceremony held in the open, in order to compel unwilling people to participate, there was the likelihood that some casual passer-by might hear the protests of the unwilling participants and report to the police or to the farmer that something was seriously wrong. This change-over to holding oath-taking ceremonies by night and inside huts instead of by day and in the open, also violated all the Kikuyu rules.

The leaders of the movement next decided to start administering the oath to women and even to children, as well as to adult males. It is not quite clear as to why this particular decision was taken, but, as we have seen, an oath taken by any member of a family was liable to bring supernatural punishment on any other member of that family. Clearly, if a woman could be persuaded, or forced, to take the Mau Mau oath, it would not bind her husband to the positive parts of the oath, i.e. it would not bind him to "kill a white man when the war horn is blown," or to do such other positive acts, but it *would act in a negative manner,* since it would prevent the husband from reporting on the ceremonies to the police. If he did so it would be tantamount to signing his wife's and his family's death warrant.

As an additional means of bringing pressure to bear upon fellow tribesmen to join the Mau Mau movement, the organizers called upon their members to have no dealings with people who had not joined. Mau Mau followers were forbidden to invite non-members to drink beer, or to attend their dances; they were not to help them in building huts or in any other tasks where it was normal for a man to call on his neighbors to give communal aid. Thus, many who had been reluctant to join the Mau Mau in its earlier days, were more easily persuaded to do so as time went on, especially in areas where the movement was strong.

A Participant's Explanation of Mau Mau
Josiah Mwangi Kariuki

Josiah Kariuki was active in the Mau Mau movement until his arrest by the British authorities in 1953. He spent the next eight years in detention camps, emerging only in 1960, after the Mau Mau Emergency was declared over. In 1963, when he wrote this explanation of Mau Mau, he was an aide to Jomo Kenyatta, who had been elected that year as the first president of Kenya. Kariuki's explanations for Mau Mau differ markedly from Leakey's, especially in their basic assumptions about the benevolence of British administration.

Josiah Mwangi Kariuki, *Mau Mau Detainee: The Account by a Kenya African of His Experiences in Detention Camps, 1953–1960.* (London: Oxford University Press, 1963), 20–23.

I must now explain the movement which was given the name of "Mau Mau." After the 1939–45 War things were changing. Our social and economic grievances were plainer to all and there were many more educated Africans who were beginning to understand that the social system was not immutable. Thousands more had recently returned from service in the King's African Rifles [a volunteer military unit composed of Africans in service to Great Britain] all over the world. The granting of Independence to India and Pakistan, the developing struggle in Ghana, and the increased publicity given to such things in newspapers and radio programmes, all contributed to the steady growth of political sensibility among the Africans in Kenya. Most of all was this happening among my own tribe, the Kikuyu.

They had long been in the van of Kenya politics; they were living in overcrowded and undeveloped Reserves [lands reserved for use by indigenous Africans, similar to American reservations or Canadian reserves for American Indians], in many places with a density of well over a thousand to the square mile; they felt deep grievances over the land which had been taken from them, land without which they could have no religious or social security. When the Europeans first came to the country the Kikuyu fought under Waiyaki Hinga to preserve their lands. Many of them were killed but the witch-doctor advising them told them to stop fighting or the whole tribe would be eliminated. He used the Kikuyu saying *Mundu ti mwahu wa irigu oragagwo oro umwe umwe* which means "people are not a bunch of bananas to be killed one by one." Waiyaki, with whom Lugard became blood brother, later died at Kibwezi on his way to the Coast to which he had been deported. It is not enough to say that the Europeans have a title to the land and had taken only uninhabited areas. The Kikuyu rightly felt that their uneducated forefathers had not understood the nature and implications of the requests forced on them by the early administrators and settlers, nor had they the weapons or power to refuse any demand that was pressed really hard. Had no Europeans come to the country they would have slowly settled in the forests and the White Highlands. When that land was finished the tribe would have considered what to do next. But as it was they had been tricked. At the same time they were suffering the humiliations of the colour bar. Many Europeans refused to talk to educated Africans in any language but their deplorably bad Swahili; old men were addressed as boys and monkeys; Africans were barred from hotels and clubs; Africans with land near European farms were not allowed to plant coffee; there was a wholesale disregard for human dignity and little respect for anyone with a black skin.

Normal political methods through K.A.U. seemed to be getting nowhere. The young men of the tribe saw that a time of crisis was approaching when great suffering might be necessary to achieve what they believed in. It is easy enough for anyone who knows my people to understand that it was a spontaneous decision that they should be bound together in unity by a simple oath. From what I have heard this oath began in the Kikuyu districts, starting in Kiambu. There was no central direction or control. The oath was not sophisticated or elaborate and initially was wholly unobjectionable. It started slowly, indeed regretfully, and was an oath of unity and brotherhood in the struggle for our land and our independence. It eventually spread all over the country among a people desperate to retain their self-respect and to prevent their subjugation in a European-dominated State. Although the situation was dangerous, even in October 1952, it was not so dangerous that it could not have been put right by a few political concessions (which would today, ten years later, seem trivial) and a little understanding. The movement could always have been extinguished in this way but the Government chose to answer it with a series of the harshest and most brutal measures ever taken against a native people in the British Empire in the twentieth century, and so the movement developed by action and reaction into a full-scale rebellion involving the soul of my people.

Although quite naturally most ex-officials of K.C.A. took the new oath it had nothing to do with K.C.A. or the old K.C.A. oath. I must, too, emphasize here that in all the statements and confessions made in my hearing by thousands of detainees in fourteen camps the name of Kenyatta was never once mentioned as being involved in an oath. *Mzee* was still trying desperately to get the Kenya Government to see sense in other ways. (*Mzee* is a Swahili word which means "an old man," and so we gave it to Kenyatta as a sign of respect.) I repeat that there was no central direction in this movement which grew from the grass roots upwards. In the years of crisis, 1952–54, it developed a system of sub-location and location committees in Nairobi, the Kikuyu Districts and the Rift Valley and these became the main instruments of the so-called Passive Wing whose job was to help and supply the fighters in the forests. In the early days the secrecy and lack of direction made it an ideal cover for the violent and criminal elements which are a menace to any state or society. Sometimes these elements would misuse the organization which had begun as a straightforward and spontaneous movement of unity among a people without hope. Had the Government given the people any prospect of justice it is possible that Kenyatta and the other constitutional fighters for freedom would have had some chance to control the Kikuyu. As it was, even Kenyatta himself became an object of suspicion to the thugs and there is strong evidence of plots to assassinate him both at a meeting in Kaloleni Hall, Nairobi, and also at the burial of Senior Chief Waruhiu, killed by a gunman on 7 October 1952.

Few people seem to know the origin of the name "Mau Mau." Kenyatta said time and time again that he did not know these words and nor did his people. In spite of the attempts to prove in the *Corfield Report* and at his trial that this was merely a very skillful piece of double-talk in Kikuyu, Kenyatta was speaking nothing more nor less than the truth.

This is the real origin of the name "Mau Mau." Kikuyu children when playing and talking together often make puns and anagrams with common words. When I was a child I would say to other children "Ithi, Ithi," instead of "Thii, Thii" (meaning, "Go, Go"), and "Mau, Mau" instead of "Uma, Uma."

The Myth of Mau Mau
Carl G. Rosberg Jr. and John Nottingham

Most scholars studying the independence movement in Kenya have concluded that Euro-Africans were fundamentally mistaken about the nature of Mau Mau and its relationship to other aspects of the independence movement. One component of their mistake was in subscribing to "the myth of Mau Mau," described and analyzed in this selection.

"Mau Mau" has been represented as a phenomenon that could not be interpreted mainly in terms of a political movement, but required a more fundamental explanation of deviant and irrational behavior. In part, reports of oathing ceremonies and the very secrecy and militancy of the movement gave support to this view, while the "Lari massacre"[1] in the early months of the Emergency tended to remove any doubt that "Mau Mau" was an atavistic flight from reason and the processes of modernization. During the Emergency, many people were brutally killed, cattle were maimed, and the discipline of men was on occasion strained to the breaking point. The siege conditions under which the poorly educated forest groups operated were conducive to acts associated with the image of "Mau Mau." They were increasingly cut off from communication with labor on European farms and kith and kin in the Kikuyu rural areas, and the organization of these groups was subjected to intense internal stresses and strains. The use of tradition with respect to symbols and organizational methods became more marked, and leadership had to rely on whatever measures it could to maintain morale in situations of increasing adversity.

But the myth of "Mau Mau" goes beyond this specific evidence of precipitating conditions and overt activity associated with the resistance movement. It claims that "Mau Mau" instigated a movement designed to achieve Kikuyu dominance, and that the symbols and traditions of the movement — its "Kikuyuism" — were not so much instrumental means as consummatory ends that were essentially evil.

1. In the Lari massacre, ex-Chief Wakahangara and 96 other people in the village of Lari were killed in a Mau Mau raid that took place on March 24, 1953. Wakahangara was loyal to the colonial government and seen as a potential rallying point for resistance to Mau Mau.

Carl G. Rosberg Jr. and John Nottingham, *The Myth of "Mau Mau": Nationalism in Kenya* (Stanford, Calif.: Hoover Institution; New York: Praeger, 1966), 320–21.

Ethnocentrism has been an important element behind the general acceptance of this myth. At a more immediate level of explanation, we may observe a concrete set of interrelated beliefs held by Europeans in Kenya. The most important of these were (1) an implicit conviction that the colonial system was perfectly capable of responding to the legitimate social and political grievances of Africans; (2) the belief that "Mau Mau" was but another manifestation of earlier African religious movements; and (3) the belief that in employing secret oaths, the African was rejecting modernity and reverting to primitive behavior patterns.

Mau Mau in Perspective
Robert B. Edgerton

This reading examines the legacy of Mau Mau and its role in the eventual independence of Kenya. In discussing the attitudes of both African and European residents, Edgerton shows that neither side of the conflict behaved irrationally. Rather, each side was reacting to what it believed to be an accurate assessment of conditions and what it perceived to be threats to its own well-being.

The rebellion of the Land and Freedom Army did not achieve its goals. When the fighting ended in 1956, white settlers still owned their farms in the highlands, and white Colonial administrators still ruled Kenya. The leaders of Mau Mau had hoped that their rebellion would become an irresistible force for freedom spreading throughout Kenya. Not only did it not unite the African peoples of Kenya, it even failed to unite the Kikuyu. Instead, it led Kenya's largest tribe into a bitter and bloody civil war. By 1956, most of Kenya's Africans had repudiated Mau Mau. The rebellion was over, its goals unmet, its legacy uncertain.

Nevertheless, even though the leaders of Mau Mau did not realize it, their rebellion inadvertently brought about one vitally important change in Kenya. Before the rebellion, Kenya's white settlers were determined to achieve a form of self-rule that would assure their continuing control. Once the Mau Mau rebels forced the settlers to call for British military support, the political dominion of whites in Kenya was over. It was obvious to everyone except the least intelligent and most intransigent settlers that Kenya's future would be decided by Britain. The British Government poured enormous resources into Kenya to defeat Mau Mau, but by 1954 the cost of intervention had become such a heavy burden that if the rebellion had not ended when it did, Britain would have had difficulty continuing its military commitment in Kenya much longer. In fact, by

Robert B. Edgerton, *Mau Mau: An African Crucible* (New York: Free Press, 1989), 236–41.

1956 British economic and military power had declined so much that Britain had to accept the humiliation of an American-imposed retreat from its invasion of the Suez Canal Zone. At the same time, Britain's African Colonies had become serious economic liabilities, and as European and American pressure to decolonize intensified, they became a political embarrassment as well. It was obvious that Britain could no longer afford the cost of holding Kenya by military might.

Yet only a few whites in Kenya seem to have understood that the end of colonialism in Africa was approaching, and only a few began to work toward the goal of economic reform buttressed by some form of a multi-racial government. If the white settlers had seized this opportunity to enhance economic and social justice, they might yet have assured a place for themselves as full partners in Kenya's future. But most would have nothing to do with reforms or African participation in government. They insisted on their economic privileges, their political power, and their racial superiority. In the fullness of their victory over Mau Mau, they overestimated their strength, and they badly misread the course of world events. "Their fierce self-interest," as Churchill had noted 50 years earlier, would bring about their final ruin.

The settlers' ruthless pursuit of their interests during the rebellion not only embittered the supporters of Mau Mau, it helped to radicalize educated young Africans as well. The white Kenyans' implacable refusal to share Kenya's future with the country's African population turned even many loyalist Africans against them just as it weakened their support in Britain. Only a few years after the fighting had ended, world developments having little to do with Kenya itself would persuade Harold Macmillan to grant independence to Britain's East African territories. But one critical event did involve Kenya, and it was a direct result of the settlers' excessive use of force against the Mau Mau. That event was the massacre at Hola.[1] For many in Britain, Hola symbolized white Kenya's lawlessness. But for Macmillan and Macleod, Hola was more than a symbol; it was a bloody reminder that white minority government could only continue in Kenya by the use of deadly force. The unlimited use of force by the white settlers and the colonial administration had given them victory over the Mau Mau rebellion, but in the end it lost them Kenya. They had only themselves to blame.

In fairness, the white settlers cannot be held responsible for everything that led to Mau Mau. The gulf between prosperous land-owning Kikuyu and their poor, landless tenants existed before the whites arrived, and the settlers were not responsible for the disease and famine that had depopulated the highlands before they arrived. Nonetheless,

---

1. On 3 March 1959, African guards under the command of a British officer beat to death 11 detainees at the Hola Camp. It is unclear whether the beatings were in response to a refusal to do farm labor or were unprovoked.

the Government of Kenya had appropriated vast tracts of African land and urged whites to settle on it. When the settlers demanded more power and extended privileges, the colonial administration chose to accommodate them instead of protecting the interests of Kenya's Africans. Even when administrative officials attempted to assist Africans with various medical, livestock, and agricultural programs, their paternalistic arrogance in forcing these measures upon reluctant and uncomprehending tribal people alienated the very people they intended to help. So did governmental favoritism of chiefs and other wealthy supporters of the administration. What is more, colonial administrators allowed African grievances to reach a flashpoint by ignoring the needs of the rapidly growing numbers of urban poor, and by refusing to permit emerging African leaders to play a meaningful part in Kenya's political life.

Whatever the failings of the colonial administration, accountability for the genesis of Mau Mau nonetheless falls primarily on the settlers. Although the white community in Kenya had varied interests that, to take one example, sometimes brought cattle ranchers into conflict with farmers, in general they were united in exploiting African labor for the lowest possible wages, and united too in denying Africans the opportunity to compete with them as farmers or stockmen. They also shared the belief that Africans were inferior, childlike beings who should be denied social equality, not to mention self-government. As a result of the settlers' racism and their demands for profit, they consistently ignored the welfare of Africans who grew poorer and more aggrieved whether they lived in reserves, labored on European lands, or gathered in the towns and cities searching for work. When African protest movements arose, the settlers demanded that the government smash them. The settlers professed to understand Africans and insisted that they were bringing the benefits of British civilization to them, but these claims were sanctimonious. What they understood was their own narrow self-interest; what they gave to Kenya's African populations was continuing social inferiority and economic exploitation. Most significant of all in accounting for the origin of Mau Mau, the white community made it absolutely clear to Kenya's Africans that the future would bring no fundamental change.

The attitudes and practices of Kenya's whites were neither pathological nor an aberration brought about by conditions unique to Kenya, as some have argued. They had deep roots in British culture and history. For one thing, British society was founded on the belief that some men were much more equal than others. The well-known bit of doggerel, "God bless the squire and his relations, and keep us in our proper stations," may have been partly derisive, but class distinctions were not merely remembrances of the nineteenth century for Kenya's whites — indeed, these distinctions gave legitimacy to white rule in Kenya. Even though the Labour Party had some success in challenging the authority of Britain's ruling class, few Britons in the 1950s disputed the idea that white people were superior to Africans. They were not unique. That black people were inferior to those of other races was taken for granted in much of Europe, Latin America, China, and Japan, as well as in the United States, which professed the equality of all yet maintained a color bar similar to the one in Kenya. It hardly needs saying that this belief is still widely-shared in many parts of the world.

White Kenyans' antipathy for Kenya's Africans was not only based on ideas of racial superiority, it was also a product of fear. Kenya's whites feared black Africans as much as white Americans in the antebellum South feared their slaves when they began to grow in number. Even though whites outnumbered blacks in the South, these Americans established a virtual police state for self-protection. In Kenya, 40,000 whites were surrounded by perhaps 6 million Africans whom white Kenyans believed were only a few years removed from bestial savagery. In such circumstances, it is not surprising that the white settlers failed to transcend their own racism as well as that of much of the developed world by working for a multi-racial society in Kenya. Yet the fact remains that the degrading racial policies they institutionalized went well beyond measures necessary for self-protection.

There can be no doubt that the settlers' racist attitudes and practices contributed to the outbreak of Mau Mau, but so did the settlers' uncompromising determination to rule Africans. Like many other Europeans who colonized Africa, Kenya's white settlers were convinced that it was not their superior weapons but their "superior civilization" that gave them an indisputable right to rule. Bolstered by their deep-seated belief in the principle that a small elite class could rightfully dominate a majority, white Kenyans from modest middle-class backgrounds eagerly joined settlers from Britain's "ruling class" in governing Kenya's Africans. Supported by the ruling-class ideology of the colonial administrators, white dominion became so deeply ingrained in the culture of Kenya's whites that even the kindest and most thoughtful of them were held in its thrall. White Kenyans understood that they could survive only as long as their economic symbiosis with Africans continued, but they chose to ensure that continuity, not by compromise or even understanding, but simply by the use of force. There were few voices of protest. Theirs was a society that left little room for dissent, and when the violence of Mau Mau struck, there was virtually no dissent at all. White Kenya was a society of masters—of "bwanas" and "memsahibs"—and, like masters throughout history who were threatened by rebellion, they closed ranks and responded ferociously.

When Mau Mau intimidation, arson, and violence first began, the settlers urged Draconian measures. When violence continued despite the government's declaration of a State of Emergency, the settlers took the destruction of the Mau Mau menace—and also took the law—into their own hands. Not all white men and women demanded the deaths of the "Kyukes," not all white Kenyans shot suspicious Kikuyu first and asked questions later, and not all whites in the Kenya Regiment or the Kenya Police Reserve tortured or murdered Mau Mau suspects. But many white Kenyans did all of these things, and those few who privately deplored what their friends and neighbors did rarely spoke out against them. Even the most liberal became entrapped in the convulsion of rage and revenge that engulfed the white community. The vicious reaction that swept through white Kenya grew in intensity as one example of brutality by whites was followed by another. White mothers whose children were cared for by Kikuyu women called for the execution of the inhabitants of entire Kikuyu "villages." Men who as children had played with young Kikuyu, and who later employed Kikuyu as servants and laborers, now thought of them as animals to be hunted, or vermin to be exterminated, while otherwise quite respectable white settlers became torturers and murderers.

The severity of the white reaction was heightened by the earliest Mau Mau killings. The first white victims, women as well as men, were chopped and slashed to death with pangas [a kind of machete or large knife] and swords. Their mutilated bodies were terrible to see or even hear about. When six-year-old Michael Ruck was killed by a flurry of panga blows, most settlers were convinced that the Mau Mau rebels were inhuman savages. Their rage was also intensified by a profound fear that African savagery, if not repressed, would engulf them all. The settlers were convinced that Africans were "primitives" whose "savage" impulses had been unleashed by the Mau Mau oaths. At best, they said, Africans were not fully human, and the Mau Mau rebels were clearly not the best of Africans. The feelings of a 31-year-old settler who had been born in Kenya were widely shared: "I was raised with Africans, you know. Kyukes mostly. I thought I knew what they were like but when the Mau Mau terrorism began I realized I didn't know them at all. They weren't like us. They weren't even like animals — animals are understandable. They're natural. The Mau Mau were . . . what's the word? Perverted, I guess. It was the oath, you see. Once they took it, life didn't mean anything to them. If we couldn't drive the (Mau Mau) poison out of them by getting them to confess, all we could do was kill them." Settlers like this one killed Mau Mau suspects in an attempt to save all that was dear to them, and to destroy all that they did not understand. Most of them killed because they believed they had no other choice.

The settlers loved Kenya's beauty, its excitement, its comfortable and privileged way of life. As they saw it, Africans had done nothing to "develop" Kenya, and as a result they deserved their roles as servants and laborers for white men and women who had brought "civilization" to them. The Mau Mau rebellion was not only a direct threat to the lives of these white Kenyans, it was an affront to their sense of the natural order of things. If the challenge to white supremacy had come from a respected "fighting" people like the Somali or Massai, these settlers would still have insisted that the rebellion be crushed. But an uprising by "warriors" might at least have been understandable. Warlike peoples were expected to fight, and while they would have had to be killed, it would have been with some regret. The Kikuyu-led Mau Mau were thought of as cowards with no military tradition who had long been the subservient employees of whites. Many settlers thought of them as little more than slaves, and for people like these to repudiate white civilization and challenge white rule was galling.

QUESTIONS TO CONSIDER

1. How does Glenda Sluga see ethnicity as a factor in the partition of Trieste? How does her interpretation differ from previous ones?

2. What were some of the differences in the ways that indigenous Africans and Africans of European descent typically saw Mau Mau and the Kenyan independence movements? Why do you think these differences in perceptions existed?

3. What are the major differences between Alvin Toffler's and Edward Wenk's viewpoints on the role of technology in social change in the current era? Using Carlo Cipolla's caution to consider whether technological change is a cause or effect, do you find Toffler's or Wenk's conclusion more compelling? Why?

4. Trieste and Kenya each had been independent at one time, but postwar developments led to the partition of Trieste and the independence of Kenya. What do you think might have been the significant differences in the situations in Trieste and Kenya that brought about these different outcomes?

ACKNOWLEDGMENTS

Part Six: The Collision of Worlds
Herman J. Viola, "Seeds of Change" from Herman J. Viola and Carolyn Margolis, eds., *Seeds of Change: A Quincentennial Commemoration*, pp. 11–16. Copyright © 1991 by the Smithsonian Institution. Reprinted with the permission of Smithsonian Institution Press.

Leland Ferguson, "Magic Bowls" from *Uncommon Ground: Archaeology and Early African America 1650-1800*, pp. 110–116. Copyright © 1992 by the Smithsonian Institution. Reprinted with the permission of Smithsonian Institution Press.

Marvin T. Smith, "Archaeological Evidence of the Coosa Reaction to European Contact" (editors title, originally titled "Indian Responses to European Contact: The Coosa Example") in Jerald T. Milanich and Susan Milbrath, eds., *First Encounters: Spanish Explorations in the Caribbean and the United States, 1492–1570* (Gainesville: University of Florida Press, 1989), Ripley P. Bullen Monographs in Anthropology and History #9, pp. 135–149. Copyright © 1989. Reprinted with the permission of the publishers.

Olive Patricia Dickason, "New Ideas in Old Frameworks" from *The Myth of the Savage and the Beginnings of French Colonialism in the Americas*, pp. 17–22. Copyright © 1984 by The University of Alberta Press. Reprinted with the permission of the publishers.

John Davis, "The Relation of the Course of the *Sunshine*," from *The Voyages and Works of John Davis, The Navigator*, ed. Albert Hastings Markham ([London]: Hakluyt Society, 1589; reprint, New York: Burt Franklin, n.d.), 30–35.

Part Seven: Europe's Global Reach
Richard Leakey and Roger Lewin, "The Greatest Revolution" from *Origins*, pp. 21–31. Copyright © 1977 by Richard E. Leakey and Roger Lewin. Reprinted with the permission of Dutton Signet, a division of Penguin Books USA Inc.

Stillman Drake, trans., excerpt from *Galileo Galilei: Two New Sciences*, pp. 11–15. Copyright © 1974. Reprinted with the permission of The University of Wisconsin Press.

Sigmund Freud, "The Premises and Technique of Interpretation" (Lecture VI), translated by James Strachey, from *Introductory Lectures on Psycho-Analysis*, pp. 122–128. Copyright © 1965, 1964, 1963 by James Strachey. Reprinted with the permission of Liveright Publishing Corporation and The Hogarth Press.

Immanuel Kant, "What is Enlightenment?," from *Critique of Practical Reason, Third Edition*, translated by Lewis White Beck (New York: Macmillan, 1956). Copyright © 1956. Reprinted by permission of the publisher.

"The [French] Declaration of the Rights of Man and the Citizen" from Paul Beik, ed., *The French Revolution*, pp. 95–97. Copyright © 1970 by Paul H. Beik. Reprinted with the permission of HarperCollins Publishers, Inc.

Olympe de Gouges, "Declaration of the Rights of Woman and the Female Citizen" from Darlene Gay Levy, Harriet Branson Applewhite, and Mary Dyrham Johnson, trans., *Women in Revolutionary Paris, 1789–1795*. Copyright © 1979 by the Board of Trustees of the University of Illinois. Reprinted with the permission of University of Illinois Press.

Hashimoto Kingoro, "The Need for Emigration and Expansion" from Ryusaku Tsunoda, William Theodore de Bary, and Donald Keen, *Sources of Japanese Tradition*, pp. 796–798. Copyright © 1958 by Columbia University Press. Reprinted with the permission of the publishers.

Mohandas Gandhi, "*Satyagraha*–Soul-Force" from Raghavan Iver, *The Moral and Political Works of Mahatma Gandhi*, pp. 244–251. Copyright © 1986. Reprinted with the permission of Oxford University Press, Ltd.

Obafemi Awolowo, "The Nigerian Youth Movement" from *Awo: The Autobiography of Chief Obafemi Awolo*, pp. 115–116. Copyright © 1960. Reprinted with the permission of Cambridge University Press, Inc.

Sun Yat-sen, "A History of the Chinese Revolution" from Julie Lee Wei, et al., eds., *Prescriptions for Saving China: Selected Writings of Sun Yat-sen*, pp. 252–255. Copyright © 1994 by the Board of Trustees of the Leland Stanford Junior University. Reprinted with the permission of Hoover Institution Press.

Part Eight: Global War and Revolution
Hans Spier, "Ludendorff: The German Concept of Total War" in Edward M. Earle, *Makers of Modern Strategy*, pp. 306–321 with cuts. Copyright © 1980 by Princeton University Press. Reprinted with the permission of the publishers.

James Laux, "The Great Depression in Europe" from *The Forum Series*, 1974 (St. Louis: Forum Press, 1974), pp. 13–14. Copyright © 1974. Reprinted by permission of Harlan Davidson.

Clarence B. Carson, "Origins of the New Deal" from *The Welfare State* (Wadley, Ala.: American Textbook Committee, 1986), 36.

"Soviet Wartime Mobilization" from John Barber and Mark Harrison, *The Soviet Home Front, 1941–1945*, pp. 96–99, 116–119, and 147–152. Copyright © 1991. Reprinted with the permission of Addison Wesley Longman Ltd.

"Chinese Women in Revolution and War" from Margery Wolf, *Revolution Postponed*, pp. 16–25 with cuts. Copyright © 1985 by the Board of Trustees of the Leland Stanford Junior University. Reprinted with the permission of Stanford University Press.

"Voices of Working Women in World War I" from Angela Woollacott, *On Her Their Lives Depend: Munitions Workers in the Great War*, pp. 5, 35, 44-45, 69, 125, and 129-130. Copyright © 1994 by The Regents of the University of California. Reprinted with the permission of the University of California Press.

"Soviet Peasants and Women in 1929" by Joseph Stalin, from Marx-Engels-Lenin Institute, *Joseph Stalin: A Political Biography* (New York: International Publishers, 1949), pp. 64–67. Copyright © 1949. Reprinted with the permission of International Publishers.

"Life in a Soviet Labor Camp" from Alexander Solzhenitsyn, *One Day in the Life of Ivan Denisovich*, translated by Max Hayward and Ronald Hingley, pp. 104–111.

Copyright © 1963 by Frederick A. Praeger, Inc. Reprinted with the permission of Henry Holt and Company, Inc.

"A Nazi Official Speaks to SS Officers" by Heinrich Himmler, translated by George Solomon, from Lucy S. Dawidowicz, ed., *A Holocaust Reader* (New York: Behrman House, 1976), pp. 130–135. Copyright © 1976 by Lucy S. Dawidowicz. Reprinted with the permission of Georges Borchardt, Inc. for the author.

Part Nine: Accelerating Change
Carlo M. Cipolla, "Technology as Cause or Effect?" from Carlo M. Cipolla and Derek Birdsall, *The Technology of Man: A Visual History*, pp. 17–19. Copyright © 1979 by Carlo M. Cipolla and Derek Birdsall. Reprinted with the permission of Holt, Rinehart, and Winston.

Alvin Toffler, "The Third Wave" from *The Third Wave*, pp. 25–30. Copyright © 1980 by Alvin Toffler. Reprinted with the permission of William Morrow & Company.

Edward Wenk Jr., excerpt from *Tradeoffs: Imperatives of Choice in a High-tech World*, pp. 6–13. Copyright © 1986 by The Johns Hopkins University Press. Reprinted with the permission of the publisher.

Glenda Sluga, "Trieste: Ethnicity and the Cold War, 1945-1954" from *Journal of Contemporary History* 29 (1994): 285–299. Copyright © 1994. Reprinted with the permission of the author and Sage Publications, Ltd.

Michael Twaddle, in collaboration with Lucile Rabearimanana and Isaria N. Kimambo, "What, Then, Was the Mau Mau?" from Ali A. Mazrui, ed., *General History of Africa, Volume 8: Africa since 1935*, pp. 237–241. Copyright © 1993 by UNESCO. Reprinted with the permission of the University of California Press.

L. S. B. Leakey, "The Growth of Mau Mau" from *Mau Mau and the Kikuyu*, pp. 95–100 (London: Methuen, 1952). Reprinted with the permission of Methuen.

Josiah Mwangi Kariuki, "A Participant's Explanation of Mau Mau" from *Mau Mau Detainee: The Account by a Kenya African of His Experiences in Detention Camp*, pp. 20–23. Copyright © 1963. Reprinted with the permission of Oxford University Press, Ltd.

Carl G. Rosberg Jr. and John Nottingham, "The Myth of Mau Mau" from *The Myth of "Mau Mau": Nationalism in Kenya*, pp. 320–321. Copyright © 1966 by the Board of Trustees of the Leland Stanford Junior University. Reprinted with the permission of Hoover Institution Press.

Robert B. Edgerton, "Mau Mau in Perspective" from *Mau Mau: An African Crucible*, pp. 236–241. Copyright © 1989 by Robert B. Edgerton. Reprinted with the permission of The Free Press, a division of Simon & Schuster, Inc.